PRESIDENTIAL ARCHIVIST

"As an archivist, David Alsobrook spent his professional life immersed in the raw materials of history, and played a central role in the creation of three presidential libraries. In this fascinating memoir, he offers a rare glimpse into the details of that work—and into the personalities of President Jimmy Carter, President George H. W. Bush, and President Bill Clinton. Alsobrook tells the story with the understated voice of an archivist: fair, respectful, meticulous. This is an important book."

—Frye Gaillard, writer in residence, University of
South Alabama and author of *A Hard Rain*

"With his trained historian's eye, archivist's sense for pertinent detail, and natural story-telling gifts, David Alsobrook cuts through the hurly-burly of his life in a fascinating memoir of his life and career in working in the Carter, George H. W. Bush, and Clinton Presidential Libraries. His memoir is at once intensely personal and highly contextualized, so readers can follow his movements and ideas as well as those of his extraordinary cast of characters. Alsobrook has penned a ground-level view of the working life of an archival professional and a bird's-eye view of the presidential library system in the late twentieth century."

—Martin T. Olliff, professor of History and
director of The Wiregrass Archives, Troy University-Dothan
and author of *The Great War in the Heart of Dixie*

"David Alsobrook loves his country and her history. After an eventful lifetime promoting each, he distills what he has learned working with presidents while fending off bureaucratic enemies, journalists in search of scandal, civic illiteracy, and popular indifference. For all the obstacles in his path, this is a story of rare accomplishment, told with wit, candor, and the narrative talent that comes with a Southern accent. Most of all, it's an antidote to the cynical treatment of public servants as dronelike 'government workers' Alsobrook knows, and shows, better."

—Richard Norton Smith, former director of five presidential
libraries and biographer of George Washington,
Herbert Hoover, Thomas E. Dewey, and Nelson Rockefeller

"There are many reasons to read David Alsobrook's memoir. His career from Carter to Clinton gives eyewitness to the transition of the presidency and the archives profession from the typewriter age to what Alsobrook calls the 'brave new world' of records in cyberspace. But in the atmosphere of 2020 the real importance of this memoir transcends the specific profession and the particular person. Alsobrook's career is a tribute to the dedication and professionalism of highly-trained, non-partisan career civil servants who work hard to serve the best interests of the public even in the face of 'treacherous political landmines.' America needs more federal employees like David Alsobrook; our leaders need to appreciate them; and we can't afford to drive them away."

—Bradley R. Rice, professor emeritus of History,
Clayton State University, and past president
of the Georgia Association of Historians

"*Presidential Archivist* is the story of one man's journey to the pinnacle of his profession—the directorship of two presidential libraries. Along the way, we learn about the politics, the intrigue, and the duplicity, but we also learn about the dedication, courage, and commitment to public service displayed by David Alsobrook and his associates. As one of the thousands of scholars who have researched their books and articles at presidential libraries, I am profoundly grateful for the men and women who have dedicated their lives to the preservation of our nation's history. This memoir is only a small part of that larger story, but it captures the significance of what it means to craft a lasting repository of our politics, our policies, and our presidents."

—Martin J. Medhurst, distinguished professor of
Rhetoric and Communication, Baylor University

"Today, students of American history, public administration and policy, the US presidency, and archival careers are the ultimate beneficiaries of David Alsobrook's phenomenal memory and meticulous documentation of his unique career in the creation of three presidential libraries/museums. His thirty-year career with the National Archives and presidential libraries is unparalleled."

—Lynn Scott Cochrane, retired director
of Libraries, Denison University

"It takes an exemplary archivist with ideal temperament to steer three presidential libraries into existence. David Alsobrook maintains that judicious temperament as he tells as much as can be told about building trust with presidents and their families, organizing millions of files, and processing reams upon reams of documents. This memoir reveals how two key skills—being an effective manager and a compassionate mediator—allowed Alsobrook, as an outsider to the former presidents' inner circles, was able to move presidential materials projects to opening day as libraries without losing the faith of his professional staff."

—Margaret E. Scranton, professor of Political Science,
School of Public Affairs, University of Arkansas-Little Rock

PRESIDENTIAL ARCHIVIST

A Memoir

David E. Alsobrook

MERCER UNIVERSITY PRESS
Macon, Georgia
2020

MUP/ H994

© 2020 by Mercer University Press
Published by Mercer University Press
1501 Mercer University Drive
Macon, Georgia 31207

25 24 23 22 21 20   5 4 3 2 1

Books published by Mercer University Press are printed on acid-free paper
that meets the requirements of the American National Standard for
Information Sciences—Permanence of Paper for Printed Library Materials.

Printed and bound in the United States.

This book is set in Adobe Caslon Pro.

Cover/jacket design by Burt&Burt.

ISBN   978-0-88146-763-5
Alsobrook, David Ernest, 1946- author.
Presidential archivist : a memoir / David E. Alsobrook.
LCCN 2020017056 | ISBN 9780881467635 (hardback)
LCSH: Alsobrook, David Ernest, 1946- | National Archives
   (U.S.)—Officials and employees. | White House (Washington,
   D.C.)—History—20th century. | Presidential libraries--United
   States—History—20th century. | Carter, Jimmy, 1924- | Bush, George,
   1924-2018. | Bush, George W. (George Walker), 1946- | Clinton, Bill,
   1946- | Archivists--Training of. | Archivists--United States—v
   Biography.
LCC CD997.A47 A47 2020. | DDC 026/.973--dc23
LC record available at https://lccn.loc.gov/2020017056

Contents

MERCER UNIVERSITY PRESS

Endowed by

TOM WATSON BROWN
and
THE WATSON-BROWN FOUNDATION, INC.

For my beloved wife, Ellen—

My North Star, who traveled every

mile of this long journey with me

Author's Note

Beginnings

The English word "memoir," a derivative of *memoria* (Latin) and *mémoire* (French), literally means "memory." Its standard definition is "a narrative composed from personal experience; an account of something noteworthy."[1]

While readers ultimately will determine if *Presidential Archivist* includes "something noteworthy," it is assuredly "composed from personal experience."

A written memoir typically appears many years after the events it documents or describes have occurred. Therefore, by the nature of its creation, a memoir is a step removed from contemporaneous personal records such as a diary or journal. A memoir thus may lack the compelling immediacy of such primary sources.

However, the passage of time provides the memoirist with an opportunity for deeper reflection on the meaning and significance of past events, which then can be placed into some sort of historical context. Although both the memoirist and novelist know in advance how the narrative will end, the former must remain true to historical facts even while expressing personal opinions.

For historians, journalists, and other nonfiction writers who strive mightily to compose objective expository prose, a memoir inherently is fraught with one potentially disconcerting stylistic characteristic. Shifting from the comfortable third-person narrator to the first-person "I" can be disorienting for any author. I first encountered this trauma in April 2018 in presenting a paper about my archival career at the Alabama Historical Association's annual meeting in Birmingham.

Introducing my topic to the audience, I recalled how President George H. W. Bush's mother always admonished him against being a

---

[1] *Webster's Seventh New Collegiate Dictionary* (Springfield MA: Merriam-Webster, Inc., 1963) 528.

"braggadocio" by speaking only of his personal accomplishments. I also cited acclaimed satirist Finley Peter Dunne's preferred title, *Alone in Cuba*, for Theodore Roosevelt's egocentric account of his combat heroics with the "Rough Riders" at San Juan Hill in 1898. Standing firmly in "braggadocio" and *Alone in Cuba* territory, I confessed that my archival memoir lacked the "safety net of a tight chronology" and the historian's traditional objectivity.[2]

My collegial audience in Birmingham refrained from hissing, booing, or throwing rotten fruit and vegetables during or after the presentation. They seemed to be genuinely interested in my narrative. After surviving this exploratory incursion into dreaded first-person narration, I seriously considered writing a more fulsome account of my life as an archivist.

In writing *Presidential Archivist*, I frequently thought about my own family's historical saga. With the exception of my maternal grandfather, barber Amos W. Starnes, all of my ancestors toiled throughout their lives in cotton mills in Eufaula, Alabama. Oma Parish Alsobrook, my beloved paternal grandmother, fueled my youthful imagination with her tales about life before World War I in Eufaula's "Southside" mill village, thereby inspiring me to write a historical account of that long-forgotten era.[3]

My parents, Thomas and Frances Alsobrook, were among the first generation of mill families to escape from the horrific, repetitious cycle of ignorance and poverty. Educated as a social worker at Alabama College in Montevallo, my mother dedicated her life to teaching and educational testing. Before I entered the first grade, she read aloud to me for hours on end, often falling asleep with the open book on her lap. While teaching me to read, she also instilled in me an abiding love for the written word, history, science, music, the arts, and nature.

Under her watchful tutelage, as a young reader, my favorite titles included the Hardy Boys amateur sleuthing series, Landmark history and science books, *Classics Illustrated*, Bobbs-Merrill's "Childhoods of Famous

---

[2] David E. Alsobrook, "A Portrait of the Archivist as a Young Man," *Alabama Review* 71/4 (October 2018): 284–85.

[3] David E. Alsobrook, *Southside: Eufaula's Cotton Mill Village and Its People, 1890–1945* (Macon GA: Mercer University Press, 2017).

Americans," and Bruce Catton's Civil War volumes. When I was nine years old in 1956, she proudly gave me a subscription to *American Heritage*, a popular illustrated history publication.[4]

Although my father also was an avid reader, he earned a living as a skilled craftsman and builder. Trained as a machinist in his early twenties at Gadsden's Alabama School of Trades, he worked alongside my mother in 1941–1942, inspecting aircraft at Brookley Field in Mobile. After overseas service during World War II with the US Navy "Seabees" (construction battalions), he attended Alabama Polytechnic Institute (later renamed Auburn University) under the auspices of the GI Bill and graduated in 1948 with a degree in Building Construction.

Despite his own successful building career, he encouraged me to pursue a profession that was less physically and emotionally debilitating. I never acquired even a small fraction of my father's skills in carpentry, metallurgy, and brick masonry. However, by observing him at construction sites, I learned how to treat other people with dignity and respect and grew to appreciate the value of hard work—whether it was manual labor or a sedentary desk job.[5]

Throughout my public school years, my parents never exerted any undue pressure on me to excel in academics or athletics. They simply expected me to work hard and do my best in class and on the playing field. Before World War II short-circuited my father's dream of playing football at Auburn, he starred on the gridiron at Eufaula High School and at Perkinston Junior College in Mississippi. Yet he never seemed to be fazed by my lack of athletic talent or the scores of the games. His only demand during my school days was not negotiable—a poor grade in conduct,

---

[4] Ibid., 95–96; Alsobrook, "A Portrait of the Archivist as a Young Man," 300.

[5] David E. Alsobrook, "The Best Years of Their Lives: Alabama Polytechnic Institute's World War II Veterans Era, 1946–1950," *Alabama Review* 70/4 (October 2017): 329, 343–44, 359–61; author's taped interview with Thomas N. Alsobrook, 31 December 1988, Mobile, AL, David Alsobrook Collection, Auburn University Special Collections and Archives, R. B. Draughon Library, Auburn, AL (hereafter cited as DA Collection); Alsobrook, *Southside*, 94, 168–69, 176–77.

"deportment," as he called it, was unacceptable. As long as I gave my best effort, average academic grades did not elicit his displeasure.

When I was not studying or playing football and baseball, I spent my early adolescence on church, Boy Scouts, and outdoor activities—singing in the choir, hiking, camping, fishing, and erecting birdhouses and feeding stations. I still found time for reading voraciously, which did not improve my extreme myopia.

My television viewing preferences gradually expanded from *The Cisco Kid*, *Gunsmoke*, *Hopalong Cassidy*, *Dragnet*, *The Life of Riley*, and *The West Point Story* to more serious fare—*Playhouse 90*, *The Twilight Zone*, and Walter Cronkite's historical productions, *You Are There* and *The Twentieth Century*. With the dawning of the Space Age and the celebration of the Civil War centennial, I became enthralled with those two topics, and my reading and TV habits shifted accordingly.

At some point in the late 1950s, I became an inveterate collector—baseball cards, scrapbooks of newspaper clippings on a wide range of topics, record albums, coins, stamps, Boy Scout patches, World War II surplus military gear, arrowheads, fossils, deer antlers, animal bones, antique bottles, seashells, and rusty Civil War projectiles that my father unearthed at construction sites. My boyhood chronicles undoubtedly would be more interesting and dramatic if there was any existing evidence that my collecting obsessions presaged my future professional archival and museum careers. But this claim would be ludicrous and bogus—as a kid I was merely a novice hoarder who liked to gather "stuff."

Based on the eclectic nature of my collections, a casual observer also might have prophesied erroneously that I was destined to be a botanist, entomologist, zoologist, or veterinarian. I identified and mounted various species of Alabama flora, fauna, butterflies, and insects. I rescued stray cats, dogs, squirrels, and birds that had sustained minor injuries. I also constructed elaborate cages for ducks, hamsters, white mice, baby alligators, turtles, frogs, and nonpoisonous snakes. My large wildlife menagerie, of course, was confined to our garage and workshop. In retrospect, I think these collections reflected my youthful fascination with everything in the world around me. Fortunately, my parents intuitively understood and tolerated my collecting mania.

From the first grade through high school, my teachers deeply structured and broadened my entire learning experience. They generally were sensitive, well-prepared teachers—dedicated to their chosen profession and enthusiastic about the curriculum. They gave me and my classmates a solid grounding in English grammar and writing, literature, history, civics, science, mathematics, geography, and "music appreciation," as it was designated in that era. Our physical education instructors taught us the mechanics of calisthenics, team sports, and folk-dancing, and our coaches insisted on clean sportsmanship.

Although I developed good study habits and earned excellent grades (except in math), standardized tests remained a mystery to me, as proven by my scores. Most importantly, my teachers believed in us and were not reticent in offering words of encouragement. For example, Bette Jean Waller, my young, vivacious eighth-grade English and social studies teacher, wrote in my yearbook in 1961, "There is, within you, the potential of greatness; I am sure that some day I shall be proud to say that I taught David Alsobrook."[6] At age fourteen, these words meant the world to me. And I am very confident that I was not the only awkward, bespectacled adolescent whom she infused with a burning desire to seek "greatness."

When I graduated from high school in May 1964, in the inaugural class of post–World War II baby boomers, the traumatic sixties loomed ahead—the civil rights movement, the Vietnam War, the counterculture, and the sexual revolution all would become dramatic mile markers for our generation. We had lost our innocence several months earlier when President John F. Kennedy was assassinated, but we faced the future with his inspirational challenge etched deeply in our hearts: "Ask not what your country can do for you, but what you can do for your country."

I am writing in the immediate aftermath of the longest shutdown of the federal government in US history. President George H. W. Bush frequently spoke with passion about "the nobility of public service." The 800,000 furloughed federal employees (and those who worked without remuneration) are emblematic of President Bush's stirring tribute to Ameri-

---

[6] Bette Jean Waller's inscription, 18 May 1961, *Eanes Teens-1961*, vol. 6, yearbook (Mobile AL: Mae Eanes Junior High School, 1961), in author's possession.

cans who are dedicated to the service of our nation. Several thousand furloughed career civil servants—deemed as "nonessential"—are employed in the National Archives and Records Administration, Presidential libraries, and various federal agencies.

For thirty years, I was a "nonessential" federal employee with the National Archives. My job was not designated as vital to our national security or public safety, but I was exceptionally proud of my career in the federal government. Sworn to support, protect, and defend the US Constitution, I occupied a position of public trust with the requisite high-level security clearance. In this position, I helped establish three presidential libraries (those of Jimmy Carter, George H. W. Bush, and William J. Clinton). In preparation for the Carter and Bush libraries, I was detailed twice as an archivist to the White House. I also participated in three transfers of presidential materials from the White House. I subsequently served as the Carter Library's supervisory archivist and as the first director of the George H. W. Bush and Clinton libraries.

Over the years, I had the unique opportunity and honor to know four former presidents, their wives, families, advisors, and associates. Only two federal entities are permanently assigned to serve first families after they leave the White House—the US Secret Service and the National Archives. I was very fortunate to be a member of the National Archives team that carried out this special duty.

Before writing my first sentence, I agonized over the contents of this memoir. After considerable thought, I decided to produce a personal account of my life as archivist, with an emphasis on my formative years; academic preparation; influential teachers, colleagues, and friends; and observations of several presidents and first ladies.

Presidential Archivist does *not* focus on monumental historical events and presidential decisions—the purview of distinguished scholars like Doris Kearns Goodwin, Michael Beschloss, Jon Meacham, Robert Dallek et al. While I have consulted published works by these and other historians, this memoir primarily is based on my personal journals, correspondence, memoranda, notes, calendars, essays, and former colleagues' reminiscences.

I had no desire to write a standard historical treatise on the presidency or presidential libraries—subjects that previous authors have mined exhaustively. Instead, I concentrated on topics that are not well publicized—the diverse roles of archivists serving in the White House, the complex logistics of moving presidential materials during transitions, and the political pressures inherent in federal employees' relationships with our first families.

I also fully exercised the memoirist's prerogative in the selection of topics to feature in my narrative. For example, I did not compile a compendium of celebrities—from Julie Andrews to Tim McGraw—whom I met during the course of my career. Moreover, I avoided verbose discussions of presidential libraries' planning sessions with architects, builders, and museum designers. While such topics are interesting and revelatory to some extent, they obscure what I wanted to highlight in this memoir—the people and events with the greatest impact on my life.

I have no illusions that my narrative rises to the level of significant presidential history. But my personal encounters with these presidents and first ladies were vitally important to me and my family. For this reason alone I have described some of these episodes—Jimmy Carter demonstrating the mysteries of fly fishing to our children, the elder Bushes' comforting words following my father's death and later in the aftermath of our daughter's traumatic automobile accident, my being briefly "lost at sea" in the fog with George H. W. Bush, Barbara Bush as a "free spirit," and my unscripted telephone conversations with Bill Clinton about whatever was of concern to him at the time.

Presidential Archivist hopefully will provide something noteworthy about our former presidents and their wives, who truly are national treasures, and archivists who silently perform their professional duties in lifelong obscurity and anonymity behind the scenes in the federal government.

Acknowledgments

I have many people to thank for their contributions to *Presidential Archivist*, and I will begin with my wife, Ellen. She and I have been together for forty-five years. Since she accompanied me on this journey and witnessed much that I have related in the following pages, this story also is hers—the wonderful, exhilarating moments and the times of heartbreak and loss. We have shared all of these experiences.

Throughout the years, she has never lost faith in me. Living with an author is no easy task; it is even more problematic if that writer is also an archivist/historian who frequently dwells in the past. Since we first met, one of Ellen's most precious gifts is the way she patiently and lovingly gives me the time and solitude to research, write, edit, and, most importantly, to compose my thoughts.

Ellen also has provided me with a realistic sense of perspective and equilibrium over the years. When Julie Andrews visited Little Rock about sixteen years ago, Bill and Hillary Clinton were in New York. I had the privilege of hosting Ms. Andrews at the Clinton Presidential Materials Project. For over two hours, I showed her presidential documents, photographs, artifacts, and memorabilia. She asked serious, thoughtful questions during our tour. Then it was time for her to leave. Pausing at the door, she said, "I'm really looking forward to returning someday to see the Clinton Presidential Library." I replied, "I'm sure that the former President and First Lady would love to give you that tour." She looked me straight in the eye and softly said, "No, David, I want *you* to do it."

I floated home on air. Julie Andrews wanted *me* to show her the Clinton Library's treasures! When I related this story to Ellen, she smiled and said, "Yes, David—that's why Julie Andrews is such a great actress." We all need someone like my wife who keeps our feet anchored on terra firma.

Four close friends graciously read the entire manuscript: Ginny Dunaway Young, Scotty E. Kirkland, Leah Rawls Atkins, and Timothy Walch. They each offered cogent recommendations for editing the final manuscript. Their careful examination eliminated a multitude of egregious errors and produced a much more informative, coherent book. Of course, any remaining errors of fact or interpretation are mine alone.

I also am deeply indebted to many former colleagues with whom I served at the National Archives and three presidential libraries: Donald B. Schewe, the late Martin I. Elzy, Robert Bohanan, Mary Elizabeth Ruwell, David Van Tassel, Lee R. Johnson, James R. Kratsas, Steve Samford, William A. Harris, David Humphrey, Dennis Daellenbach, James Hastings, Jay E. Hakes, Jimmie Purvis, Deborah Bush, Keith Shuler, John Laster, Sharon Fawcett, and Cindi Fox. They all endured my persistent questions about events that transpired many decades in the past. Their generosity in sharing recollections, insights, documents, and factual data contributed significantly to this memoir.

I extend my sincere thanks for their archival expertise to the following National Archives professionals: Keith Shuler, the Jimmy Carter Presidential Library and Museum; Mary Finch, the George H. W. Bush Presidential Library and Museum; John Keller, Deborah Bush, and Dana Simmons, the William J. Clinton Presidential Library and Museum; and Emily Robison, the George W. Bush Presidential Library and Museum.

I also wish to express my deep appreciation to Paul M. Pruitt, Jr., and Kathy Tomajko, friends of many years, who generously furnished informative commentaries on librarians' professional preparation; and to Hugh Thomas Taggart, Jr., who formerly served in the White House Office of Records Management, for his invaluable analysis of electronic records systems.

Edwin C. Bridges, who served as director of the Alabama Department of Archives and History in 1982–2012, provided extensive background information about the innovative archival, museum, and educational programs that evolved during his tenure in Montgomery, Alabama.

Presidential Archivist, of course, owes much to Marc Jolley, the gifted editor of Mercer University Press, and his magnificent staff, including Mary Beth Kosowski and Marsha Luttrell. Their professionalism, forbearance, and encouragement were instrumental throughout the entire production process—from inception to publication.

Finally, *Presidential Archivist* also benefitted substantially from the wise counsel, guidance, and support from my faithful Auburn family—Wayne Flynt, Leah Rawls Atkins, Paul M. Pruitt, Jr., Robert J. Jakeman, Allen W. Jones, Debbie Pendleton, Marlene Rikard, and David Rosenblatt.

PRESIDENTIAL ARCHIVIST

Prologue

The Archivist's Life

[T]he sad truth seems to be that the American archivist simply has not the made the grade yet. His activities have not yet captured the imagination of the American people so as to make him a qualified subject for the columns of the Saturday Evening Post, to say nothing of full-size novels and m usical comedies.
—Ernst Posner, presidential address,
Society of American Archivists, October 1956

I vividly remember spirited debates in scholarly circles four decades ago about whether an archivist should be categorized as a "professional" along with students of history, political science, and other academic disciplines. One professed article of faith among academics that I found particularly galling was that an archivist was merely "a bearer of water and hewer of wood" for "true scholars" such as historians. While archivists generally are no longer second-class citizens in academe, government, and society at large, ignorance and confusion stubbornly persist about their chosen careers. Before relating the details of my own circuitous journey as an archivist, I want to discuss some of the common misunderstandings surrounding this profession, requisite academic and practical training, standard duties, and the ideal archival temperament.

Anyone who takes the vows of poverty and solitude to pursue the introspective, sedentary archival lifestyle quickly discovers that this job title is totally mystifying for the uninitiated. For example, archivists frequently are mistaken for archaeologists and anthropologists. Identifying myself as an archivist often elicited this response from friends and relatives: "It really must be fascinating to study dinosaur bones, human skeletons, fossils, and ancient civilizations." [1]

Even august institutions like the National Archives and the Library

---

[1] Alsobrook, "A Portrait of the Archivist as a Young Man," 287.

of Congress have exacerbated this confusion. Professional staff in the Library of Congress's Manuscript Division who perform a variety of archival duties, from basic processing to reference, are designated as "manuscript librarians," "curators," and "subject area specialists." The National Archives' presidential libraries contain relatively small volumes of books and other published materials. With their massive collections of presidential and federal records and personal papers, these "libraries" inarguably are archives. Yet, thanks to President Franklin D. Roosevelt's precedent, they will be known in perpetuity as "libraries."

Differentiating between librarians and archivists traditionally has focused on their respective collections' formats. Books, magazines, periodicals, and other published items are librarians' purview. Archivists primarily deal with original unpublished documents and manuscripts. Yet even this basic distinction has become blurred as librarians *and* archivists have acquired collections of photographs, film, audiotapes, and digitized records.[2]

This confusion over nomenclature reminds us of the apocryphal tale of an archivist's earnest young son who struggled to describe his father's job to classmates. During multiple "show and tell" sessions, the child explained in excruciating detail the basic archival procedures of preservation, arrangement, and description. After disquieting responses equating his father to an atheist, agnostic, or the Antichrist, the exasperated youngster shrugged and sadly said, "My Daddy's dead."[3]

Even those archivists who have ascended to the profession's most heralded ranks are not exempt from cases of mistaken identity. Don W. Wilson, former Archivist of the United States, once remarked that he "often received some very strange introductions" because "most people did not know how to pronounce the word archivist—let alone know what it meant." He was "introduced as Ar*chiv*ist of the US—a couple of times as the Anarchist of the US—once as the Alchemist of the US, and perhaps

---

[2] Ibid.; William E. Leuchtenburg, "R. D. W. Connor and the Creation of Presidential Libraries," *Carolina Comments* 51/4 (October 2003): 133–39; Raymond Geselbracht and Timothy Walch, "The Presidential Libraries Act After 50 Years," *Prologue* 37/2 (Summer 2005): 49; Don W. Wilson, "Presidential Libraries: Developing to Maturity," *Presidential Studies Quarterly* 21/4 (Fall 1991): 771–72, 778–79.

[3] Alsobrook, "A Portrait of the Archivist as a Young Man," 287–88.

most memorable of all…as the Archbishop of the United States."[4]

Despite such malapropisms, archivists have been "hiding in plain sight" in the United States since the earliest days of our republic. Today we find them deeply embedded throughout the strata of our society and government—in public and private archival organizations, libraries, museums, courts, corporations, and ecclesiastical institutions. Befitting our nation's diverse historical, ethnic, and cultural tapestry, specialized archives are devoted to women, African Americans, Native Americans, Latinos, agriculture, art, aviation, architecture, literature, outer space, photography, film, and music. Furthermore, unlike forty years ago, archivists now have to contend with the "brave new world" of cyberspace. The unprecedented proliferation of electronic and digitized records has demanded more sophisticated technical training and greater cooperation among archivists, records managers, librarians, and information specialists.[5]

During and after my archival career, whenever I spoke publicly about presidential libraries, someone in the audience inevitably asked, "How can a student prepare for a job like yours?" While obviously flattered that civilians found my work interesting, I usually responded that many different pathways could lead to a very fulfilling professional life as an archivist. I added that although archival work is fascinating and intellectually stimulating, particularly for a historian, it also at times is incredibly monotonous, boring, and mentally debilitating. I thus tried to remove some of the glitter and sheen from a job that I obviously loved.

My own archival preparation was not remarkably unique. After about

---

[4] Don W. Wilson, "Presidential Records: Evidence for Historians or Ammunition for Prosecutors," Samuel Lazerow Lecture, Simmons College, Boston, MA, 3 April 1997, typescript in DA Collection. Dr. Wilson subsequently published a revision of his remarks under the same title in the *Government Information Quarterly* 14/4 (October 1997): 339–49. Wilson emphasized the second syllable of the word "archivist."

[5] Alsobrook, "A Portrait of the Archivist as a Young Man," 288–89; Edward Weldon, "Archives and the Challenges of Change," *American Archivist* 46/2 (Spring 1983): 125, 131–32; Gerald Beasley, "Curatorial Crossover: Building Library, Archives, and Museum Collections," *RBM: A Journal of Rare Books, Manuscripts, and Cultural Heritage* 8/1 (Spring 2007): 20–28; Conrad De Aenlle, "Digital Archivists, Now in Demand," *New York Times*, 8 February 2009, http://nytimes.com/2009/02/08/jobs/08starts.html (accessed 15 February 2009).

four years toiling as a high school social studies instructor, I earned a master's in history at West Virginia University. Although I thoroughly enjoyed teaching, because of a huge surplus of history PhDs in the early 1970s, the university job market was extremely bleak. I had to find a nontraditional history niche outside the classroom. In 1972 I discovered Auburn University's new Archival Training Program for history graduate students. Auburn's program—the only specialized collegiate training of this genre at the time in the Deep South—combined formal academic studies in history and archival administration with practical experience, highlighted by a summer internship at the National Archives regional branch in East Point, Georgia.[6]

My three years at Auburn thoroughly prepared me for my first archival job in 1975 at the Alabama Department of Archives and History (ADAH) in Montgomery, the sepia-toned "Cradle of the Confederacy." I launched my presidential libraries career in January 1977 at the National Archives (the "Mothership") in Washington, DC. After about ten months of archival classroom instruction and practical training, I was detailed for three years to the National Archives liaison office in the White House. Afterward, I served in three presidential libraries for thirty years until my retirement in 2007.[7]

Unlike my archival training pathway, several of my presidential libraries' colleagues went directly from history graduate programs to the National Archives. Donald B. Schewe, after combat duty in Vietnam as an Army infantry officer, earned an MA in history at the University of Nebraska in June 1968. He then left his native state and enrolled in Ohio State University's PhD history program.[8]

---

[6] David E. Alsobrook, "The Auburn University Archival Training Program," paper presented at conference, "Archives by Degree: Academic Preparation for the Archival Profession," Society of Georgia Archivists Fall Meeting, Emory University, Atlanta, GA, 17 November 1983, typescript in DA Collection. The author later published this paper under the same title in *Provenance: Journal of the Society of Georgia Archivists* 2/2 (Fall 1984): 49–53. Further citations hereafter will be to the published article.

[7] Alsobrook, "A Portrait of the Archivist as a Young Man," 289–91, 295–99, 310–18.

[8] Donald B. Schewe email to DA, 19 February 2019, DA Collection.

In late winter or early spring 1971, Daniel J. Reed, Assistant Archivist for Presidential Libraries, traveled to Columbus, Ohio, to recruit new archivists for the National Archives training class. Don Schewe later wrote about that occasion:

> I was interviewed by Dan Reed at Ohio State. His daughter was a student there at that time. I really think it was a trip to see his daughter, thinly disguised as a recruiting trip. Jon Heddesheimer and I and at least ten other graduate students were in one ten-minute (if that) interview. All I remember...was his showing us how to apply. After that, I was the only veteran on the list—they had to take me to get to the people below me on the list. I had a telephone interview later, and they asked me about Eisenhower and Kansas— They really needed someone who would go to NLE [the Eisenhower Library] and stay.[9]

Dan Reed selected Schewe and Heddesheimer to join the new class of National Archives trainees who gathered in Washington, DC, in September 1971. Two other classmates were Tom Gedosch and Ron Swerczek. Reed quickly nicknamed Schewe, Heddesheimer, Gedosch, and Swerczek the "German Mafia." Schewe recalled, "We were somewhat unique because we all were either Ph.D.'s or ABD [All But Dissertation] when we arrived. I don't believe any of the other classes before us had more than one Ph.D."[10] Six years later, when I was a National Archives trainee, my supervisor Trudy Huskamp Peterson fondly recited the names of the "German Mafia," much like a tongue-twisting pronunciation exercise.

After completing his training in autumn 1972, Schewe weighed three job options: the Nixon Presidential Papers Staff in the White House, the Eisenhower Library in Abilene, Kansas, and the nation's first presidential library established by Franklin D. Roosevelt in Hyde Park, New York. Schewe had visited the FDR Library as a trainee and decided to begin his career as an archivist in the bucolic Hudson River Valley. Between 1972 and 1981, he held positions as archivist, supervisory archivist, and assistant director at the FDR Library. In 1981 he became the director of the Carter Presidential Materials Project in Atlanta, Georgia, and subsequently

---

[9] Ibid. For biographical information about Daniel J. Reed, see ch. 2, 45n.1.
[10] Donald B. Schewe email to DA, 19 February 2019, DA Collection.

served as the Carter Library's first director.[11]

Another trained historian, Martin I. Elzy, a native son of Sullivan, Illinois, earned his undergraduate and master's degrees in the late 1960s at Eastern Illinois University. Around 1970 Elzy entered graduate school at Miami University (Ohio). He taught world history at Franklin High School in Ohio in 1972–1973 and completed his PhD in American diplomatic history three years later. Following his National Archives training in 1973–1974, he was assigned as an archivist to the Lyndon B. Johnson Library in Austin, Texas, where he coordinated the declassification of documents. In January 1981, Elzy transferred to the Carter Presidential Materials Project, later serving as the Carter Library's first assistant director, a position he held until his retirement in 2003.[12] Elzy, Schewe, and I were colleagues for ten years (1981–1991) at the Carter Project and Library.

Our mutual friend, Dennis A. Daellenbach, was working on his PhD history dissertation when he joined the Eisenhower Library staff as a young archivist in August 1972. His recollections of that time include a precise delineation between librarians and archivists:

> I was an ABD historian, but my archives training was "On the Job"…and then being sent to…the Introduction to Modern Archives Administration class in October 1973.…One thing that sticks with me to this day,…is Frank Evans making it emphatically clear that librarians and archivists were two very different players.… Librarians work with individual published items, non-unique, with many extant copies, all of them already appropriately numbered and in order. Archivists, on the other hand, work with aggregates of related unpublished records and documents and papers, unique in character and requiring judgments about appraisal, preservation, arrangement, review for legal issues, full descriptions, and specialized

---

[11] Ibid.

[12] Martin I. Elzy oral history interview by Albert Nason, 20 April 2004, Oral Histories, Jimmy Carter Presidential Library and Museum, Atlanta, GA (hereafter cited as Carter Library), https://www.jimmycarterlibrary.gov/research/oral_histories (accessed 3 March 2019); Martin I. Elzy, "Recollections of My Presidential Libraries Career," email typescript, 15 December 2018; Martin I. Elzy, vita, email typescript, 17 February 2019, DA Collection.

reference.[13]

If there exists a more accurate description of the variation between the basic responsibilities of librarians and archivists, I have not seen it. After his departure from Abilene, Daellenbach held senior supervisory positions at the Ford and Reagan libraries.[14]

The "historians' portal," exemplified by the careers of Daellenbach, Elzy, and Schewe, was one popular, well-traveled avenue for aspiring archivists. Some of my friends and colleagues, however, unintentionally became archivists. When Mary Elizabeth Ruwell graduated in 1970 with a BS in French from Georgetown University, she applied for entry into the United States Foreign Service. Since she also had studied Russian as an undergraduate, her immediate, ulterior motive was to accompany a State Department exhibit that was scheduled to travel to the Soviet Union. Meanwhile, INA Corporation (formerly known as the Insurance Company of North America and now as CIGNA) in Philadelphia hired her to track financial data on several French companies. After rejecting an INA secretarial job offer, Ruwell transferred as a trainee to the company's small museum and archives. INA agreed to fund her graduate school tuition expenses and fees for Frank Evans's Modern Archives Institute at the National Archives. "So, I had a new career, and loved it," she later declared.[15]

She also chronicled the progress of her academic and archival training in the mid-1970s:

> In addition to enrolling in graduate school (American Civilization dept. at the University of Pennsylvania), I learned a lot from the two-week program at the National Archives and at the week-long workshop at the Ohio Historical Society. But my real inspiration was Penny Alum, who taught me about preservation, arrangement and description and to appreciate business archives. I also became active in the Mid-Atlantic [Regional] Archives Conference (MARAC) which was just starting up. After I finished my M.A. at Penn, I put in an application for the National Archives....Then I was offered a job as a GS 07-09-11 in Presidential Libraries [in]

---

[13] Dennis A. Daellenbach email to DA, 18 October 2018, DA Collection.
[14] Dennis A. Daellenbach email to DA, 31 December 2018, DA Collection.
[15] Mary Elizabeth Ruwell, "Internship at National Archives, 1977–79, Reminiscences," email typescript, 29 January 2019, DA Collection.

1976! I was part of a group of new hires, who were interns targeted at eventually working on the Nixon Presidential papers.[16]

Ruwell and I served together as National Archives trainees in 1977. Following three years as an archivist at the Nixon Presidential Materials Project, she returned to Philadelphia in 1981 and established an archives at her alma mater's anthropological and archaeological museum. That fall I greeted her from my posting at the Carter Presidential Materials Project: "I hope that you don't think I've forgotten you since we both went in opposite directions from Washington. I trust that you're happily settled into your position at the University of Pennsylvania, [and] your job allows you time to work on your dissertation. I know it's good to be back close to your sources, professors, etc."[17]

Ruwell ultimately published her dissertation as a historical monograph on eighteenth-century American marine insurance. Combining her diverse academic interests and archival and museum experience, she pursued an interdisciplinary career. She formerly led the Smithsonian Institution's National Anthropological Archives and the Peterson Air and Space Museum in Colorado. Since 2004, she has served as Archivist and Chief of Special Collections at the United States Air Force Academy.[18]

These brief career vignettes provide a cursory glimpse into how a few of my colleagues and I became archivists. This miniscule sampling of "archival lives" obviously does not produce any quantifiable results that might be found in a larger survey. During my thirty years as an archivist, I participated in several nationwide studies relating to training, career goals, and job satisfaction. I responded to multiple questionnaires on these topics and later read the published findings. All I can remember today about these surveys is that they revealed that archivists came from many different academic backgrounds and were often dissatisfied with their salaries—

---

[16] Ibid.

[17] DA to Mary Elizabeth Ruwell, 26 October 1981, DA Collection.

[18] Mary Elizabeth Ruwell email (with attached vita) to DA, 15 January 2019, DA Collection; Regina Reynolds and Mary Elizabeth Ruwell, "Fire Insurance Records: A Veritable Resource," *American Archivist* 38/1 (January 1975): 15–21; Mary Elizabeth Ruwell and Eleanor M. King, "From the Archives: Rediscovering the Eskimo," *Expedition* [Journal of University of Pennsylvania's University Museum of Archaeology and Anthropology] 25/2 (Winter 1983): 2–4.

"revelations" that were well-known within our profession.[19]

I am unaware of the existence of any "best practices" formula for academic and practical preparation that guarantees a felicitous, productive archival career. Although no single academic discipline is essential for *all* archivists, undergraduate and graduate degrees in history can provide a basic foundation for entry-level positions in the field. Robert Bohanan, a veteran archivist with the Eisenhower and Carter libraries and at the National Archives, asserts: "My [history] M.A. taught me how the history profession worked. How historians did research, and what they did...to turn it into historical literature. That helped me in dealing with researchers, but my experience has taught me that some of the best reference archivists I've known never had a degree in history—bachelor's, master's, or Ph.D."[20]

Similarly, Charlaine Burgess McCauley, who was an eighteen-year-old freshman music major at Oglethorpe University when she joined the Carter Presidential Materials Project staff in the early 1980s, was one of the best processing archivists I ever supervised.[21] Martin Elzy, who also supervised her, views a history master's as a solid entry-level basis for recruitment but adds, "I know a scientific archives (and many other specialties) might prefer something else."[22]

Other examples abound in the archival universe that support Elzy's point about specialization. Very early in my supervisory experience, I recognized the difficulty of identifying archivists whose expertise perfectly matched specific assignments. Nevertheless, speaking about the "ideal archival world" in 1983, I briefly noted: "[A] major in American literature would prove invaluable to an archivist processing the papers of literary figures like Thomas Wolfe and William Faulkner. Likewise, a mathematics,

---

[19] Misc. archival career surveys and questionnaires, ca. 1974–1998, Archival Professional Activities File; Jimmie Purvis email to DA, 26 February 2019, both in DA Collection.

[20] Robert D. Bohanan email to DA, 7 February 2019, DA Collection.

[21] DA to Charlaine Burgess, 21 October 1991, 22 November 1992, 27 July 1993; DA to James R. Kratsas, 20 May 1992, DA Collection. Ms. McCauley later earned an MA in history and pursued an archival career at the LBJ Library. However, she never lost her love for music.

[22] Martin I. Elzy email to DA, 7 February 2019, DA Collection.

physics, or engineering background might aid an archivist working on the papers of Werner von Braun. In dealing with the papers of a German immigrant in Nebraska, a reading knowledge of the language would be necessary."[23]

I once asked Mary Elizabeth Ruwell at the Air Force Academy to weigh in about academic preparation for archivists. A staunch proponent of archival training "as a combination of academic and practical experience," she responded, "For Presidential libraries and the National Archives, it makes sense to me to have the American history requirement."[24] I immediately recalled that performing my duties at ADAH and presidential libraries would have been exceedingly problematic without an academic background in Alabama and US history.

Ruwell also cited a specific example from her own professional experience in which another academic specialty rather than history was more appropriate for an archivist. She reminded me that during the 1990s, the Academy of Certified Archivists, following protracted discussions, "settled on an M.A. in any discipline and a test for knowledge specialized for archives." "I always felt a good example of someone who was a good archivist," she further noted, "was Willow Powers, an anthropologist (Ph.D.), but who attended enough workshops and read enough material to pass the certified archivist exam. Since she works mainly with anthropology museums and Native American archives, she really needs the academic background."[25]

Any balanced, substantive discussion of archival training assuredly must include some assessment of graduate programs in librarianship. Over the past thirty years or so, archivists have enhanced their knowledge, résumés, and job prospects by supplementing graduate degrees in history and other academic fields with a master's in library science (MLS). As these programs gained popularity, the American Library Association (ALA) formulated standard accreditation criteria for universities that granted the MLS.

In the mid-1970s, when Robert Bohanan was considering an archival

---

[23] Alsobrook, "Auburn University Archival Training Program," 50.
[24] Mary Elizabeth Ruwell email to DA, 6 February 2019, DA Collection.
[25] Ibid.

career, his job market research revealed that the two "best degrees" for entry-level positions in the field were a history MA and an MLS. After earning his master's in history at Memphis State University, he enrolled in the ALA-accredited MLS program at Peabody College in Nashville, Tennessee. Although the Peabody curriculum lacked any archival courses, he worked in the Vanderbilt University Archives in a position similar to his part-time undergraduate job at Memphis State University.[26]

In his estimation, this melding of academic and "hands-on" experience was invaluable: "By the time I hit the job market I knew how to process,...to do reference, and I had a basic understanding of the principles of archival science. [T]he M.L.S. [gave] me a broader understanding of information science and information technology....This helped me out tremendously as automation and cybernation changed society in the 1980s and changed archives in our careers."[27]

While his MLS studies expanded Bohanan's familiarity with the new field of "information technology," the 1980s were unsettling, traumatic years for archival antediluvians like myself who learned our craft before the advent of computers. The vast federal bureaucracy, including the National Archives and presidential libraries, systematically replaced typewriters with "clunky" word processors and experimental automated systems. Martin Elzy, who transitioned more smoothly than I did to electronic equipment at the Carter Library, pragmatically embraced computerization as a modernized means of facilitating our basic archival tasks.[28]

Thirty-five years ago, Robert Bohanan tagged me and other archivists who stubbornly resisted the onslaught of the electronics revolution as "Neo-Luddites"—philosophical heirs of the crazed, wild-eyed, early nineteenth-century foes of British industrialization who sabotaged textile equipment.[29] I personally thought at the time that we more closely re-

---

[26] Robert D. Bohanan email to DA, 7 February 2019, DA Collection.

[27] Ibid.

[28] Alsobrook, "A Portrait of the Archivist as a Young Man," 292.

[29] Ibid.; Robert D. Bohanan, "The Presidential Libraries System Study: The Carter Project's Experience," *Provenance: Journal of the Society of Georgia Archivists* 2/2 (Fall 1984): 37–38; Steven Levy, "The Luddites Are Back," *Newsweek*, 15 June 1995, 55; Catherine C. Mitchell, "Computers Are Only Machines," *Chronicle of Higher Education*, 16 January 1985, "Opinions" page;

sembled the genteel "Vanderbilt Agrarians" of the 1920s, who nostalgically yearned for a simpler, less mechanized society, than the earlier British industrial saboteurs. Clutching my IBM Selectric typewriter, in March 1984 I anxiously informed a friend in Texas: "No doubt the next generation of archivists will adjust more readily to computerization than I have,…[but] I'm not sure if I want to…. I think we'll always have to rely on the human touch in archival work, especially in processing and reviewing documents. Also, I think most researchers like to deal with a human being rather than [with] a terminal."[30]

Although my "Neo-Luddite" moniker firmly stuck to me, I eventually acquired a basic literacy in computer usage. I vividly remember, however, that Bohanan, observing my ink-stained fingers as I perused the *Atlanta Journal-Constitution*, boldly prophesied a time in the future when most daily news consumption would be delivered via a small, handheld electronic device. Bohanan proved to be remarkably prescient, but I never abandoned my belief that, regardless of new electronic innovations and equipment, the solitary archivist, girded with academic and practical expertise, would never become obsolete. Even the most powerful automated system could not replace the archivist's intellectual powers of reason and logic.[31]

The computer revolution of the 1980s severely jolted librarians as well as archivists. MLS programs of that era emphasized instruction in the basic principles of cataloging and reference, supplemented with courses in specialized libraries, audiovisual technology, bibliographical compilations, collection acquisitions and development, and children's literature. Prior to her librarian's career, Ginny Dunaway Young grew up in New Hope, Alabama, and studied history and sociology in earning her undergraduate degree at the University of Montevallo.

She later discovered that the University of Alabama's MLS curriculum in 1974–1975 was virtually devoid of computer issues: "I can remember one class that was taught by the chairman of the department, …about

---

Richard Conniff, "What the Luddites Really Fought Against," *Smithsonian Magazine* (March 2011), https://www.smithsonianmag.com/history/what-the-luddites-really-fought-against-264412/ (accessed 16 February 2018).

[30] DA to Estelle Owens, 26 March 1984, DA Collection.

[31] Alsobrook, "A Portrait of the Archivist as a Young Man," 292.

the libraries of the future. It really was incredulous to hear him tell of the technology that was 'probably' on the way and sounded ridiculously complicated." She wondered, "Who in the world would ever consider books not being all important and the source of most information in a library?"[32]

Like archivists who had to absorb computerization's "shock to the system" in the 1980s, Ginny Young forged ahead into this strange, alien world without any preparatory academic training. During her prolific tenure as a school librarian between 1982 and 2011 in Fort Worth, Huntsville, and Willis, Texas, she became a self-taught wizard in online research and a master genealogist in her spare time. She later offered a brief summary of that era: "I was fortunate to work with two other librarians [in Huntsville, Texas] who had more recent degrees, and technology had been stressed in their classes. I learned from them, but I never felt intimidated by the 'new library,' …[and] because of my love for research, I became the expert librarian that faculty members came to for advice."[33]

The career arc of Paul M. Pruitt, Jr., is slightly different from Ginny Young's. Before enrolling in the University of Alabama's MLS program, he completed his PhD in history at the College of William and Mary. Currently the Special Collections Librarian at the University of Alabama's Law School Library, he has produced an impressive array of scholarly publications on Alabama history and jurisprudence. Today his duties include coordinating collection development and special collections. Reflecting on the powerful electronic tools now available, Pruitt writes, "Of course, research in the legal world has been so completely transformed by WestLaw, Lexis, and Hein Online that it is hard to remember the pre-computerized days."[34]

His MLS training featured "minimal computer instruction—maybe a few hours in all." He initially learned how to catalog books manually and to respond to reference queries solely with printed sources. This entire process "was hopelessly out of date," he readily admits, "but it had the advantage of grounding us, forcing us to think like librarians without any

---

[32] Ginny Dunaway Young email to DA, 21 February 2019; Ginny Dunaway Young misc. text messages to DA, 23–24 February 2019, DA Collection.

[33] Ginny Dunaway Young email to DA, 21 February 2019, DA Collection.

[34] Paul M. Pruitt, Jr., email to DA, 22 February 2019, DA Collection.

help from a machine."[35]

After finishing his MLS, Pruitt participated in the grueling task of converting the old card catalog into an online system (ATTICUS)—"an agonizing sequence of inventory, bar-coding, and computer installation." After ATTICUS was fully implemented, he marveled at its streamlining effect on collection development procedures—instantaneously allowing him to identify and purchase titles. "In my own research," he adds, "I've been able to mix conventional print/archival research with the unrivaled ability of the Internet to pluck specific facts out of millions of scanned pages."[36] His only fear about online research is that it may deprive current students of "that 'feel' for context that has always been the mark of the scholar."[37]

Similar to the academic preparation of Paul Pruitt and Ginny Dunaway Young, when Ohioan Kathy G. Tomajko studied librarianship at the Georgia Institute of Technology in the late 1970s, her formal training included "a rudimentary programming class" and instruction in using multimedia and audiovisual equipment. She later concluded, "On-the-job training…provided most of my exposure to library technology."[38]

During this formative portion of her lengthy, productive career, she helmed the Georgia Tech Library's Information Exchange Center, which processed interlibrary loans and coordinated research services for faculty, students, and other corporate and nonprofit clientele. Utilizing a shared computer system, she relied on OCLC (the Online Computer Library Center) and two topical databases, Dialog and ORBIT, in serving her patrons. These two databases basically were early electronic prototypes of the World Wide Web. In that era before the availability of online, full-text sources, her computer queries produced topical bibliographies of published articles and research papers, "printed on a roll of thermal paper."[39]

Over the course of her forty-five years at Georgia Tech, Tomajko

---

[35] Ibid.

[36] Ibid.

[37] Ibid.

[38] Kathy Gillespie Tomajko, "Thoughts about the Effects of Technology on Library Education and Libraries," email typescript, 26 April 2019, DA Collection.

[39] Ibid.

witnessed the computer revolution's unprecedented impact on librarianship. She recently recalled: "I can remember to this day when it dawned on me, as I sat in my office in the Georgia Tech Library in the early 1980s, …it would be so wonderful and more efficient to have a computer on my own desktop."[40] Her librarian's dream soon became a reality. In the late 1980s and early 1990s, Georgia Tech purchased and downloaded magnetic tapes of bibliographical data into the library's computer system, thereby providing direct access to faculty, students, and staff. "Considerable librarian time" immediately shifted from performing online searches to instructing "end-users" in accessing these new databases and technologies.[41]

Echoing Paul Pruitt's experience, Tomajko concludes that among the most significant effects of computer technology on librarianship over the previous five decades was the conversion from the standard card catalogs to "online public access catalogs (OPACs)." Librarians' traditional roles quickly expanded beyond basic research services—they developed software and MARC (MAchine-Readable Cataloging) records standards; selected, purchased, and operated the computers; and taught their patrons how to use this innovative technology.[42]

After distinguished service as head of the Georgia Tech Library's Reference Department, Tomajko retired in 2015 as Associate Dean of Libraries. Four years later, she reflected on how computerization "altered the traditional academic library beyond recognition": "Many librarians provide virtual reference services (via web-based chat, instant messaging, text messaging, and e-mail), work in digitizing initiatives for publications in the public domain, teach information literacy and technology classes to their users,…develop the information architectures for improving access and research functionality,…[and] have continually adapted to new formats for information, such as electronic journals and e-books."[43]

---

[40] Ibid.

[41] Ibid.

[42] Ibid.

[43] Ibid. Academic libraries' accelerated production of digital content to ensure greater online accessibility for their specialized collections has demanded that their personnel become proficient in new technologies, including digital library architecture and software, database design and management, HTML coding, and

Perhaps one obvious lesson to be drawn from the Tomajko, Pruitt, and Young careers is that the computer revolution has significantly altered the traditional chasm between librarians and archivists, thereby enhancing cooperative efforts between the two professions. As more original documents and manuscripts (such as US census and military records) are digitized online, this collegial spirit hopefully will accelerate.

Moreover, the proliferation of public history programs with archival components and online MLS curricula has produced more enlightened approaches to antiquated concepts about training librarians and archivists. Mary Elizabeth Ruwell, who personally has observed many dynamic changes in training over the past three decades, offers cautionary but encouraging commentary: "I am somewhat appalled by the plethora of library programs that have one course on archives and encourage graduates to work in archives. On the other hand, I have been very lucky to have some great interns from online library M.A. programs, one of whom is working for me and another who just became head of our library reference department."[44]

Although the "ideal" archivist's résumé still remains elusive today, my former colleagues generally believe that practical experience is the most essential qualification. Robert Bohanan, for example, offers this succinct guidance on hiring: "So, if I was recruiting an entry-level archivist today, I would look for someone with a master's in information science from an ALA-accredited library school that had an archival program. There are a lot of those around these days. I would also look for evidence of internships in archives, because you really learn to be an archivist by doing. A master's in history would be nice, but I wouldn't make it a requirement."[45]

Jimmie Purvis, who has served as an archivist at the Carter, George H. W. Bush, and Clinton libraries, concurs with Bohanan's assessment of the importance of internships, workshops, and practicums. Purvis also

World Wide Web mark-up languages like SGML and XML. For further reading on this topic, Kathy Tomajko recommends Youngok Choi and Edie Rasmussen, "What Qualifications and Skills Are Important for Digital Librarian Positions in Academic Libraries?" *Journal of Academic Librarianship* 35/5 (September 2009): 457–67.

[44] Mary Elizabeth Ruwell email to DA, 6 February 2019, DA Collection.
[45] Robert D. Bohanan email to DA, 7 February 2019, DA Collection.

believes that "a heavy dose of introspection,…careful consideration and much thought" are essential for archivists in addressing problems that seldom arise during training.[46]

Carter Library archivist Keith Shuler argues that archivists must be "detail-oriented," well organized, and intellectually rigorous, with strong written communication skills. Shuler also stresses that archival tasks seemingly never are finished: "There will always be another collection to process, so if you're looking for a big payoff in the end, don't bother. The victories are small, sweet and disappear the next day when you start on the next project."[47]

These two veteran archivists thus suggest that certain personality characteristics are vitally conducive to archival productivity. According to Bohanan, the only "born archivist" he has ever known is Brittany Parris, whom he recruited to the Carter Library: "She self-identifies as OCD [Obsessive Compulsive Disorder]. She is compulsively organized. She loves to make order out of chaos. And I think that is the defining personality trait for any good archivist. You just have to love to put things in order!"[48]

Bohanan also relates the intriguing details of his lunch several years ago with Martin Elzy and Carter Library Director Jay Hakes and his wife. Anita Hakes was "amazed and amused" that Elzy and Bohanan, after paying the cashier, neatly arranged the bills in their wallets in ascending order, from ones to twenties. In response to her reaction, Bohanan said, "Money is paper and therefore it must be arranged."[49] Sweeping generalizations about the entire archival population's personality traits obviously are quite risky and easily can descend into excessive "psychobabble." Regardless of our disparate ancestries, DNA, and environmental influences, I personally think that the solitary nature of our work as archivists tends to make us more introspective and introverted than the general population.[50]

---

[46] Jimmie Purvis email to DA, 7 February 2019, DA Collection.

[47] Keith Shuler email to DA, 15 February 2019, DA Collection.

[48] Robert D. Bohanan email to DA, 7 February 2019, DA Collection.

[49] Ibid.

[50] For further reading on this topic, see Charles R. Schultz, "Personality Types of Archivists," *Provenance: Journal of the Society of Georgia Archivists* 14/1 (January 1996): 15–35.

After peeling away and weighing the layers of training, experience, and temperament that go into the making of an archivist, what remains for our consideration? I doubt that I can answer this question with any degree of specificity or certainty. However, in reflecting on my own life as an archivist, I perhaps can offer a few comments that may be illuminating. I firmly believe that, like archivist Jennifer Davis McDaid, we all are "lifelong learners." Furthermore, I strongly agree with her that "a good archivist is patient, organized, persistent, and thoughtful, ...likes working with people, is excited by a challenge, is open to change, and appreciates variety. It's not really like [the movie] *National Treasure*—but it is rewarding, and often exciting, work."[51]

I will let others who know me well and have worked with me over the years determine if I was "a good archivist." From the time I became an archival student at Auburn University in 1972 until my retirement in 2007 as the Clinton Library's director, I continued my pursuit of knowledge about the profession. Along the way, I was very fortunate to be mentored and guided by many wise, talented role models—teachers, supervisors, colleagues, and friends. Each of them—in ways great and small—inspired me and taught me the value of hard work, dedication, and preparation. Throughout my entire career, my greatest joys were passing on my knowledge to a younger generation of archivists and watching their growth and maturation, and personally witnessing researchers' excitement of discovery in collections that we had sweated over and opened to them.

I am deeply indebted to my dear friends and esteemed colleagues—all members in good standing of a relatively small archival fellowship. Their recollections and comments have given me a fresh perspective and deeper appreciation of our profession and shared experiences. We undoubtedly can ruminate *ad nauseum* about best practices in archival education, the various nuances of our jobs, and exactly what is this strange creature known as an archivist.

Regardless, beyond such philosophical musings, I think we all have experienced certain "Eureka!" moments in our lives as archivists. For me,

---

[51] Jennifer Davis McDaid, "Alternatives to the Academic Job Market—Archival Work," August 2006, http://thesawh.org/wp-content/uploads/2012/06/Alternatives_to_the_Academic_Job_Market.pdf (accessed 26 February 2019).

that particular realization occurred during an oppressively hot afternoon in mid-summer 1973. I climbed into the loft of a barn in rural Chambers County, Alabama, to retrieve and "triage" the records of a defunct cotton and mercantile company.[52] Sweating profusely and covered with dirt, hay, and cotton lint, at that precise moment I knew I had found my life's work.

---

[52] Alsobrook, "Auburn University Archival Training Program," 53; Angie Lowry, "All the President's Stuff," *Auburn Magazine* 5/1 (Spring 1998): 15.

Chapter 1

"The Loveliest Village":
The Auburn University Archival Training Program

Sweet Auburn! The loveliest village on the plain...
—from Oliver Goldsmith's poem,
"The Deserted Village," 1770

My earliest, most distinctive memories are of living in World War II surplus housing around 1949 in Chickasaw in Mobile County. My parents came to Mobile in 1942 to work in the defense industry at Brookley Field. Six years later, after my father's service in the US Navy and completion of his studies at Alabama Polytechnic Institute (API) in Auburn, they returned (with me) to Mobile. Growing up in Mobile between 1948 and 1964, I always considered the Port City to be my hometown. Although my younger sister was the only member of our small family who was born in the city, we all thought of ourselves as Mobilians.[1]

Our family's roots lay about 250 miles northeast of Mobile in Eufaula, where my parents and I were born. I spent many idyllic summers and holidays with my grandparents in this small town in East Alabama. Historically, Eufaula had thrived first as an antebellum cotton port on the Chattahoochee River, and then from the early 1890s into the mid-twentieth century as the site of two textile mills. During my boyhood in the 1950s, Eufaula was still a prosperous cotton mill town—a significant "jewel in the crown" of the Comer family's vast textiles empire in Alabama.[2]

Although I first saw the light of day in Eufaula in September 1946, my birthplace easily could have been sixty miles north, in Auburn's API Infirmary. My father was in the first wave of World War II veterans who

---

[1] Alsobrook, "The Best Years of Their Lives," 343–44, 359–60; Alsobrook, *Southside*, 93–94, 189–90; Thomas N. Alsobrook interview; DA notes, ca. September 1977; "My Father," n.d., DA Collection.

[2] Alsobrook, *Southside, passim.*

enrolled in colleges under the auspices of the GI Bill. He and my mother decided that she would return before my birth to Eufaula, facilitating access to her physician and my grandparents' free babysitting services. I thus became the first member of my family who was born in a hospital rather than at home. While my father finished his degree in Building Construction at API, I spent the first two years of life in a modest, sparsely furnished apartment on West Glenn Avenue in Auburn. I have no personal memories of those early years in Auburn, but my parents later pointed out where we lived in Professor E. W. Camp's "veterans' enclave."[3]

I returned to Auburn in June 1964 at age seventeen as a frightened incoming freshman, just a few weeks removed from high school graduation. With the exceptions of weeklong Boy Scout camps and summer vacations in Eufaula, my freshman year at Auburn University (AU) was the first time I was away from home for any appreciable period of time. Although I occasionally visited with my grandparents in Eufaula and my aunt and uncle in nearby Alexander City, like many college freshmen, I was extremely homesick in 1964–1965.

Auburn proved to be the ideal location for a callow freshman who had an adequate high school academic preparation, below-average ACT scores, and only a vague understanding of the overall collegiate experience's demands. The campus was small and self-contained. Moreover, the blurring of the traditional boundaries between "town and gown" produced an environment that was remarkably informal and cordially welcoming for newcomers.

Eighteen years after API's World War II veterans "invaded" the campus and forever altered the university's future evolution, their children, the baby boomers, arrived in early autumn 1964. API's ambitious postwar building program, the "Greater Auburn" plan, was woefully inadequate by 1964. With the student population rapidly approaching 11,000, classrooms and lodging were at full capacity.[4]

Auburn's congested campus certainly was no worse than during the

---

[3] Alsobrook, "The Best Years of Their Lives," 316–18, 329; DA birth certificate, 17 September 1946, Bureau of Vital Statistics, Alabama Department of Public Health, Montgomery, AL; DA notes, "My Father," DA Collection.

[4] Alsobrook, "The Best Years of Their Lives," 316, 338, 345.

postwar boom years. I believe that we generally were excited to have an opportunity to study at AU. If our parents' generation had not revolutionized the concept of a college education via the GI Bill, many baby boomers could not have enrolled at AU in 1964. Our families had bequeathed a precious legacy to us; we were determined to take full advantage of their gift.[5]

With few outside distractions, AU's quiet campus and town allowed me to concentrate on academics. All of my classes and the library were within easy walking distance of the dormitories and apartments where I lived. I did not own a vehicle until the last quarter of my senior year. Since I had no interest in fraternity-sorority life, my closest friends were roommates, classmates, and other students who frequented the Wesley Foundation adjacent to the Auburn First Methodist Church. I carved out my own preferred campus niche, with a heavy emphasis on classwork in preparation for a high school teaching career.

Despite the lack of any basis for comparison with professors on other campuses, I was impressed with my AU instructors, particularly those in English, history, political science, and physical education. Many of these teachers had settled in Auburn during the postwar boom years—like English professors Eugene Current-Garcia, Paul Haines, Walton Patrick, and Ruth Faulk. Several of my best teachers were young English graduate students, such as Albert Bekus and William Koon.[6]

However, the AU instructor who undoubtedly exerted the most dramatic impact on my life was a brilliant, lovely young woman from Birmingham—Leah Rawls Atkins. A world champion water-skier, she was married to George Atkins, who played and coached football for AU's legendary Ralph "Shug" Jordan. How she skillfully balanced her hectic schedule as a wife, mother, graduate student, and history instructor always remained a mystery to me.

Leah Atkins was a magnificent lecturer—she demonstrated an innate, God-given talent for infusing life into the driest, most mundane historical topics. I enrolled in her two world history courses in 1964–1965. Although I loved both of her classes, my most serious problem was an

---

[5] Ibid., 361–62.
[6] Ibid., 332, 338, 346.

23

acute case of homesickness. I missed my family and friends back in Mobile.

Near the end of fall quarter 1964, I told her after class one day of my plans to leave school and go home. She was not pleased. Without waiting for any further explanation about my decision, Atkins said, "No, you're not going home. It will ruin your life,…and if you quit you may not ever come back."[7] She simply refused to let me drop out of school in 1964. She patiently said, "Just get through the next quarter and see how you feel then about quitting." She gently nursed me though spring 1965, when my bout of homesickness finally abated, and I decided that perhaps AU was the best place for me. Over the next fifty-five years, while continuing to nurture and mentor me as a historian, she became a trusted friend.

Because of the positive influence of Leah Atkins and other instructors, my AU undergraduate years were vitally instrumental in preparation for the future. I learned how to study, conduct library research, write coherently, and think critically. For the first time in my life, I also acquired an ability to budget my time. These basic skills would be invaluable in my future graduate studies and career development.

My ascetic lifestyle suited me well in 1964–1968—when one quarter of poor grades meant immediate reclassification of one's draft status from 2-S (student deferment) to I-A (eligible for induction). During the Vietnam War, draft-eligible collegiate males had three choices: enlist, defer, or evade military service. AU was a politically conservative campus during the war; very few students or professors publicly opposed US involvement in Southeast Asia.

We all reached fateful decisions during those years. Many of my friends joined the Alabama National Guard, Reserve units, or Advanced ROTC (Reserve Officer Training Corps) programs. I do not recall any AU students who went to Canada or otherwise evaded induction. Several friends grew weary of the pressure to maintain good grades each quarter and enlisted, usually in the US Navy or Air Force. Both military branches offered attractive training and educational benefits, and enlistees were less likely than Army and Marine Corps recruits to serve in combat.[8]

---

[7] Leah Rawls Atkins email to DA, 20 August 2019, DA Collection.

[8] The obvious exceptions were pilots and US Navy corpsmen who were assigned to US Marine Corps combat units.

Soon after registering for the draft in September 1964, I began thinking about my military obligation. I decided to defer my service until after graduation in four years. After completing two years of mandatory Army ROTC in 1966, I failed a US Air Force physical for entry into the Advanced Officers' program, due to "unwaiverable extreme myopia." The medical technician at Maxwell Air Force Base in Montgomery who examined my vision was shocked at the results: "You can't read this line? Jesus Christ!" Immediately following my physical, an AU Army ROTC recruiter phoned me in Auburn and said, "Although the Air Force rejected you, we'll be happy to have you in our program. We need officers with your academic credentials." While flattered by his compliment about my grades, I wondered if any non-military service options were available to me.

Since the early inspirational days of President Kennedy's "New Frontier," I had been enthralled with the concept of serving overseas in the Peace Corps. In April 1967, I was selected for the Peace Corps Advanced Training Program to teach English in Thailand. The first phase of training was conducted that summer at Northern Illinois University, northwest of Chicago in DeKalb. A second training session was scheduled in Hawaii for the following summer after graduation. My Peace Corps introductory training, especially in mastering the complexities of the Thai language, was intensive. During that intellectually stimulating summer in rural Illinois, I joined about eighty other young men and women from across the US. We all shared a fervent, idealistic desire to serve our nation. However, unlike myself, the majority of our training class unequivocally opposed the war. Several were veterans of VISTA (Volunteers in Service to America) and had taught in Appalachian and Native American schools. Other trainees were active in the era's civil rights and anti-war movements. Being immersed in this diverse group deeply influenced my rapidly evolving views about the war.[9]

In July 1967, John West, an AU friend from Andalusia, Alabama, wrote to me, "What have you decided to do about that fungus on the toilet

---

[9] Misc. correspondence and notes, ca. June–August 1967, Peace Corps—Advanced Training Program (ATP) for Thailand, Northern Illinois University (DeKalb, IL) File, DA Collection.

bowl—the draft?"[10] West already had staked out his pathway to medical school, with the possibility of fulfilling his military obligation with the US Air Force or a deferment through the US Public Health Service. His question haunted me for several months after my return from Illinois. That fall I discovered that the Mobile draft board very likely would issue my induction notice during my Peace Corps stint in Thailand or immediately afterward. I found the prospects of serving two years in the Peace Corps, followed by active military duty, totally unappealing. In autumn 1967, I officially withdrew from the Peace Corps training program.

During my senior year at AU in 1967–1968, I decided to concentrate on academics, regardless of what happened with my draft status. However, after the Tet Offensive in 1968 and the escalating public opposition to the war, my enthusiasm for enlisting after graduation significantly waned. By that time, even my most politically conservative friends and my own parents thought that the war was a lost cause and not worth further sacrifices of "blood and treasure."

Furthermore, in spring 1968, several former classmates returned to Auburn with debilitating physical and emotional combat wounds. Associating with these traumatized young veterans ultimately led me to this decision: "If the Army calls, I'll do my bit for two years as a 'grunt' (enlisted man)."[11]

With green combat officers' casualty rates skyrocketing, I figured that serving in the enlisted ranks provided a greater chance of survival. Unless assigned to a desk or "in the rear with the gear," however, combat infantrymen's casualty rates were not appreciably lower than those of their young officers. Meanwhile, drawing upon their personal experiences

---

[10] John West to DA, ca. mid-July 1967, DA Collection.

[11] When I returned to Auburn for history graduate studies in 1972, many Vietnam veterans were finishing their coursework that had been interrupted by the war. For example, one of my high school and AU classmates, Bob Williamson, was a brilliant engineering student. He suffered a severe gunshot wound to his hand and spent his remaining months in the Army "pushing recruits" through basic training at Fort Benning, Georgia. When our paths crossed again at Auburn in the early 1970s, he said that the most positive result of his military service was meeting his future wife, who was a nurse, at the Martin Army Hospital in Columbus, Georgia.

during World War II, my parents urged me to enroll in OCS (Officer Candidates School) after graduation in June 1968. Their recommendation was based primarily on a belief that officers traditionally received better pay, food, and quarters than enlisted men. Although my parents meant well, they obviously had not seen the soaring casualty statistics for combat officers.

Within a few weeks after receiving my diploma in June 1968, my 2-S deferment was replaced with a 1-A notification. I spent the summer as a counselor at Blue Lake Methodist Camp, deep in the tranquility of the Conecuh National Forest of South Alabama. Throughout the summer, I anxiously anticipated receiving "Greetings from Uncle Sam," but my induction notice never arrived. In August 1968, after being hired as a high school instructor, I was granted a teaching deferment. When I enrolled in the AU graduate history program in 1972, the draft lottery system already had been implemented. With a high lottery number and the war incrementally winding down, I was unlikely to be drafted unless, in the words of an AU friend, "the North Vietnamese and Viet Cong were marching on Chattanooga."

Of course, in the late 1960s and early 1970s, the war's impact on an entire generation of Americans was no joking matter. My own draft history was not remarkably different from those of thousands of other young men. Of our three baby boomer presidents, also born in 1946, one enlisted in the Texas Air National Guard, and the other two held deferments. We all knew that the draft was grossly inequitable, and non-college whites and minorities were inducted disproportionately to those citizens with student, medical, and teaching deferments. If I did not serve in the military, somebody else had to take my place in the Army's "big green machine."

The Vietnam conflict barely resembled World War II, when virtually every young able-bodied American male either volunteered or was drafted for military duty. During the Vietnam era, an individual's future longevity depended on a combination of random factors such as income, political influence, education, and the roulette wheel of the draft and lottery system. As sardonically memorialized in song by the Creedence Clearwater Revival's lead vocalist, John Fogerty, each of us spared from Vietnam's horrific combat truly was a "Fortunate Son."

Like many other baby boomers, I actively searched for my particular calling in life; in the self-absorbed jargon of the day, this process was dubbed "finding myself." Perfectly happy and contented in the classroom, I thought that teaching would be my life's work. Yet, by 1970–1971, as a slightly burned-out high school instructor, I was eager for a career change. After four years of teaching English, Alabama history, civics, and social studies and monitoring study halls, cafeterias, and bus pickup zones, my creative and intellectual energy was atrophying.

To enhance my classroom performance, I wanted to pursue history graduate studies. Mobile County Schools reserved its financial aid for graduate study in educational administration for teachers and coaches who aspired to be principals. Since I lacked any interest in such graduate work, I paid my own tuition over three summers and earned an MA in history in 1972 at West Virginia University.[12]

In late 1971 or early 1972, while writing my thesis, I discovered a printed flyer about AU's new graduate-level history program with a specialty in "Archives Administration." At age twenty-five, I knew virtually nothing about the archival profession—academic prerequisites, duties, current and projected job markets, salary ranges, and working conditions. I could not distinguish between a Hollinger box or a Federal Records Center carton. I was even unsure of the preferred pronunciation of "archivist."

Yet, from the archival research for my thesis, I had acquired a deep fascination with primary sources—the raw, unpublished, original material that constituted the bedrock of historical study. Regardless of the history muse Clio's dulcet, seductive tones, I admittedly was enthused by AU's promise of *paid* assistantships for "qualified candidates." During winter 1972, I submitted an application to the AU Graduate School and expressed my particular interest in an archival assistantship. I was selected as a PhD history candidate and the first enrollee in the new AU Archival Training Program.[13]

---

[12] Alsobrook, "A Portrait of the Archivist as a Young Man," 300; misc. correspondence and academic transcripts, 1970–1972, West Virginia University Graduate School File, DA Collection.

[13] Misc. correspondence, applications, and notes, ca. 1971–1972, Auburn University Graduate School File, DA Collection; Alsobrook, "A Portrait of the Archivist as a Young Man," 300; David E. Alsobrook, "William Dorsey Jelks: Alabama Editor and Legislator" (MA thesis, West Virginia University, 1972).

In July 1972, about two months before the fall quarter, I moved from Mobile back to "The Loveliest Village" and began working under the vigilant tutelage of Dr. Allen Woodrow Jones, an intense forty-one-year-old son of Andalusia, Alabama. His official title was Associate Professor of History and University Archivist. He exulted in his new archives training program—the only one of its type then in existence in any college or university in the Southeast.[14]

Although Jones was not one of my undergraduate professors, his reputation as an academic perfectionist and self-avowed liberal firebrand preceded him. He abhorred laziness, intellectual slovenliness, and inadequate preparation and exhorted us to seek excellence in our academic and archival work. Whenever we fell short of *his* expectations, Jones typically unleashed a blistering compilation of our deficiencies. He usually laughed, cleared his throat, and delivered an impassioned sermonette along these lines: "God knows, I'm doing everything that I can to make y'all into decent historians and archivists."[15] These were not hollow words; he firmly believed in his message.

As to his attitude toward his graduate students, I once heard Jones colorfully described as an "equal-opportunity hard-ass." He treated everyone the same, regardless of their academic pedigrees, undergraduate honors, hometowns, or family connections. William A. Harris, originally from Searight, Alabama, about thirty miles north of Jones's birthplace, studied archival administration at Bowling Green State University in Northern Ohio before returning to Alabama to secure his teaching credentials through AU's College of Education. Recognizing Harris's exceptional talents and potential for an archival career, Jones expedited his transfer to the AU graduate history program.[16]

Harris had accrued an outstanding academic record and felt that he was well prepared for his first tutorial with Jones on assigned archival readings. Harris "had admittedly lazily" read the material, and Jones quickly gauged his level of unpreparedness. While he had been forewarned by

---

[14] Allen W. Jones email to DA, 13 March 2018; "AU Archivist Replies to Tuskegee Letter," (Auburn University) *Plainsman*, 7 November 1974, clipping, both in DA Collection.

[15] Alsobrook, "A Portrait of the Archivist as a Young Man," 301–302.

[16] William A. Harris email to DA, 3 June 2019, DA Collection.

other graduate students about "the explosive Dr. Jones," that evening Harris personally experienced this side of his new professor:

> It started off with a little grin and some shuffling of papers on his desk, and he leaned back in his chair.... [H]is office in Haley Center faced west looking towards the stadium or at least away from most of campus. I had been impatient and wanted to get home for some reason or the other and kept glancing out the window.... [H]e got himself more worked up as he spoke about the need to be prepared and the importance of the work. He was roaring by the time it was over, observing that I "had what it takes but...won't waste his time on laziness" and "there are plenty of students who would beg for this chance and maybe I mistakenly thought you were serious." ...[H]e closed the evening early and said, "[Y]ou come prepared next time or you don't come at all."17

This memorable tutorial with Jones shocked Harris because previously he "had found school fairly easy and never thought twice about it." This was the first time in his college career that a professor had "laid down the law" to him in this manner. Harris saw that Jones expected much more than a light reading of the material; he demanded a comprehensive, thoughtful understanding of the relevant issues and their practical applications. Jones carefully monitored Harris's performance during successive tutorials. "I buckled down and did the work," Harris remembers. "I didn't need to be told twice, that's for sure, and I wanted the career. I had always wanted this career. He knew that well enough, but knew that I needed a kick in the pants, too."18

Jones's written critiques of our work were equally withering and intimidating and clearly conveyed his exasperation or disappointment. During my tenure in the AU Archives, my major processing assignments included the voluminous papers generated by Alabama Congressman George W. Andrews, who served the state's Third District for over twenty-five years. Jones sequestered me within a secluded, caged basement corner of the Draughon Library. This project was ideal for a rookie archivist because I had to deal simultaneously with an array of preservation,

---

17 Ibid.
18 Ibid.

arrangement, description, and provenance issues.[19] Because of the collection's sheer bulk and repetitious subject matter and my own inexperience as an archivist, this processing task became increasingly debilitating. As my productivity precipitously declined, I hoped that Jones would commiserate with me and offer some comforting words of encouragement.

Jones, however, addressed my situation in a startlingly different manner. When I returned from the Christmas and New Year's holidays in January 1974, this note, emblazoned in blood-red ink, awaited me: "While you are away on vacation, I have been 'snooping' around down here! I must *confess* that I am *much depressed* on the *slow* 'progress' we are making on this collection. At the rate we are going, it will take another 2 years, and this *can't be!* I want some *positive suggestions* from you on how to get on with this job and get it completed by next year. Allen W. Jones (S.O.B.)."[20]

While Jones's fury definitely aroused my own ire, I also was saddened that my performance had disappointed him. I did not respond in kind to Jones's angry words; I cannot recall any follow-up discussion with him. Yet his wife, Grace Preiss Jones, privately said, "David, just don't fret about it too much. Allen actually is impressed with your work and is proud of you." She always intuitively knew when we needed her compassionate encouragement. We called her "Amazing Grace." More impatient notes and letters from her husband followed over the next two years, prodding me to finish this task. I finally produced a finding aid for the Andrews Collection in 1976.[21]

Perhaps Jones could have been more conciliatory or dealt directly with me rather than relying on his wife to convey his true feelings. But that was not his personal supervisory style. Nevertheless, I learned a hard lesson about the necessity of finishing archival projects that was invaluable throughout my career. Overtly or subconsciously, I incorporated this processing standard in guiding a later generation of young archivists.

As a student himself at API and later at the University of Alabama,

---

[19] DA email to Paul M. Pruitt, Jr., 7 February 2019, DA Collection; Alsobrook, "The Auburn University Archival Training Program," 52–53.

[20] Allen W. Jones to DA, 28 December 1973, DA Collection.

[21] Misc. Jones notes and correspondence, ca. 1974–1976, AU Archives—Cong. George W. Andrews File, DA Collection.

Jones was the product of a rigid academic system that discouraged collegial relationships with professors. I suspect that this hide-bound barrier inhibited Jones from lavishing effusive praise upon us while we labored in his archival vineyard. Yet this seemingly impermeable wall began to erode after we left the AU Archives.

Debbie Pendleton, one of Jones's graduate students in the early 1980s, remembers him in this way: "I first encountered the force that is Allen Jones in Historical Methods class, where he did all he could to separate the wheat from the chaff…. In that class and later in archival reading classes, I found Allen Jones to be an extraordinary advocate for his profession and his students. He had the big gruff grizzly bear exterior, but inside he was a loyal teddy bear who cared deeply for his students."[22]

William Harris, despite a rocky start in his first archival readings tutorial, largely agrees with Pendleton's view of Jones:

> He was to me generous and supportive and unflinching in his assessments, …and he was suspicious of anything that would seem to come between me and my career. He opened his home to me and counseled me not only professionally but personally as I know he did many others. He could be hard, and I never wanted to cross him. But I knew at the end of the day, for all the bluster and criticism and bold, readily shared opinions, that he wanted me to succeed. Of that, once he saw I was committed, I never doubted. It gave me real confidence. I had never had support like that before. It was personal and real.[23]

As faithfully revealed by Harris and Pendleton, our relationships with Jones were decidedly personal and matured with the passage of time. His obstinate, relentless demands in the pursuit of perfection yielded mixed results—he literally ran off any students he perceived as unwilling to pay the price for seeking academic and archival excellence. Among those who survived his rigorous gauntlet, several students rebelled in varying degrees—I certainly did. I am quite sure that when our lives first intersected in 1972, Jones accurately sized me up as rebellious, somewhat arrogant, and in his own distinct South Alabama vernacular, "full of piss and

---

[22] Debbie Pendleton email to DA, 14 February 2018, DA Collection.
[23] William A. Harris email to DA, 3 June 2019, DA Collection.

vinegar." Yet, as the final chapters of our training were written, he beamed with pride and satisfaction.[24]

Most memorably, when we all were financially destitute and frantically seeking archival jobs, Jones was our staunchest advocate. For example, his formal recommendations usually featured some variation of these words: "Mr. Alsobrook is dedicated to archival work and is not just merely another displaced, unemployed historian."[25] Such full-throated advocacy was vital to us during an era when traditional academic sinecures for historians were disappearing rapidly.

After he retired, Jones continued to seek archival positions for his former students. In late autumn 1992, for example, he contacted me: "I have a young man who is a great archivist and he is now with the UAB [University of Alabama-Birmingham] Archives. He would be interested in a job with you because his present appointment is for one year and will end in April '93.... His name is Bill Harris and is one of the brightest students I've had in several years. Received his M.A. last March and wrote a splendid thesis on the Mississippi massacre of 1886 in Carrollton."[26]

I am not suggesting that Jones miraculously morphed into Auburn's version of the beloved, avuncular "Mr. Chips" as portrayed in print and on the silver screen. However, as the years passed, our calcified professor-student relationships gradually shifted. And, to be fair, we all mellowed with age.

In November 1997, I received this warm, congratulatory note from Jones: "What a delightful time Grace & I had with all you folks at the Bush Library dedication. It was a great reward for me personally to see my students doing such a grand job. I'm really proud of you and the staff for doing such a professional job. It made all my years as a professor and archivist worthwhile to see you in action."[27]

Several months later, I labeled Jones in an *Auburn Magazine* interview as "one hell of a hard task master," whose archival program prepared me

---

[24] Alsobrook, "A Portrait of the Archivist as a Young Man," 303–304.

[25] Ibid., 303; misc. Jones recommendation letters for DA, ca. 1974–1977, DA Collection.

[26] Allen W. Jones to DA, 18 November 1992, DA Collection.

[27] Allen W. Jones to DA, 17 November 1997, DA Collection.

for a fulfilling career.[28] After reading my remarks, he quickly replied: "I am very proud to have had a little part in helping you all to develop the talents you have. This is what teaching is all about. No one will remember all this crap we publish, but they will never forget the…teachers who inspired and worked them the most."[29]

Lacking formal training in the profession, Jones basically was a "self-taught" archivist who acquired a wealth of technical and practical knowledge through his own historical research in primary sources at ADAH, the Tuskegee University Archives, and the National Archives. He also absorbed a steady diet of the published archival literature of the day. After he succeeded Thomas Belser as the second AU Archivist in the late 1960s, Jones began building his training program. He consulted with professors at American University and Wayne State University and analyzed their training regimens, which carefully balanced archival academic studies with hands-on applications. Jones applied this basic template in establishing his AU program.[30]

Under Jones's direction, we delved deeply into the standard archival principles—appraisal, preservation, arrangement, and description. Reminiscent of Professor George Petrie's "History Laboratory" at Auburn sixty years earlier, the AU Archives provided an environment in which students could experiment with theories and procedures—utilizing and refining them based on actual processing experience.[31]

By 1973 the AU Graduate School had approved the two academic components of Jones's program—"Directed Study in Archival Procedures, HY 628," and "Archival Internship, HY 650." Therefore, from its

---

[28] Lowry, "All the President's Stuff," 18.

[29] Allen W. Jones email to DA, 17 May 1998, DA Collection.

[30] Allen W. Jones emails to DA, 13 March 2018, 15 September 2019; DA notes, 15 September 2019, telephone conversation with Allen W. Jones, DA Collection.

[31] Jimmie Purvis emails to DA, 12 February 2018, 16 May 2019; Debbie Pendleton email to DA, 14 February 2018; Mary Swenson Stewart email to DA, 16 February 2018; DA notes, 6 September 2019, telephone conversation with Robert J. "Jeff" Jakeman, DA Collection; Alsobrook, "The Auburn University Archival Training Program," 52; Mike Jernigan, *Auburn Man: The Life & Times of George Petrie* (Montgomery AL: The Donnell Group, 2007) 48–49, 53–54, 201, 209.

inception, the AU program's strength lay in simplicity, flexibility, and an emphasis on practical applications of archival principles. Moreover, Jones unapologetically promoted his new training endeavor as a viable "alternative career portal" for history graduate students. His nationwide recruiting campaign attracted many talented young historians to Auburn, such as Robert J. "Jeff" Jakeman, a US Air Force pilot who had earned an MA at Valdosta State University in South Georgia. Jakeman viewed the AU program in 1980 as "another career pathway" beyond traditional research and teaching.[32]

Mary Swenson, a bright, soft-spoken young woman from Canby, Minnesota, who studied history at Iowa's Coe College, also was intrigued by AU's archival preparation opportunities. After finishing her BA in 1973, she weighed whether to pursue a career as a museum curator or an archivist. Her Coe College department chairman was a friend of AU history professor Robert R. Rea. "Before I knew it," she recalled, "I was on my way to Alabama."[33]

As the first two AU archivist-trainees, Swenson and I worked closely together in 1973–1974. Her processing assignments paralleled mine; she worked on the papers of Alabama Congressman Bill Nichols and the Alabama League of Women Voters. After she completed her MA requirements, Swenson's professional career was highlighted by service at the Birmingham Public Library in cataloging and collections management. Following her retirement in 2017, she credited the AU program for laying a foundation for her knowledge of "research methods, organization, and writing...." "[W]e were exposed to great primary sources," she later wrote, "and given the opportunity to 'really get into' the archival world."[34]

---

[32] Alsobrook, "The Auburn University Archival Training Program," 49–50, 52; "An Introduction to Graduate Study in History: A Handbook of Regulations, Requirements, and Advice to Graduate Students," unpub. typescript, Auburn University, 1984–1985; "Directed Study in Archival Procedures, HY 628," unpub. typescript, ca. 1973–1974; DA notes, 6 September 2019, telephone conversation with Robert J. "Jeff" Jakeman, DA Collection. Jakeman's major professor at Valdosta State University was historian Linda Hines McMurry, who completed her PhD at AU in the early 1970s under the guidance of Allen W. Jones.
[33] Mary Swenson Stewart email to DA, 16 February 2018, DA Collection.
[34] Ibid.

Since the AU Archives was Allen Jones's experimental laboratory, Mary Swenson and I subsequently became his "lab rats." This terminology may seem harsh, but I think it is accurate. While I am reluctant to characterize Jones as a "crazed archival scientist," he was an inveterate bibliographical compiler, and our required reading list grew exponentially larger as new publications appeared in print. In our periodic tutorials with Jones, we dutifully fulfilled these "lab rat" obligations by critiquing his reading list, thereby sparing future trainees from treatises that we deemed were redundant, pedantic, or inordinately technical. Despite our conscientious efforts to delete such material, approximately twenty-five books and seventy-five articles remained on the list.[35]

Swenson and I also were the first trainees to complete a summer internship in 1974 at the Federal Archives and Records Center (FARC) in East Point, Georgia. Regional Archivist Gayle Patrick Peters patiently supervised our individual training assignments in preservation, accessioning and disposal (A&D), and description. For the first time in our nascent archival careers, we also were assigned each day to research room duty. This task, I reported, required us to utilize "a wide diversity of archival skills" and to become more comfortable in our personal interactions with genealogists, historians, and other researchers, and it reinforced our appreciation of the archivist's role as a civil servant. We learned that processing was only one essential task performed by archivists—the final step was ensuring that the material was easily accessible to researchers.[36]

Our archival horizons now expanded far beyond Auburn to encompass the federal government's records holdings. As a historian, I especially relished digging into the "virginal" documents that scholars had never seen—akin to an explorer who stumbled upon previously unmapped territory. This experience was thrilling and exciting for a rookie archivist—a feeling that remained with me throughout my career.

For my A&D project, I examined a sprawling series of Immigration and Naturalization Service (I&NS) records, spanning the 1890s through

---

[35] Archival reading lists, ca. 1974–1975, AU Archival Training—Graduate Courses—Readings in Archival Procedures (HY628) & Archival Internship (HY650) File, DA Collection.

[36] David E. Alsobrook, "Summary of Activities at the FARC [Federal Archives and Records Center]," East Point, GA, Summer 1974, DA Collection.

the early 1950s. Analyzing this material within the guidelines of federal retention and disposal schedules, "I had to project myself into the future and attempt to determine the value of I&NS records to historians of the twenty-first century and beyond."[37] This assignment was not merely a training exercise. Gayle Peters and his staff approved my recommendation that this entire records series merited permanent retention.

In addition to the practical hands-on experience I gained from the FARC internship, it linked me with National Archives personnel across the nation—from Washington, DC, to regional branches in Boston, in Chicago, and on the West Coast. Later generations of archivists, of course, labeled this process as professional "networking," a term that I was not familiar with in 1974.[38]

Gayle Peters, who previously served as an archivist at the LBJ Presidential Library in Austin, Texas, became a seminal link in my professional network. I was enthralled with Peters's recollections of his archival sojourn in the Lone Star State several years earlier, when President Johnson was actively involved in the LBJ Library's programs.

I decided after our discussions that working with presidential papers would be an exciting opportunity for any archivist, including a neophyte like me. Peters introduced me via letters and telephone calls to Dr. Daniel J. Reed, Assistant Archivist for Presidential Libraries, and his deputy, Richard A. Jacobs, at the National Archives. Reed and Jacobs indicated that they might offer archivist-trainee positions over the next year. In the meanwhile, they recommended that I submit applications to the Office of Presidential Libraries (NL) and the various libraries in their domain.[39]

Returning to Auburn at summer's end in 1974, I had no idea how pivotal this internship would be in determining my future archival career. Nevertheless, I understood the internship's contribution to my own training portfolio and its value to future AU students. I reported to Allen Jones in my FARC evaluation, "I think it is fair to say that this experience was a

---

[37] Ibid.

[38] DA comments, quoted in Mark Samuelson, "Interns Help Out, Discover Careers," *On the Record: A Newsletter for the National Archives and Records Service* (April 1978): 4.

[39] Misc. correspondence, memos, and notes, ca. 1974–1976, Presidential Libraries Personnel File, DA Collection.

terrific success, considering…it was Auburn's premiere effort in archival training. Now maybe we can figure out a way to pay the next interns enough to keep them from starving."[40]

Jones was attentive to his students' most problematic needs while serving as interns, like stipends for food and housing. AU did not fund off-campus internships at that time. So Jones devised a reciprocal arrangement with FARC officials by which Georgia State University paid us a modest allotment for our living expenses and received a reimbursement from the federal government. Several future interns like Jeff Jakeman paid for their own meals and lodging, which were exorbitantly expensive in the Atlanta area, especially in comparison with the costs of living in Auburn.[41]

Jones also carefully assessed the FARC assignments to ensure that his students were not misused as archival "beasts of burden" because of a shortage of federal employees. Consequently, Gayle Peters assigned projects to us based on their substantive training value rather than his own processing priorities. In the early 1980s, Jones eventually expanded internship venues beyond FARC to the Carter Presidential Library in Atlanta and to ADAH in Montgomery after Edwin C. Bridges assumed the directorship.[42]

The AU program clearly was on the rise. During the decade between 1973 and 1983, twenty-seven trainees completed the program, fourteen of whom landed archival positions. Mary Swenson, Dowe Littleton, Bev Watkins, Paul Martin, Jeff Jakeman, Deborah Hay, and I were among this first group. After 1983, a larger wave of graduate students followed—Marty Olliff, Norwood Kerr, Steve Murray, Debbie Pendleton, Mary Finch, John Hardin, David Stanhope, Laura Spencer, Jimmie Purvis, William Harris, Mary Jo Scott, John Laster, and many others. They all embarked on highly productive careers with ADAH, presidential libraries,

---

[40] Alsobrook, "Summary of Activities at FARC," DA Collection.

[41] DA notes, 6 September 2019, telephone conversation with Robert J. "Jeff" Jakeman, DA Collection.

[42] Allen W. Jones to DA, 3 September 1981, 22 July 1985, 30 October 1986, 18 November, 18 December 1992; DA to Allen W. Jones, 10 September 1981, 31 July 1985, 5 November 1986; memo, DA to Donald B. Schewe, 5 August 1985, RE: "Pendleton, Gatlin, & Stanhope," DA Collection.

and other archival institutions.[43]

This steady production of well-trained archivists continued through Allen Jones's retirement in 1991 and Jeff Jakeman's tenure afterward. Building on Jones's foundation, Jakeman expanded academic course offerings to include seminars on archival history and additional specialized topics. He opened up selected classes to advanced undergraduates. He bolstered the internship with financial support from ADAH, the AU College of Liberal Arts, and the history department. Jakeman also partnered with archival programs at LSU and the Universities of Kentucky and South Carolina in creating a cooperative teaching lecture/seminar that was available via a live cable television feed at these campuses.[44] Debbie Pendleton praises Jakeman as "a wonderful teacher—kind, patient, encouraging and collaborative," adding that AU training "opened the world of archives to me and prepared me for a wonderful career of thirty-one years" at ADAH.[45]

Perhaps most notably, Jones and Jakeman built and nurtured the AU archival program with inconsistent financial and institutional support from the history department. Malcolm C. McMillan, the department chairman who tapped Jones to become the AU Archivist, reduced his history teaching load to two courses per quarter (in addition to the archives readings tutorial) but without any extra compensation for administrative duties. Taylor Littleton, the Vice President for Academic Affairs, later approved funding for three archival graduate assistantships and several under-

---

[43] Allen W. Jones, "Grad Students at AU who Completed Archival Training Program," handwritten list, August 1983; Steve Murray email to DA, 8 February 2018; DA email to Martin T. "Marty" Olliff, 24 April 2018; Martin T. "Marty" Olliff email to DA, 24 April 2018; DA notes, 4 February 2018, telephone conversation with Allen W. Jones, DA Collection; Alsobrook, "The Auburn University Archival Training Program," 53. The AU program attracted enrollees from throughout the nation. The initial wave of graduate students included eleven from Alabama, five Georgians, two North Dakotans, and one each from Florida, Mississippi, Minnesota, Arkansas, Illinois, Ohio, Wisconsin, California, and Arizona.

[44] DA notes, 6 September 2019, telephone conversation with Robert J. "Jeff" Jakeman, DA Collection.

[45] Debbie Pendleton email to DA, 14 February 2018, DA Collection.

graduate work-study positions.[46]

Despite the proven successes of Jones's archival program, Auburn suffered from a pernicious strain of academic snobbery that inspired historians to snipe condescendingly that archivists were blue-collar mechanics, technicians, and "bearers of water and hewers of wood" for "pure" scholars who upheld their discipline's traditions through teaching and research. AU's version of the "pure versus practical or applied history" schism periodically erupted with ferocity. Since Auburn's history department already was deeply factionalized in the 1960s and 1970s, internal squabbling over an archival program was analogous to fighting a raging inferno with jet fuel.[47]

When the indomitable Southern historian Wayne Flynt ascended to the chairmanship in 1977, he inherited a department that was deeply riven by internecine struggles over criteria for academic promotions and tenure and funding for "tangential" programs such as folklore studies, historical editing, oral history, and archival training.[48] Flynt compared the feuding parties to "cliques of adolescent girls tattling to the principal": "On occasion one or the other would come in the office, close the door, and report to me all the craven, unprofessional conduct and miscreant behavior of the other faction."[49] Blinded by their fierce infighting, they "tragically" failed from Flynt's perspective to visualize what was obvious to him: "We had a really fine faculty, with diverse skills, instincts, philosophies, priorities; and it was the composite of ALL of them which gave us strength and the endless sniping which weakened us internally and externally."[50]

Debbie Pendleton, who finished her MA about ten years after Flynt's baptism under fire as department head, hails his unique presence among other professors because he "valued wider life experiences and was very encouraging." As "a fairly non-traditional," slightly "older" graduate student, employed as a Huntingdon College librarian, Pendleton enrolled on

---

[46] Allen W. Jones emails to DA, 13 March 2018, 15 September 2019; DA notes, 4 February 2018, 15 September 2019, telephone conversations with Allen W. Jones, DA Collection.

[47] Alsobrook, "A Portrait of the Archivist as a Young Man," 308.

[48] Allen W. Jones to DA, 23 March 1978, DA Collection.

[49] Wayne Flynt email to DA, 10 January 2019, DA Collection.

[50] Ibid.

a part-time basis at AU. "I think that most of the AU history faculty felt all those factors worked against me," she asserts, with this powerful addendum: "I don't think the AU History Department as a whole has ever valued the contributions of that [archival] program on the students, the history profession, or the world at large.... They wanted young minds that they could 'own' and who lived and breathed the traditional academic life."[51]

In 2016, eleven years after Wayne Flynt retired and Debbie Pendleton and many other graduates of the AU archival training program had completed their lengthy careers, the history department became fixated on a "bright new shiny ball" in a reprise of the ancient academic debate over "pure" and "applied" history. The department, following protracted discussion and debate, voted to abolish the archival training program in lieu of new studies in "digital history." An amorphous archival option would remain available within AU's public history program. However, the archival training program that had launched so many successful professional careers now officially ended.[52]

Despite being an archival Neanderthal who learned and practiced my craft prior to the electronics era, when the earth was still cooling, I eventually learned to welcome new technology to our profession. I have become an enthusiastic devotee of digitization and any electronic innovations that facilitate archival tasks and procedures and expedite public access to historical data and analyses. I remember experiencing the same burst of excitement when an IBM Selectric replaced my battered old manual typewriter.

I am aware that today the bulk of archival coursework is offered within the curricula of SLIS (School of Library and Information Science) programs rather than through history departments. However, SLIS graduate study, accompanied by minimal academic archival instruction, will not necessarily produce "better" archivists. A basic grounding in historical knowledge, research, writing, and practical experience in the archival field

---

[51] Debbie Pendleton email to DA, 14 February 2018, DA Collection.

[52] Wayne Flynt emails to DA, 17 December 2018, 10 January 2019; Leah Atkins email to DA, 17 December 2018; Kathryn Braund email to DA, 16 December 2018; Steve Murray email to Kathryn Braund, 16 August 2016, DA Collection.

also are required. A wealth of theoretical expertise, without these vital pre-requisites, is simply inadequate preparation for any prospective archivist. I concur strongly with ADAH Director Steve Murray that SLIS graduates "arrive in the workplace with technical abilities, but not necessarily the ability to think historically, to understand the perspective of a record creator, or to put themselves in the shoes of a scholar who relies on thoughtful archival practice to facilitate research."[53]

In December 1983, after eleven years as a working archivist, I confided to Jeff Jakeman in Auburn: "I'm quite prejudiced, but I think the AU program stacks up favorably with most of the other[s]…in the entire nation, …[and is] as good as any in the South."[54] Thirty-six years later, I still stand by my statement. My AU archival training thoroughly prepared me for my future career—at ADAH, the National Archives, three presidential libraries, and the History Museum of Mobile. I rarely encountered any archival problem or issue I had not seen at Auburn. I cannot speak for other AU program graduates, but anecdotal evidence suggests that their experiences mirror my own. As for legacies, I think one that will stand the test of time is that those AU graduates who earnestly sought archival careers were universally successful in their quest and remained in the profession or a related field until retirement.

Additionally, I am personally aware of three former US presidents who have high regard for Auburn-trained archivists. For example, in December 1996, President George H. W. Bush asked me why seven of the thirty-two staff members working in his library were Auburn graduates. I briefly related the history and evolution of the AU archival program, which six of us had completed. He grinned broadly and replied, "Well, I see, and

---

[53] Steve Murray email to Kathryn Braund, 16 August 2016, DA Collection.

[54] DA to Robert J. "Jeff" Jakeman, 6 December 1983, DA Collection. AU's archival program blazed the trail for similar academic instruction during the 1980s and 1990s. For example, by the early 1980s, the University of Alabama, Emory University, and Georgia State University offered courses in basic archives administration. LSU and the Universities of South Carolina and Kentucky eventually developed comprehensive training programs that more closely resembled the AU model.

War Eagle!" Then he repeated the famous Auburn battle cry.[55] President Bush apparently filed away this fact for future reference. In April 1999, when PBS (the Public Broadcasting System) interviewed him at the library, he said to Jim Lehrer, "Now I have a trivia question for you; which school in the US has produced more archivists than any other?" President Bush slyly glanced at me, and I told Lehrer, "He's just piling on me a little bit."[56] While I never *actually* told the President that Auburn had trained the largest number of archivists in the entire nation, if he wished to say so, I had no desire to contradict him. He was quite proud of the Auburn Tigers who helped build the Bush Library, and that was good enough for me.

Those special moments with President Bush occurred over twenty years after I survived my PhD preliminary written and oral examinations in 1975 and joined the burgeoning ranks of unemployed history graduate students (ABDs) who still lacked finished dissertations. My far-flung Auburn family of graduate school colleagues and former professors like Rick Halperin, Estelle Owens, Bill Morrison, Leah Atkins, and William Warren Rogers sustained and buoyed me during that difficult time. That spring and summer, I dabbled at my dissertation research and played on an intramural softball team, "The Phoenix," primarily composed of history graduate students who were at loose ends after passing their "prelims." In my plentiful spare time, I cast a wide net in my archival job search—the University of North Carolina-Chapel Hill, Texas Tech, the Rockefeller Foundation, the Montana State Historical Society, the US Air Force Historian's Office, and ADAH. I also frequently corresponded with Daniel Reed regarding my pending job application with the Office of Presidential Libraries. As a last resort, I dusted off my teaching credentials and applied for high school positions in Auburn, Opelika, Eufaula, and Mobile.[57]

Although Allen Jones retained me as a graduate assistant at the AU

[55] DA email to Allen W. Jones, 24 December 1996; DA memo for the record, 2 December 1996, RE: "President and Mrs. Bush's Visit to Library Construction Site"; President George H. W. Bush to DA, 19 May 1998, DA Collection; Lowry, "All the President's Stuff," 16–17.

[56] DA email to Jean Becker, 12 April 1999, DA Collection.

[57] Alsobrook, "A Portrait of the Archivist as a Young Man," 309; misc. correspondence and vitae, ca. 1974–1976, Jobs/Personnel File, DA Collection.

Archives as long as possible, that modest stipend eventually vanished. My parents graciously invited me to return home during my protracted unemployment. However, at age twenty-eight, I did not want to move in with my parents and live in the bedroom of my adolescence. I began to regret ignoring my father's advice in 1964 about the future value of a brickmason's apprenticeship.

At that time, I lived in unit 19 at Village Court Apartments in Auburn. Ellen Lester, a senior in the School of Home Economics from Homewood, Alabama, resided next door in apartment 20. Her academic studies focused on designing and creating residential and office environments, including the selection of requisite furnishings, fixtures, and equipment. She quickly corrected my erroneous assumption that she was preparing for a career as an interior decorator. That profession, she indicated, did not require collegiate coursework in engineering drawing, organic chemistry, physics, calculus, microbiology, textiles manufacturing, and consumers' issues.

On the surface, Ellen and I seemed to have few common interests. However, living in close proximity to each other for over two years, we discovered that we shared many similar views about politics, education, religion, marriage, and life in general. Our casual association as next-door neighbors eventually evolved into a deeper relationship based on mutual love, respect, and trust. We decided to spend the rest of our lives together and planned to marry after her graduation in March 1976. Ellen later recalled, "I literally married the boy next door." However, since I had no viable employment prospects, even that joyous future event was fraught with uncertainty for both of us.

Subsisting largely on my parents' "care packages" and financial generosity, I expected that living as a transient vagabond in "The Loveliest Village" would be my fate for the foreseeable future. Since Auburn was my initial destination after departure from home a decade earlier, at least I was in familiar surroundings, among close friends with similar lifestyles and financial woes. In short order, however, unexpected events during summer 1975 completely altered the course of my life and career.

Chapter 2

Toiling in Milo Howard's Vineyard:
The Alabama Department of Archives and History

David, if you don't try to accommodate yourself to the other staff
members, you shall make my life a living hell.
> —Milo B. Howard, Jr., conversation
> with the author, ca. September 1975

In 1974–1975, I periodically exchanged letters with Daniel J. Reed at the Office of Presidential Libraries in Washington, DC. He strongly urged me to drop by his office for a visit if I was in the area on vacation or for dissertation research. With my parents' financial assistance, I flew to Washington for a meeting with him on 10 June 1975. I was impressed with Reed—a trim, white-haired gentleman in his early fifties. He was articulate, scholarly, and courteous, immediately reminding me of several former professors in Auburn, Alabama, and Morgantown, West Virginia.[1]

He asked why I wanted to be an archivist. I explained that an archival career would unite my passionate interest in history with a desire to preserve primary sources and assist researchers. He next asked which

---

[1] Daniel John Reed (1922–2012), a native of Springfield, Illinois, served in the US Coast Guard during World War II. He earned his bachelor's and master's degrees in 1947–1948 at St. Louis University, and a PhD at the University of Chicago in 1958. He taught history at St. Louis University and the University of Detroit. He served in three positions with the federal government: Assistant Chief of the Library of Congress's Manuscript Division (1959–1965), Chief Historian of the Smithsonian's National Portrait Gallery (1965–1968), and Assistant Archivist for Presidential Libraries at the National Archives (1968–1980). After retiring from the government in 1980, he became the Director of Historic St. Mary's Museum in Maryland, where he remained for five years. He died in February 2012 at age eighty-nine. See "Dr. Daniel John Reed." (1922–2012), *Find a Grave*, memorial no. 98429639, https://www.findagrave.com/memorial/9842-9639 (accessed 23 September 2019).

presidents were of special interest to me, and I answered several of the "modern ones"—FDR, Truman, JFK, and LBJ. Although I cannot recall the specific details, the remainder of our brief conversation was consumed with discussing each of these men and their historical contributions; Reed knew a lot about them, and I tried not to contribute anything trivial to the discussion.

As we concluded our brief meeting, Reed encouraged me to submit an application directly to the US Civil Service Commission, which hopefully would rank me on an official register of eligible archivist-trainees. I thought that our meeting went well, but Reed indicated that the current federal hiring freeze would delay his hiring any new archivists; he told me to be patient. That evening, two of my unemployed AU history comrades, Rick Halperin and Bill Morrison, met me at the airport in Columbus, Georgia, for the short drive back to Auburn. I thought to myself, "Nothing ventured, nothing gained."

Three days after my meeting with Reed, he dictated a private message for his file:

> On June 10 Mr. Alsobrook visited me in my office and after a conversation of perhaps 20 minutes I judged him to be a candidate of considerable promise for either the NL training program or direct employment by a Library. I say this also on the basis of his record and recommendations that we have from people who know him. He has one outstanding qualification—he has experience...as an archivist in the NARS Regional Archives in East Point, Georgia. He is a powerfully built young man—actually a smaller version of Will Jones [Truman Library Curator] in appearance and style. He is engaging, forthright, direct, and conveys strength of personality. He is quick, alert[,] and has a record of being an effective archivist. He also insists he has a strong personal commitment to archival work. This is what he very much wants to do.[2]

Back in Auburn, I was completely unaware of my interview's positive impact on Reed. For that matter, I did not learn of the existence of his written record until over fifteen years later, when NL purged our trainee personnel records and allowed us to keep any extra copies as souvenirs. By

---

[2] DJR [Daniel J. Reed], "Memo of Interview with Mr. David Alsobrook," 10 June 1975, Presidential Libraries Personnel File, DA Collection.

then Reed had retired from the National Archives. Although slightly embarrassed by his comments about our first meeting, this interview had launched my presidential libraries career, and for the first time I understood the value of my FARC internship in 1974.

Throughout June and early July 1975, I received a heavy flow of rejection letters in response to my various archival job applications—usually because I was an ABD or lacked the requisite supervisory experience. As I agonized over my fading employment opportunities, in mid-July I was summoned to Montgomery for an interview with ADAH Director Milo Barrett Howard, Jr. Since I had applied for a vacancy in the Manuscripts Division several months earlier, I assumed that this interview was for that job. Allen Jones and Milo Howard were not professional or personal friends; therefore, I did not anticipate my being hired at ADAH. However, Howard knew me from our earlier correspondence regarding my thesis research in 1971–1972.[3]

This interview was my first substantive private meeting with Milo Howard in his palatial office. Ramrod straight, seated behind his desk, attired in his customary immaculately tailored dark suit with matching vest, tightly knotted tie, starched white shirt with ornate gold cuff links, Howard *in situ* resembled a portrait of a genteel, antebellum Alabamian. The only visual accoutrement absent from this tableau was his stylish walking stick. A ubiquitous grey sheen of cigarette smoke floated above us as we casually conversed for over an hour.[4]

He politely inquired in his deep baritone voice about "my people"—their ancestral roots and occupations, and then asked about my career goals and marital status. In response to his two latter questions, I expressed an interest in someday working in a presidential library and identified myself as "engaged to be married." "When were you born?" he then asked. When I replied, "September 1946," he peered over his glasses at me with a whimsical smile on his face and revealed that another twenty-eight-year-old "baby archivist," Winston Walker, from Albertville, Alabama, soon would

---

[3] Misc. correspondence, ca. 1974–1975, Jobs/Personnel File; Alabama state employment application, 1975, ADAH Personnel File; misc. correspondence, ca. 1971–1972, West Virginia University—MA Thesis File, DA Collection.

[4] Alsobrook, "A Portrait of the Archivist as a Young Man," 310.

join the Records Management staff.[5]

Howard then described the Civil Archivist's duties as the custodian of official state records and newspapers. Since I had applied for the Manuscripts Division's vacant position, this revelation surprised me. He quickly clarified, "Oh, no—you'll be the Civil Archivist; Mrs. Jones [Miriam "Mimi" Jones] will move upstairs to private papers." He reiterated, "The job is in the Civil Archives," to remove any misunderstanding. I thus realized that he was offering me a job on a "take it or leave it" basis, largely on the recommendation of his former AU professor, mentor, and friend, Robert R. Rea. Although this job offer actually was a clever "bait and switch" maneuver to appease Mimi Jones, who wanted to "move upstairs," I gratefully accepted it and reported to duty in September 1975. I remained at the archives for about fifteen months.[6]

When I arrived in autumn 1975, Milo Howard was in the eighth year of his tenure as director—only the fourth person in that position for over seventy years. My office, the Civil Archives, was situated in the secluded southwest corner. Like a claustrophobic, dusty old curio shop, the Civil Archives was cluttered with compact rows of steel file cabinets and shelving, all bulging with legislative records and ledger books. The funereal air literally reeked of the combined odors of brittle, yellowing newspapers, manuscripts, and ancient leather book bindings.

A vintage photograph of Marie Bankhead Owen, prominently affixed to the wall near my desk, greeted me each morning. "Miss Marie" had succeeded the archives' founder, her late husband Thomas McAdory Owen, as director in 1920. She reigned with a paternalistic, authoritarian iron hand for over three decades. Her framed, spectral presence on the wall served as a perpetual reminder of the preordained succession of the four directors since 1901—Tom Owen, Miss Marie, Peter Alexander Brannon, and Milo Howard. The "Old Hands" in the various divisions and departments, several of whom had served since Brannon's day, acquired their status among their colleagues according to which directors they personally

---

[5] Ibid., 310–11.
[6] Ibid., 311.

knew.[7]

While Miss Marie undoubtedly wished to perpetuate her husband's memory in the state's historical annals, she gradually drifted away from his vision for the nation's first state archives. During the 1920s and 1930s, while bemoaning the dispersal and loss of Alabama's archival treasures, she became increasingly absorbed with her own personal projects—historical novels, plays, patriotic festivals and pageants, and genealogical studies.

Owen's complex, problematic relationship with the Historical Records Survey (HRS) in the 1930s provides a glimpse into her management style and vision for the archives' future. As a New Deal Works Progress Administration (WPA) program, the HRS employed hundreds of displaced, dispirited Alabamians whom the Great Depression had eliminated from gainful employment. HRS workers conducted county records surveys, transcribed original "at-risk" documents, prepared church histories, and contributed to Alabama's version of the WPA *State Guides* series. Miss Marie, however, viewed HRS positions as a source of "free labor" for ADAH and as political patronage sinecures for her friends. She assigned many of the HRS employees who staffed the department in the 1930s to genealogical tasks, such as clipping newspaper articles for the family history files.[8]

As the daughter of Alabama's veteran US senator, John Hollis Bankhead, Miss Marie inherited and wielded sizable political influence as the second director. For example, she energetically led a campaign to acquire federal funds for the construction of the state's "War Memorial Building" to honor Alabamians who died during the Great War. Tom Owen originally proposed in 1919 that the structure would serve dual purposes—as a memorial to those who "made the ultimate sacrifice" in World War I (and by extension the Civil War) and to house the state's historical records and artifacts. When the building was dedicated in 1940, Miss Marie was barely mentioned, despite her prodigious lobbying efforts in behalf of federal

---

[7] Ibid., 313–14; Richard J. Cox, "Alabama's Archival Heritage," in *Assessing Alabama's Archives: A Plan for the Preservation of the State's Historical Records* (Montgomery AL: Alabama Historical Records Board, 1985) 35–63; DA notes, telephone conversation with Allen W. Jones, 4 February 2018, DA Collection.

[8] Cox, "Alabama's Archival Heritage," 41–45, 49–55.

largess over the previous twenty years.[9]

ADAH's new home in reality was a monument that memorialized Tom Owen's unfulfilled dream of preserving Alabama's historical treasures. Only the second woman to lead an Alabama state agency, from 1940 until her retirement in 1955, Miss Marie reigned like a widowed queen over a hollowed-out department that lacked adequate funding and staffing. While ensuring that her husband's *History of Alabama and Dictionary of Alabama Biography* remained in print, she failed to move the needle forward on any substantive records or museum projects. She continued to pursue her own patriotic and genealogical ventures and tried in vain to resuscitate the archives' antiquated museum exhibits.[10]

When Miss Marie retired in her eighties, Peter Brannon, who was only about ten years younger, succeeded her as director. The least well known of the directors, Brannon was born in 1882 in Seale, a small East Alabama village in Russell County. Like Tom Owen, the balding, dour Brannon belonged to "The Thirteen," Montgomery's exclusive men's literary club. Trained respectively as a lawyer and as a pharmacist, Owen and Brannon had acquired their knowledge of Alabama history through voracious personal reading habits. Brannon also studied anthropology and ornithology in his leisure hours. He faithfully served as Tom Owen's aide-de-camp from 1911–1920 and then seamlessly transferred his fealty to Miss Marie. Although Brannon was a meticulous researcher and scholar, he lacked a deep interest in professional archival issues.[11]

Milo Howard was the next in line in the department's orderly succession. Since he squired "Old Peter Brannon" around Montgomery and the state until the elderly man's final days, Howard earned the "blessings of

[9] Ibid., 40–43; Robert J. Jakeman, "Memorializing World War I in Alabama," in *The Great War in the Heart of Dixie: Alabama during World War I*, ed. Martin T. Olliff (Tuscaloosa AL: University of Alabama Press, 2008) 201–11, 216–19.

[10] Jakeman, "Memorializing World War I in Alabama," 216–17; Cox, "Alabama's Archival Heritage," 45, 48–49, 58–59.

[11] Thomas McAdory Owen, *History of Alabama and Dictionary of Alabama Biography*, 4 vols. (Chicago: S. J. Clarke Publishing Company, 1921) 3:1210–11; 4:207; DA notes, 4 February 2018, telephone conversation with Allen W. Jones, DA Collection; Cox, "Alabama's Archival Heritage," 47, 60–63.

the king" as the next ADAH director. After his appointment in 1967, Howard patterned his management style on everything he had observed and learned from his predecessors' eras. Although Howard initiated some rudimentary records management functions, he devoted much of his time to chairing the Alabama Historical Commission and overseeing the construction of the new east wing.[12]

Like the archives' founder, Howard was an articulate, erudite, charming champion of Alabama's past. He and Tom Owen were members of the same state and local historical, civic, and social organizations, including "The Thirteen." After his marriage into the powerful Bankhead family, Owen became a skilled political operative in his own right. Howard was well versed in the state's political culture, but he deftly eschewed partisan causes whenever possible. Educated as a historian at Auburn, he seemed at times to yearn for the scholar's contemplative life. I once heard him wistfully remark that one of his greatest regrets as director was failing to ask the ADAH Board of Trustees for an extended leave of absence to earn a doctorate in history at Johns Hopkins University.[13]

Not surprisingly, Howard perpetuated the organizational structure that had existed since the time of Miss Marie. In the words of Edwin C. Bridges, who became the fifth director in 1982, the previous staff was organized along the lines of a "medieval kingdom," with all of the various divisions and departments subservient to the top of the hierarchy. The entire staff reported to the director, without any intermediate supervision. Each unit had its own eccentric quirks as to administrative and archival procedures, such as the production of finding aids. A central research room did not exist. Historians, genealogists, and other patrons conducted their research in each office—Maps and Manuscripts, Military Records, the Civil Archives, State Publications, and the Library. ADAH also had no centralized registration system for soliciting historical records, manuscripts, photographs, and artifacts. Records management schedules for official state records were seldom enforced systematically. This management schematic existed without any extensive alterations between 1940 and

---

[12] Cox, "Alabama's Archival Heritage," 63–65.
[13] Alsobrook, "A Portrait of the Archivist as a Young Man," 314.

1982.[14]

At the beginning of each workday in the 1970s, the staff assembled for a lengthy coffee klatch in the lounge. Howard delivered informal lectures or vignettes about Alabama history. On one occasion he recounted a cherished family tale about a day in April 1865, when Union General James H. Wilson's cavalry troops rode through Montgomery. One of Howard's ancestors, a diminutive young woman, was standing in her front yard when the federal horsemen arrived. After a trooper asked for permission to water his horse at the trough, she drove the "Yankee marauder" away with her riding crop. An extremely talented raconteur, Howard had a large repertoire of such historical lore, and we all listened attentively to his entertaining narratives.

Another daily ceremonial event was Howard's opening the mail in his office. All incoming and outgoing letters, regardless of their importance, passed across his desk. He personally signed the bulk of outgoing correspondence, including routine research queries. He or his secretary, Patricia Sweet, delivered incoming research letters to each unit, where the staff handled the requests and produced the relevant information and photocopies. We were expected to bring our research products to Sweet to be mailed under the director's signature. Since researchers usually contacted me by phone or letter, I found this procedure to be unduly inefficient and time-consuming. Consequently, after about three months on the job, without fanfare, I ignored this policy and personally handled all of the Civil Archives' research queries, thereby expediting our response time.

I enjoyed my research duties in the Civil Archives. During my first weeks on the job, Mimi Jones provided invaluable guidance and expertise. She was one of the few "Old Hands" who exhibited an interest in following basic archival procedures. She became a trusted mentor and a friend.[15] Each day I trundled the heavy bound newspaper volumes to eagerly awaiting historians and genealogists. I wore a knee-length grocer's apron to protect my clothing from the thick layers of grime that coated the newspaper

<hr />

[14] DA notes, 17 September 2019, telephone conversation with Edwin C. Bridges, DA Collection.

[15] Miriam "Mimi" Jones to DA, 11 March 1977; DA to Miriam "Mimi" Jones, 14 March 1977; DA notes, 17 September 2019, telephone conversation with Edwin C. Bridges, DA Collection.

bindings. My blue-collar wardrobe elicited howls of disapproval from many "Old Hands" who thought I should dress "more professionally." They unleashed a barrage of complaints about my personal appearance and demeanor.[16]

I usually ignored their incessant carping about such trivial matters and focused on my researchers in the Civil Archives. I greeted several regulars who appeared daily—a weather-beaten Alabama State Trooper sergeant who devoted his lunch hour to genealogy; genial Julia Dozier, whose historical "Yesterdays" column was carried in Montgomery newspapers; and sweet, whispering Lela Legaré, an aficionado of Bartlett's Botanical Trail in Alabama. In recognition of my love of the written word, she gave me a tiny ceramic bookworm figurine for my desk, which I treasure to this day.[17]

Perhaps my most unforgettable researcher was the brilliant young historian, J. Mills Thornton III—on sabbatical from the University of Michigan—grinding away at the fragile, highly acidic newspaper pages in feverish preparation for his definitive monograph on the civil rights movements in Montgomery, Birmingham, and Selma. Courtly, chivalrous, and impeccably gracious, Thornton to me epitomized the ideal of the Southern gentleman-scholar.

He also was the quintessential "Professor Iron-bottom," who became completely transfixed with his research and seldom took lunch breaks, unless Milo Howard bounded down the marble stairs and absconded with him for a quick meal. Fortunately for Thornton, the men's restroom was just outside the Civil Archives. I believe a small nuclear device could have been detonated beneath his chair without seriously disturbing his concentration. He greatly expanded my knowledge, understanding, and appreciation of Alabama history; we subsequently became very good friends and corresponded in the future on many scholarly, political, and personal topics.[18]

---

[16] Alsobrook, "A Portrait of the Archivist as a Young Man," 312.

[17] Ibid.

[18] Ibid.; J. Mills Thornton III, *Dividing Lines: Municipal Politics and the Struggle for Civil Rights in Montgomery, Birmingham, and Selma* (Tuscaloosa AL: University of Alabama Press, 2006); DA to J. Mills Thornton III, 10 October 1977, 12 June 1980; J. Mills Thornton III to DA, 7 June 1980, DA Collection.

I learned a great deal about my professional responsibilities in the Civil Archives. Like all archival institutions, ADAH had been victimized by theft for many years. Since we did not have any security guards in our building, I was particularly vigilant when researchers were at work. I cannot guarantee that no thefts occurred on my watch. However, several times I prevented the destruction or defacing of records and newspapers. Late one afternoon, I noticed a researcher who appeared to be busily writing in ink on an original newspaper. When I confronted him, he said, "My grandfather edited this paper; I'm annotating some of the articles to correct typos and factual errors for the benefit of other researchers." I explained that his "helpful" edits were not necessary and that, in the future, only a pencil would be permissible for his use in the Civil Archives.

On those rare occasions when my office was uninhabited by researchers, I tried to establish better intellectual control over my holdings by creating finding aids such as descriptive notes and container inventories for each collection and series. I also performed some basic preservation measures—like the removal of rusty metallic fasteners—in the official governors' papers, which were largely unprocessed.

In addition, I explored several less accessible nooks and crannies. In the Civil Archives' neglected file cabinets and "under the terrace" in the dank, gloomy northern quadrant, I discovered a small forgotten cache of Tom Owen's personal papers, bound with rough burlap cord. My other explorations yielded additional "fugitive" papers relating to the "Scottsboro Cases," Georgia Populist leader Tom Watson, and Civil War and Reconstruction historian Walter Lynwood Fleming, one of Professor George Petrie's prized pupils at Auburn. I inventoried, described, and transferred these files to more accessible locations and notified Dan T. Carter, C. Vann Woodward, and other historians about replevining these lost treasures.[19]

My extracurricular archival explorations further inflamed the "Old Hands," who accused me of "poking around" in places outside my domain. I naively believed that despite their woeful lack of curiosity about history

---

[19] Alsobrook, "A Portrait of the Archivist as a Young Man," 316; DA to Thomas Belser, 3 January 1976; DA to Paul M. Pruitt, Jr., 3 September 1979, DA Collection.

and archival principles, they would appreciate any efforts that produced better access to our holdings. I was wrong—my presence mysteriously threatened them in some inexplicably perverse, passive-aggressive manner. I suspect that they jealously thought I was attempting to curry favor with our director by such archival "antics."

As a "baby archivist," I harbored no illusions whatsoever about my niche within the staff hierarchy. From my earliest days on duty, the "Old Hands" openly branded me as "a typical cocky, hotshot graduate student," which I probably was. They vociferously groused to our boss and the ADAH Board of Trustees that I required close supervision because of my dearth of "broad-based experience" and that I spent too much time on my dissertation research. This latter allegation perhaps contained a kernel of truth. Instead of reading books and newspapers during breaks like the "Old Hands" did, I searched for records about Mobile during the progressive era. Their former charge, however, was patently bogus. I found that complaint especially ironic and disingenuous, since few "Old Hands" had any formal archival training or practical experience outside of ADAH. In the wake of the "Old Hands" uprising, Milo Howard sadly counseled, "David, if you don't try to accommodate yourself to the other staff members, you shall make my life a living hell."[20]

He was not being overly dramatic, and I deeply empathized with him. I was a constant irritant for his "Old Hands"—that was a certainty. But I refused to dumb down my own understanding of archival principles and practices to placate anyone who was somehow angered or aggrieved simply by observing my daily work schedule. Rather than attempting to defend myself against their tirades and snitching to our boss, I rededicated myself to archival work and gravitated toward younger colleagues who shared my views on professional archival and museum standards. Moreover, the "Old Hands" were not totally united in their opposition to my presence on the staff. Archivist Mimi Jones, bookkeeper Judy Perdue, and docent Marguerite Pearce, who adored and respected our director, became like surrogate

---

[20] DA to Milo B. Howard, 26 September 1976; DA to Jill Levin, 28 October 1976; DA to Miriam "Mimi" Jones, 27 February, 14 March 1977; DA to Paul M. Pruitt, Jr., 28 September 1993; misc. correspondence and notes, ca. 1981–1982, ADAH Personnel File; DA notes, 23 June 1977, telephone conversation with Allen W. Jones, DA Collection.

mothers to Ellen and me after our marriage in May 1976.[21]

Since ADAH's moribund organizational structure blocked any reasonable opportunities for professional advancement or supervisory experience, I did not wish to remain on the staff any longer than necessary. A future career in presidential libraries still beckoned to me. After the federal hiring freeze ended, Dan Reed and I shared our mutual frustrations that my name had not appeared on any archivists' selection registers. In late summer 1976, over a year after my interview with Reed, I contacted US Senator John Sparkman and my local congressman, Jack Edwards, for assistance in determining the status of my applications. At the end of September, Senator Sparkman's staff notified me that the US Civil Service Commission had misinterpreted the selection guidelines for qualified archivist candidates. Soon afterward, my name appeared on an archivists' register, and Reed selected me and three other candidates as archivist-trainees.[22]

Several days after Reed offered me the job by phone, I received my official letter which specified the terms of my appointment, starting salary, and reporting date of 10 January 1977. When I proudly shared my job offer with Milo Howard, he appeared to be genuinely saddened by my upcoming departure from his staff. Noting that my annual salary would increase from $9,000 to approximately $14,000, he said, "That's a very handsome offer." His own salary in 1976 was about $25,000. He also said that if it were just a matter of paying me more money, that would be possible. Then he added, "But I know that this is the job that you've always wanted. From the time I hired you, I realized that you would leave us someday."

I was gratified by Howard's gracious response to my leaving—I did not want to dynamite any bridges behind me. He had risked alienating his "Old Hands" by hiring me in the first place and had given me my first real archival job. At times he undoubtedly regarded me as somewhat of an enigma; however, from the outset he knew I was a "short-timer" because

---

[21] DA memo for the record, 21 October 1976, RE: "Conversations with Winston Walker and Bob Cason," DA Collection; Alsobrook, "A Portrait of the Archivist as a Young Man," 316.

[22] Misc. correspondence, memos, and notes, 1975–1976, Presidential Libraries Personnel File, DA Collection.

of my goal to serve in presidential libraries.

Nevertheless, he invested considerable personal time and department mental financial resources in my professional development. He generously authorized my travel to historical conferences, avoided any micromanagement of my work, and shielded me as much as humanly possible from the depredations of the "Old Hands." When Ellen and I were married, he attended our wedding in Birmingham. He treated me well; under different circumstances, I probably would have devoted the rest of my archival career to ADAH.

We engaged in many discussions in his inner sanctum about the historical and archival professions and ADAH improvements that were badly needed. He was not defensive or upset regarding any of my negative comments about his beloved department, and he intimated that someday I might be a legitimate candidate for the directorship or other leadership positions. Although I appreciated his encouraging words, we both truthfully knew that was not a realistic possibility given the current staff situation. While I hoped that we would remain friends after I left in January 1977, that was not destined to be.

In June 1979, Allen Jones solicited my thoughts about ADAH's deficiencies and possible solutions. Jones did not specify precisely how anything I said or wrote on these topics might be utilized in any public debates about the archives' future. However, I was not a political naif and understood the risk of accepting Jones's invitation. Furthermore, as a career federal employee, I was strictly prohibited from any involvement in partisan political matters. Thus, I had to exercise extreme caution in wading into any potentially turbulent political waters back in my native state. My deep concerns as an archivist and historian about the disposition of Alabama's records also weighed heavily on me, and I finally agreed to write a brief statement for Jones.[23]

In my written remarks, I generally concentrated on ADAH's failure to perform standard archival procedures in pursuit of Tom Owen's original vision for preserving historical records. I recommended several corrective administrative measures to upgrade the department's staff recruitment and

---

[23] DA to Allen W. Jones, 5 July 1979, DA Collection.

hiring policies and overall management procedures.[24] I also included several specific proposals: hire an administrative assistant to the director to coordinate reference services, personnel actions, and routine paperwork; reorganize the staff and reallocate personnel based on the workload; produce comprehensive finding aids for collections; utilize federal grants to fund archival and museum projects; hire security personnel to protect the collections from theft; expand the records management program; and finally, solicit personal papers and memorabilia of African Americans and other minorities who played pivotal roles in Alabama history.[25]

I did not consider my statement to be radical in any way or a personal attack on Howard's service. I carefully avoided blaming him for any current problems or failures. However, my conclusion infuriated him and his supporters: "[T]he State Archives needs stronger leadership and legislative assistance. With just a small amount of energy and imagination, the State Archives can become a viable, productive institution.... I hope that my remarks will help bring about some positive results."[26]

My comments surfaced in the midst of a bitter political struggle over ADAH's future. Milo Howard and his circle of friends were deeply offended by my remarks. While he personally felt betrayed by my disloyalty and never forgave me, I seriously doubt that my words surprised him. I had not been reticent in the past about openly sharing my views on these topics with him. Furthermore, after his death, my statement quickly ceased to be perceived by the ADAH Board of Trustees and their allies as incendiary, the way it was two years earlier.[27]

I admittedly was an imperfect advocate to promulgate any ADAH

---

[24] "Statement by David E. Alsobrook," 5 July 1979, unpub. typescript, DA Collection.

[25] Ibid.

[26] Ibid.

[27] DA memos of telephone conversations with Allen W. Jones, 22 August 1978; and Robert R. Rea, 8 August 1979; DA to Allen W. Jones, 5, 15 July 1979; Allen W. Jones to DA, 12 July, 17 August 1979; Robert R. Rea to DA, 6, 9 August 1979; DA to Alden N. Monroe, 5 August 1993; "Patterson Backs Archives; House Approves Ed Budget," *Opelika-Auburn News*, 11 July 1979, n.p., clipping, all in DA Collection; Frank Bruer, "Archives historical outlook aired," *Birmingham Post-Herald*, 12 July 1979, B8.

improvements and reforms. Other than any personal discomfort that my commentary inflicted upon Howard, I had no regrets about publicly articulating the desperate need for sweeping, innovative changes in the archives' management and future direction. Regardless of any personal repercussions or recriminations, I believed that, as an Alabamian *and* as a professional archivist, my duty was clear—provide objective recommendations without engaging in political partisanship.

A new era of ADAH renovations and innovations began in 1982 with the appointment of Director Edwin C. Bridges. A native of Bainbridge, Georgia, Bridges completed his undergraduate studies at Furman University and earned a PhD in history at the University of Chicago. He previously served as the Georgia Department of Archives and History's assistant director under Carroll Hart.

Bridges inherited a department "with a soul" and a "memory of early days," but also one that was decidedly anachronistic in its management and organizational structures, staffing, and adherence to the original mission. Bridges found that his staff, despite their lack of formal archival training, were "articulate and literate." While still grieving over Milo Howard's premature death to cancer, they looked to Bridges for leadership and guidance. Yet, before addressing a myriad of management and personnel issues, he immediately faced the exigencies of the archives' aging infrastructure—a leaky roof, antiquated lighting, crumbling ceiling plaster, and widespread mold and mildew.[28]

Bridges systematically dealt with these architectural and environmental anomalies and also implemented ADAH's first security plan to safeguard the staff and their collections. Between around 1982 and 1997, his archivists concentrated on establishing comprehensive intellectual control over their records. This monumental task left minimal time to deal with museum artifacts and exhibits. They prepared preliminary records inventories and instituted archival triage priorities for the retrieval and preservation of fugitive historical materials that had been dispersed haphazardly since the 1920s. In early 1983—thanks to a $150,000 legislative appropriation—Bridges began recruiting a cadre of experienced archivists,

---

[28] DA notes, 17 September 2019, telephone conversation with Edwin C. Bridges, DA Collection.

including Alden N. Monroe, Richard J. Cox, Tracey Berezansky, Dowe Littleton, and Debbie Pendleton.[29]

Bridges also acquired National Historical Publications and Records Commission (NHPRC) funding to supplement the department's annual budget for staffing and special projects. Debbie Pendleton, whose first ADAH position was created by an NHPRC grant, joined the team in late September 1985. She was thrilled to discover the practical value of her academic studies: "My job was to review the backlog of collections processing and make recommendations on processing priorities. I found my experience and coursework at Auburn prepared me well for this challenge. Later I would call upon my library school training for basic management techniques…as the worlds of archival and library cataloging merged."[30]

Pendleton and her colleagues relied on RLIN (Research Libraries Information Network) for manuscripts and records cataloging, and ADAH eventually developed partnerships with the state archives in New York, Minnesota, and Wisconsin that employed similar software systems. Relying on professional partnerships, NHPRC grants, and a collegial relationship with state officials, Bridges reconstituted the archives' core records function and established an innovative management system that laid a solid foundation for the future. Utilizing NHPRC funding, he created an archival advisory committee of legislators who traveled to South Carolina and Kentucky to observe how other archivists performed their duties. Additional NHPRC support for a "self-assessment" study brought the "radically brilliant" David Bearman from the Smithsonian Institution to Montgomery as a ADAH consultant. Bearman coached the staff in the basic principles of strategic planning. Bridges deployed Bearman's guidance in organizing a management team concept to facilitate quarterly progress reports to the Board of Trustees and to engage in decision-making. Strategic planning today is still an invaluable management tool at the Alabama Department of Archives and History.[31]

Several seminal initiatives evolved from the staff's strategic planning

---

[29] Ibid.

[30] Debbie Pendleton email to DA, 14 February 2018, DA Collection.

[31] DA notes, 17 September 2019, telephone conversation with Edwin C. Bridges, DA Collection.

sessions. During staff retreats in 1996–1997, they discussed the need for additional storage and staging areas for records and artifacts and identified logistical problems with the research room's current configuration. They also envisioned future needs for integrated educational and museum programs. Bridges recalls that because of "serious mildew" infestation in their major storage areas, his staff "felt a sense of urgency about doing something that would alleviate these problems": "[T]he construction of new, high quality storage space would address our conservation needs. We would then be free to do repairs to the older part of the building once records were moved into the new spaces."[32]

These staff meetings formed the genesis for a massive, unprecedented building expansion over the next two decades. With a combination of state and private funds that approached $25 million, Bridges launched the construction of the west wing, featuring a spacious research room, expanded storage and processing areas, staff offices, and interactive museum exhibits, highlighted by "Alabama Voices."[33]

In 2012, Bridges passed the leadership torch to Steve Murray, one of his talented supervisors, who was a graduate of the AU Archival Training Program. Murray built upon the archival and museum bedrock that Bridges had laid over the past thirty years. For example, the Smithsonian-quality, award-winning "Alabama Voices" exhibit opened to the public in February 2014. Murray also expanded scanning of primary sources through the Digital Assets Section. Thousands of digitized documents and photographs became readily accessible to researchers around the world.[34]

Murray also secured the largest donated collection in ADAH history—the Alabama Media Group's three million photographic negatives. These rare historical images—which provide a unique glimpse into "everyone's story, not just our leaders"—currently are being scanned daily by the Digital Assets team to expand their public accessibility. Since many of these images were not published previously in the *Huntsville Times*,

---

[32] Ibid.; Edwin C. Bridges emails to DA, 27, 28 September (quote), 1 October 2019, DA Collection.

[33] DA notes, 17 September 2019, telephone conversation with Edwin C. Bridges; Edwin C. Bridges emails to DA, 27, 28 September, 1 October 2019, DA Collection.

[34] Scotty E. Kirkland email to DA, 27 September 2019, DA Collection.

Birmingham News, and *Mobile-Press-Register*, they provide fresh views of significant historical events, particularly from the civil rights era. This collection may prove to be among ADAH's most important archival holdings.[35]

During the Alabama Bicentennial commemoration, Murray selected education as one of his top priorities. Under the auspices of the Bicentennial Education initiative, ADAH dispensed special grants to 200 local schools and sponsored Alabama History Institutes, which trained 1,500 classroom teachers in 2017–2019. These institutes, combined with teaching resources packets produced by Murray's educational team, empowered classroom instructors in history, social studies, and other curricula. Murray also guided the development of Montgomery's Bicentennial Park, one of the largest government-funded public art installations in Alabama since the New Deal, and "We the People," an exhibit on the state's constitutions. ADAH produced an exquisite companion piece for this exhibit—a beautifully illustrated historical monograph with the same title.[36]

Thirty-seven years have elapsed since Edwin Bridges unveiled his ambitious plans to reinvigorate the department—beginning with a return to Tom Owen's visionary archival roots. Under the creative, productive stewardship of Bridges and Murray, ADAH has not only fulfilled Owen's dream but has evolved into one of the finest state archives in the United States. With innovative educational and public outreach programs, it is now much more than an archives and a museum. I think that Tom Owen, Miss Marie, Peter Brannon, and Milo Howard all would be amazed and proud to see this magnificent facility—a fitting tribute to their pioneering efforts and to the dedicated directors and staff members who followed.

---

[35] Ibid.

[36] Ibid.; Scotty E. Kirkland, *We the People: Alabama's Defining Documents* (Montgomery AL: Alabama Department of Archives and History, 2019).

Chapter 3

"Are You from Georgia?":
My National Archives Initiation Rites

Where are you from? You sound like something in a "Shake 'n Bake" Commercial!
—unidentified Library of Congress staffer,
ca. June–July 1977

On New Year's Day 1977, Ellen and I left Montgomery and spent two nights with her parents in Birmingham. On 3 January, we embarked on the first leg of our northward trek on the icy interstate—bypassing Atlanta and overnighting in Greenville, South Carolina. The next day was bright and sunny, and the frozen glaze on the highway had melted away. Since our apartment in Gaithersburg, Maryland, would not be available for another two days, we decided to drive leisurely on the fourth as far as Fredericksburg, Virginia.

We soon regretted this fateful decision. We awoke early on 5 January to find Fredericksburg blanketed in heavy snow. Driving cautiously north on I-95, we saw several abandoned cars and tractor trailer trucks along the highway and in the median. Our truck skidded on an icy patch into the steel roadside guardrail. A Good Samaritan motorist stopped and helped us steer the truck back onto the asphalt. As we continued on our slow, tedious journey, the snowfall grew increasingly heavier, forcing us into a single, narrow, middle lane. Congealed brown ridges of slush—the residue of salt and sand trucks—lay on each side of our pathway. We seriously considered jettisoning our relocation plans and returning to Alabama.

After losing our way several times in the heavy snow, we finally reached Gaithersburg at 1:30 p.m. We spent the afternoon unloading our truck and Volkswagen in the freezing cold. Our two cats, Squeaker and Muffin, were chilled, famished, and disoriented in their strange, new environment—just like us. As winter darkness descended upon us, Ellen and

I sought refuge in a nearby pizza parlor, Mario's, where we ate our first meal in suburban Maryland.[1]

We first considered Gaithersburg for our new home based on the enthusiastic recommendation of Jim and Karen Kershner, two of my friends from graduate school at West Virginia University in Morgantown. Situated about twenty miles northwest of Washington, DC, Gaithersburg, originally a remote farming community in the late eighteenth century, was incorporated as a town around 1878. A century later, it had evolved into a suburban mecca for federal employees who were unable to afford the exorbitant housing costs in the District of Columbia and contiguous neighborhoods in Northern Virginia and Maryland.

As a GS-9 archivist earning an annual salary of $14,071, I had limited housing options. Apartment rental prices were much lower in the distant Virginia and Maryland suburbs, and our budgeted housing figure was $300 per month. Owning only a single vehicle, we also needed reliable public transportation for my daily trip to and from the National Archives. With these factors in mind, we carefully weighed our choices.

Not surprisingly, given our meager income, we selected the far Maryland suburbs, and "G-Burg" was an ideal location for us over the next four years. Our apartment complex at 412 North Summit Avenue lay within a half-mile of Gaithersburg's shops and restaurants. We lived adjacent to a dairy farm and a Methodist retirement home. To describe our neighborhood as "quiet and peaceful" was a great understatement. The only noises that occasionally disturbed our overnight slumber were the mooing of cows and random freight trains rumbling through downtown Gaithersburg.

Most importantly to us, the Baltimore and Ohio (B&O) Railroad depot was only about a ten-minute walk from our apartment. The B&O's daily schedule included nine passenger trains with stops in Gaithersburg. Each morning I boarded either the 7:11 or 7:31 a.m. train, which arrived at the District's Union Station within an hour. In the evening, I usually caught the 5:55 p.m. train and would be home by 7:00 p.m. My total daily commuting time was approximately 2.5 hours for the nominal monthly

---

[1] DA Journal, 1–5 January 1977, DA Collection.

cost of $42.70.[2]

My B&O commute was relatively short, especially in comparison with those of passengers who lived farther up the tracks in Martinsburg and Harper's Ferry, West Virginia. Rail commuting also spared me from the daily trauma and expenses of driving to and from the District with all of its vehicular congestion. On the train, I could read or chat with friends and arrive refreshed at work or home. After hearing horror stories of passengers who slept through their stops in Rockville and Gaithersburg and ended up in West Virginia, I seldom napped during my evening commute. In a transient, heavily populated area that did not encourage personal interactions, B&O commuting also offered a rare opportunity for socializing among the passengers. Spirited card games and Christmas parties were commonplace aboard the evening trains, and many lifelong friendships were forged over years of rail travel.[3]

During our first month in Gaithersburg, the B&O train proved to be a godsend because of the abysmal weather—bitterly cold (from zero to fifteen degrees) with sleet and snow on "warmer" days. Our frozen Volkswagen was entombed for several days beneath a heavy shroud of ice and snow. Having rarely seen any snow in Alabama, I was traumatized by the frigid winter of 1977. As my reporting date at the National Archives drew inexorably closer, Ellen and I, accompanied by Squeaker and Muffin, were snowbound in our apartment. Fortunately, severe winter weather did

---

[2] "Commuter Rail Survey, Gaithersburg Station," printed form, ca. 1978–1979; B&O Railroad Schedule, 1977, typescript, both in DA Collection. When the Metroline from Washington, DC, later was extended to its northwestern terminus at the Shady Grove Station in Gaithersburg, the commute to and from the District was speedier but at least twice as expensive as a B&O ticket.

[3] Over the years, a colorful trove of history, legend, and lore became associated with B&O commuter trains and their passengers. For example, according to one possibly apocryphal tale, James McCord, the infamous CIA operative and Watergate burglar, supposedly was a daily B&O daily commuter out of Rockville, Maryland, during the early 1970s. Aboard the train he acquired a close circle of friends, who later were shocked by revelations in 1972 of his role in the Watergate scandal. True to his CIA oath and trade craft, he apparently never discussed his clandestine activities with his fellow commuters.

not significantly alter the B&O's schedule.[4]

On 10 January 1977, I slogged through the "tundra" from Union Station to the National Archives at 7th and Pennsylvania Avenue. Dim yellow lights lit the circular row of windows below the shimmering, icy Capitol dome. In preparation for the Carter Presidential Inauguration parade, US Army troops, bundled up in Artic weather gear and armed with jackhammers, were slicing away thick slabs of ice on the sidewalks along Pennsylvania Avenue. Inside the steamy warmth of the National Archives personnel office, I filled out a ream of paperwork and was fingerprinted, photographed, and issued a laminated identification badge embossed with the acronym "NARS" (National Archives and Records Service). I also swore and signed an oath "to support, protect, and defend the Constitution of the United States...."[5] My thoughts briefly flashed back to my benighted Confederate ancestors who had signed a similar oath of allegiance in regaining their rights of citizenship after the Civil War. I now was officially a career federal civil servant—a title I proudly bore for the next thirty years.

I then reported to the Office of Presidential Libraries (NL) on "Mahogany Row" (a casual nickname derived from the offices' wood trim), where the archives' senior officials resided. Almost two years had elapsed since my interview with Dr. Daniel J. Reed, Assistant Archivist for Presidential Libraries. Susan Borkowski, Reed's affable, highly efficient receptionist, ushered me into his office suite. Smiling and welcoming me aboard, he briefly revisited details of the breaching of the bureaucratic logjam that finally had brought us to this moment. He proudly recalled that my hiring had corrected a glitch in the US Civil Service Commission's interpretation of standard qualifications for archivists, thereby expediting his filling additional vacancies. Over the next few weeks. I met my fellow archivist-trainees, including George T. Mazuzan, Mary Elizabeth Ruwell, and Byron A. "Scott" Parham. We subsequently became very good

---

[4] DA Journal, 7–19 January 1977; DA notes, 22 June 1977, "Impressions of DC after Five Months"; David E. Alsobrook, "A Southerner in Washington, DC, 1977," unpub. typescript and handwritten draft, all in DA Collection. In 1977, if Ellen and I had suspected that the next two winters would be even worse, we probably would have returned to Alabama.

[5] DA Journal, 10 January 1977, DA Collection.

friends.[6]

After our conversation, Reed introduced me to his deputy, Richard A. Jacobs, and Supervisory Archivist Trudy Huskamp Peterson. A tall, thirty-two-year-old Iowan, Trudy Peterson had coordinated the administrative details of my hiring throughout the previous autumn. Among her "other duties as assigned," she was responsible for the "care and feeding" of all NL trainees. She was supportive of archival rookies like myself and dubbed us "Trudy's Trainees," distinguishing us from the much larger NARS training class in 1977.[7]

Dick Jacobs appeared to be about ten years older and five inches shorter than Trudy Peterson. Everything about him bespoke "squared away"—from his neatly groomed light brown hair to his spit-shined shoes. He was decidedly gregarious, ebullient, and engaging. I noticed that several stacks of documents and briefing books encircled his desk. Gesturing with a golf putter toward this archival clutter on the floor around him, he said, "Dave, you're coming on board during a very busy time in NL; there's a lot going on right now."[8]

Although Jacobs failed to elaborate any further, I eventually determined that multiple tasks were weighing heavily on him and the entire NL staff: the legal and logistical disposition of President Richard Nixon's papers and audio recordings, the movement of President Gerald Ford's historical materials from the White House to Michigan, and the urgent demands of the "Georgians"—President-elect Jimmy Carter's transition team.[9]

Any one of these missions easily could have absorbed NL's staff resources, and the clock was ticking relentlessly toward the Carter Inauguration. In 1977 the National Archives was under the management aegis of the vast General Services Administration (GSA) bureaucracy. However,

---

[6] Misc. correspondence, memos, and notes, ca. 1975–1977, Office of Presidential Libraries File; Alsobrook, "A Southerner in Washington, DC, 1977," both in DA Collection.

[7] Alsobrook, "A Southerner in Washington, DC, 1977," DA Collection.

[8] Ibid.

[9] Ibid.; Robert M. Warner, "The Prologue Is Past," *American Archivist* 41/1 (January 1978): 10–11; Stephen Klaidman, "9 Trucks Convey Ford Presidential Papers to Mich.," *Washington Post*, 21 January 1977.

NARS depended on annual congressional appropriations for the bulk of its operations and programs. Presidential transitions are especially chaotic during a change in political parties, as occurred in 1976–1977. Each of the transition stakeholders had different agendas, goals, and expectations. Archivist of the United States James B. "Bert" Rhoads, Reed, and Jacobs thus had to deal simultaneously with multiple political exigencies—from GSA, Congress, the outgoing and incoming presidents and their advisers, and an army of attorneys who were involved in various Nixon lawsuits.

Moving the Ford materials from the White House to temporary storage in Ann Arbor, Michigan, within ten days was obviously a top priority. All of the other gears, levers, and complex moving parts in the transition equation depended on the Ford mission's success. Further complicating this situation, Gerald Ford, like his incumbent predecessors who were embroiled in heated political campaigns, delayed a final decision on the disposition of his presidential and vice presidential papers until after the 1976 election. He already had donated his congressional files and other personal papers to the Bentley Library at the University of Michigan. Almost two months after Jimmy Carter's victory, President Ford finally agreed that his White House materials also would be deposited at his alma mater.[10]

With the determination of the archival storage site for the Ford papers, Reed and Jacobs could focus on the logistics of the move and various Carter and Nixon matters. They urgently needed to provide the Carter team with guidance on a range of complex archival issues and furnish courtesy storage for their transition records. Jimmy Carter's state senate, gubernatorial, and 1976 campaign records all were in the custody of the Georgia Department of Archives and History (GDAH) in Atlanta. Questions and decisions about these records' future disposition could be deferred until later.

The Nixon materials, however, secured in the Old Executive Office Building (EOB) and the National Archives, were the proverbial "fly in the ointment." Attorneys representing the former president and the federal

---

[10] Warner, "The Prologue Is Past," 8–10. Dr. Robert M. Warner, the veteran director of the Bentley Library's Historic Michigan Collections, played a seminal role in resolving all Ford papers issues during the transition in 1976–1977. He succeeded James B. Rhoads as Archivist of the United States in 1980 and later led the National Archives' successful battle to achieve independence from GSA.

government, respectively, demanded access to the papers and audiotapes for ongoing litigation that had arisen since 1974. But the Georgians insisted on an expeditious removal of all Nixon materials from the EOB. Reed, Jacobs, and GSA attorney Steve Garfinkel adroitly negotiated an agreement with these contentious factions that authorized the relocation of the Nixon materials after the Carter Inauguration festivities. Removing the Nixon conundrum as a political pressure point freed NL to concentrate their resources solely on the Ford-Carter transition.[11]

Such thorny issues were far above my GS-9 pay grade in winter 1977. Having literally just entered the National Archives' portals, I was completely oblivious of the Nixon, Ford, and Carter imbroglios. Yet, after participating in three presidential transitions since 1980, I often have thought about that earlier era when I first arrived at the archives. I firmly believe that Rhoads, Reed, Jacobs, and Garfinkel exhibited exceptional leadership, diplomacy, and political acuity in solidifying the gold standard for the National Archives' role during transitions.[12]

In January 1977, lacking even a rudimentary grasp of the historical context of presidential transitions and their political dynamics, I was blissfully unaware of everything that Dick Jacobs described as "a busy time in NL." While awaiting the arrival of other trainees during my first week on the payroll, Trudy Peterson dispatched me to Stack 2W-2 to process a series of Democratic National Committee (DNC) records from the early 1970s. Stack 2W-2 was the archival base of operations for Douglas Thurman and his staff.

They collected and maintained presidential papers, audiovisual materials, and domestic and foreign gifts that were retired for storage by the White House. Thurman, Fynnette Eaton, and the rest of his staff retrieved these archived items as requested by the White House and also provided a wide range of archival support and assistance to all of the presidential libraries. This office, ordinarily awash with frenetic activity, was very quiet that week. Since Thurman was on leave, I processed the DNC records

---

[11] Alsobrook, "A Southerner in Washington, DC, 1977," DA Collection.

[12] For a historical overview of this topic, see David McMillen, "Moving Out, Moving In: The National Archives' Important Role when the Presidency Changes Hands," *Prologue* 48/4 (Winter 2016): 36–46.

without an onsite supervisor. My first NL archival project was relatively routine; I completed a draft finding aid by the end of the week. On 14 January 1977, I noted some early impressions of my job and location: "First week was pretty tough—new environment, new people, new responsibilities, etc. Ellen & I are both homesick."[13]

One obvious reason we missed living in Alabama was the brusque, intrusive manner in which strangers responded to us as Southerners. Since Washingtonians supposedly were proud of their sophisticated, cosmopolitan ways, I was dumbfounded by their typical reactions to a Southern accent: "Are you from Georgia?" "Are you with the Carter transition team?" At first I attributed such queries to honest curiosity and coyly responded, "Where do you think I'm from?" After enduring numerous variations of these questions, I began to lie unashamedly, "Yes, I'm from Georgia," joining the ranks of Jimmy Carter's illustrious "Peanut Brigade."[14]

This was not the first time in my life that I was singled out as "different" because of my distinct Southern dialect, but those earlier episodes ordinarily were casual, genial, or flirtatious. For example, ten years earlier, during my Peace Corps training in rural Northern Illinois, a teenaged cafeteria worker summoned one of her friends and pointed toward me in the serving line: "That's him—he's the one I was telling you about." Then she said to me, "Go ahead say something, anything." I replied, "What do *y'all* want me to say?" They giggled, deeply blushed, and retreated to the kitchen. Sitting in a barber's chair in Rockford, Illinois, I silently acquiesced as he incorrectly assumed, based on my being an Alabamian, that I was an ardent devotee of George Corley Wallace and droned on about the governor's "political genius."[15] However, neither of these incidents in the American heartland was particularly offensive to me.

My similar encounters in Washington, DC, in 1977 were quite different, both in their tone and underlying meaning. That summer, a Library of Congress archivist in the Manuscript Division loudly inquired, "Where

---

[13] DA Journal, 14 January 1977, DA Collection.

[14] DA notes, 22 June 1977, "Impressions of DC after Five Months"; misc. DA notes, 13 September 1977, DA Collection.

[15] Peace Corps—Peace Corps Advanced Training Program (ATP) for Thailand, Northern Illinois Univ. (DeKalb IL), June–August 1967, file in DA Collection.

are *you* from? You sound like something in a 'Shake 'n Bake' commercial!" The other researchers in the room paused and stared at us. Deeply embarrassed by his rudeness, I wondered if he also ridiculed foreign scholars' awkward English usage. On another occasion in 1977, I was on a training assignment in the National Archives stacks. Carmen Delle Donne, a diminutive, bearded employees' union representative, suddenly appeared at my desk to use the telephone. After his lengthy call, we exchanged pleasantries, which I fully anticipated would lead to the inevitable query about my place of birth. As expected, he asked, "Where are you from? You sure do talk funny!" Halfway through my response, he interjected, "Well, I'm from Rhode Island—we all have perfect diction." He uttered these words without the slightest trace of good-natured humor or irony. Both of these episodes deeply troubled and disappointed me because of their stereotypical implications that drawling, slow-talking Southerners were inherently stupid and backward.[16]

In retrospect, I admittedly was overly sensitive to such perceived personal slights. Nevertheless, because of my acute self-consciousness about my dialect, I often was reticent to speak very much in public or tried to enunciate my words more precisely. While awkwardly attempting to camouflage my natural speech, I remembered the lessons I had learned as a child. My parents taught me that it was morally reprehensible and unacceptable to mock anyone with a physical or mental disability or a speech impediment. Perhaps subconsciously I modified this code of personal conduct to include individuals with distinct regional or foreign dialects. I definitely became more sensitized about anyone who was unfairly stereotyped and categorized simply because of his or her speech patterns.

As I gradually became somewhat less self-absorbed and more comfortable with my new surroundings and colleagues, I used my accent to generate self-deprecating humor. In 1978 Iowan John T. Fawcett transferred from the LBJ Library to an NL supervisory position. When we were first introduced, he asked where I was from, and in my most exaggerated inflection, I drawled, "Boston." He briefly looked at me with puzzled

---

[16] Alsobrook, "A Southerner in Washington, DC, 1977"; DA notes, 22 June 1977, "Impressions of DC after Five Months"; DA notes, 13 September 1977, "Southerners & Northerners," all in DA Collection.

skepticism and then laughed uproariously. With the passage of time, however, I realized that my obsession with being "different" was also a matter of personal perspective. My colleague, Mary Elizabeth Ruwell, later offered her views on this topic as a transplanted Northerner: "I only moved two hours south, but working in Washington, DC, was very different. One of my earliest recollections was going to the cafeteria in the Federal Trade Commission next door and seeing grits, collard greens, and fried okra, and feeling like I had moved to the Deep South."[17]

As other new NL trainees came on board, I felt much less isolated and alone. By late January 1977, George Mazuzan, Mary Elizabeth Ruwell, Scott Parham, Christopher Beam, and several others had joined our training class. Two additional archivists, David Humphrey and David Van Tassel, hired in 1976, were further along in their training progression but also were members of our class.[18]

I was the only new trainee from the Deep South; my new colleagues hailed from Maine, Maryland, Minnesota, New York, Pennsylvania, Vermont, Washington, DC, and Texas. We were predominantly white males in our thirties and forties. About half of our training class had earned doctorates in history or other social sciences; several had completed all of their PhD studies except dissertations. Mazuzan, Humphrey, and Parham had distinguished academic credentials as university historians and administrators. I was one of the few class members with any substantial archival training or work experience. We all had been displaced or eliminated from traditional classroom or research careers by the massive "PhD glut" of the 1970s. Nevertheless, we shared a common goal—turn the pages on our previous lives and launch new careers with the National Archives or elsewhere in the federal government.[19]

---

[17] Alsobrook, "A Southerner in Washington, DC, 1977," Mary Elizabeth Ruwell, "Internship at National Archives, 1977–79, Reminiscences," email typescript, 29 January 2019, DA Collection.

[18] Alsobrook, "A Southerner in Washington, DC, 1977," DA Collection.

[19] Misc. correspondence, memos, and notes, ca. 1975–1977, Office of Presidential Libraries File; DA to J. Mills Thornton III, 10 October 1977; Martin I. Elzy, "Recollections of My Presidential Libraries Career," email typescript, 15 December 2018, all in DA Collection; David Sarasohn, "Zero Historian

We spent many hours training and socializing in 1977. Like military recruits who share the rigors of boot camp, we closely melded together, acquiring a special *élan* and *esprit de corps* based on our growing knowledge of presidential libraries' history and traditions. While we were not elitists, we were an undeniably closely knit, collegial group. When we were folded into the larger NARS training class in May 1977 and bussed on a field trip to the FDR Library, we still retained our own distinctive identity.[20]

Our training fell into two categories—classroom lectures by NARS "senior professionals" and practicums ("rotations") in "records custodial units," in administrative offices, and in the Library of Congress's Manuscript Division. George C. Chalou, the chief of reference services at the Washington National Records Center in Suitland, Maryland, was the Archives Training Course's coordinator. As outlined in Chalou's syllabus, the seventeen lectures would "introduce to new professionals the various theories of archives and...examine how those theories have been implemented" by the National Archives.[21] In other words, we would glean from these lectures the NARS method of performing our archival duties. Since I logged a heavy dose of readings in archival theories during my Auburn University graduate school training, I was skeptical about the value of these upcoming lectures. I anticipated daydreaming and doodling during my classroom hours.

To my surprise and relief, our senior officials—each of whom had extensive experience in his or her area of expertise—emphasized the practical application of archival theories in their lectures. Our classroom sessions were informative, featuring lively discussions on the basic archival principles of preservation, arrangement, and description, and specialized types of records—audiovisual, cartographic, architectural, security-classified, and "machine-readable" (electronic). As an archival neophyte, I was eager to learn everything about the National Archives and its methods and missions. I found five lectures especially compelling: James W. Moore, "Audiovisual Archives"; Mabel Deutrich, "Archival Arrangement"; Edwin

Growth," *Harper's Magazine*, July 1975, 92: Gil Sewall and Elliott D. Lee, "The Ph.D. Meat Market," *Newsweek*, 4 February 1980, 74.

[20] DA Journal, 4–6 May 1977, DA Collection.

[21] Syllabus, misc. notes, Office of Presidential Libraries—National Archives Training Course, Part 2, February–June 1977, file in DA Collection.

Alan Thompson, "Records Declassification"; Dick Jacobs, "Archiving and Political Controversy"; and James E. O'Neill and Trudy Peterson, "Access and the Law."[22]

Several trainees openly balked at George Chalou's academic format for his course, such as a mandatory written final examination. Since we were all products of the graduate school academic "grind," I empathized with their recalcitrance in response to the course's regimented format. Yet, since we came from disparate archival backgrounds (if any), Chalou had to impose some measure of organizational structure upon our classroom work. Regardless, I thought our classroom sessions were intellectually invigorating and challenging. I also was extremely impressed with the lectures' depth and applicability to our future careers. As a nascent archivist, I was inspired by our instructors' professional stature and bearing, technical knowledge, practical experience, and spirited advocacy for the National Archives.

Our rotations in records units and offices ran concurrently with the classroom lectures between February and May of 1977. After successfully completing Chalou's final examination, we continued our rotations through the summer and fall. Trudy Peterson meticulously planned each trainee's rotations schedule and tried to match individual research interests with these assignments. She contacted me about my research preferences two months before my arrival date. Since I listed urban history as one of my interests, she scheduled my first rotation in the Industrial and Social Branch, which was the custodial unit for large series of records relating to this topic. As I left for my rotation, Trudy Peterson wished me luck and ominously warned, "It's a troubled branch."[23]

Her cryptic description initially did not resonate with me. However, a week into my rotation, I observed several archivists typing job applications (SF-171s), filing grievances, conducting union business, reading the *Washington Post*, and knitting. Even from my limited perspective, this bizarre scene reinforced every negative stereotype of lazy, dysfunctional federal employees. Surely, I thought, they once were conscientious, highly

---

[22] Ibid.

[23] DA Journal, 18 January 1977; misc. correspondence, memos, and notes, ca. 1976–1977, Office of Presidential Libraries File, DA Collection.

motivated archivists. What had happened to them over the years? For reasons unknown to me, they had washed up, like so much archival driftwood, on the shore of this "troubled branch."

Since Jerome Finster, the beleaguered branch chief, apparently lacked confidence in his archivists, he seldom delegated any of his supervisory or administrative responsibilities. As my only supervisor, he personally drafted copious critiques of my finding aids ("Preliminary Inventories"). He obviously preferred written over oral communications.[24] I never fathomed why this unit was so deeply "troubled." Yet this experience instilled in me a lasting appreciation for the nexus between staff morale and productivity. This lesson served me well for the rest of my career.

After three or four months, I realized that the quality of my rotations—which fluctuated significantly—depended largely on the supervisors' management skills and levels of interest in the training regimen. For example, in my rotations in Analysis and Planning and Educational Programs, supervisors Adrienne Thomas and Leslie Buhler, respectively, carefully selected and organized my projects, inserted me into their office's daily operations, and delegated other staff to monitor my progress. Both supervisors also were accessible when I needed their guidance. I consequently learned a great deal about NARS' administrative, budgetary, and educational outreach procedures.[25]

In contrast to these two rotations, the Records Appraisal and Disposition supervisor asked each of her archivists, "Do you have any work for this trainee?" This was the ad hoc procedure by which I received assignments. Without any preliminary planning by the supervisor, I primarily worked on projects that had been left unfinished by other archivists or trainees. After examining descriptions and accessioning schedules for a US Coast Guard records series from World War II, based on its unique historical importance, I recommended permanent retention. I then discovered that the NARS regional branch in East Point, Georgia, had destroyed these records several years earlier. Since whoever had begun this project

---

[24] Jerome Finster's typed and handwritten comments, ca. January 1977, Office of Presidential Libraries—Training Assignments File, DA Collection.

[25] Misc. correspondence, memos, and notes, ca. May–June 1977, Office of Presidential Libraries—Training Assignments File; DA Journal, 13 May, 10, 13, 20 June, 5 July 1977, DA Collection.

failed to indicate in the file that the records already were scheduled for shredding, I wasted about three weeks of my time. The National Archives only had a small volume of US Coast Guard records from that era; the loss of this series for future World War II historians was inestimable.

At this stage in my rotation, an experienced, perceptive archivist, Jerry Wallace, intervened and took me under his wing. He skillfully guided me through an appraisal of US Army criminal investigation records. As a Vietnam veteran, Wallace had a personal stake in ensuring that this records series was considered for retention. This project was the most substantive portion of my rotation. He also arranged an informative luncheon meeting with two of his mentors, Mary Walton Livingston and Leonard Rapport, who were legendary figures in the archival profession. With two weeks remaining in my posting, I had completed all of my assigned projects. Several trainees, who had rotated earlier through this office, warned me against requesting any additional assignments, which invariably would lead to more "scut work," like my Coast Guard records debacle. So I kept quiet and pretended to be busy for two weeks. Without Jerry Wallace's timely intervention, this rotation probably would have been worthless.[26]

My extended rotation in the Library of Congress's Manuscript Division was interesting and highly instructive. After multiple conferences with supervisor Rick Bickel and various subject area specialists, I began processing the Jedediah Hotchkiss Papers—a massive cache of correspondence and cartographic materials produced by General Thomas "Stonewall" Jackson's preeminent topographical engineer. This collection included letters from Jackson, Robert E. Lee, and other Confederate officers and scores of exquisite, hand-drawn maps of the Shenandoah Valley campaigns. At one time, these papers were in the possession of historian Douglas Southall Freeman, and he had annotated many of the documents in heavy, black ink. Although as an archivist I was appalled to see permanent alterations to priceless manuscripts, Freeman's incisive comments traced the evolution of his assessments of Confederate leaders that he later

---

[26] DA Journal, 8, 16, 20–22, 26–28 September 1977; misc. DA notes, 7, 8, 13, 19, 22–23 September 1977, DA Collection.

incorporated into his seminal monograph, *Lee's Lieutenants.*[27]

Working in the Manuscript Division more closely resembled a real archival job than any of my other rotations. For two months, for the first time since my training began, I had my own desk and work space that I did not share with other archivists. Instead of being isolated deep within the NARS stacks, I was surrounded by experienced archivists with whom I communicated throughout each day. The informal camaraderie of this working environment resembled a small history department—strikingly different from some of the National Archives' more bureaucratic units. Since my rotation overlapped with those of David Van Tassel and George Mazuzan, sharing this experience with two colleagues contributed significantly to my own morale and productivity.

Perhaps the most invaluable legacy of this rotation was my gaining a better understanding of the distinct differences between official federal records and personal manuscripts. While NARS' Preliminary Inventories provide generic information about records groups and series, the Library of Congress's intricate descriptions drill down into the specific contents of individual file folders. The levels of description in presidential libraries' finding aids more closely resemble those of the Library of Congress than the National Archives. Therefore, I understood why this particular rotation was mandatory for all NL trainees.[28]

Our other required rotation was with the National Historical Publications and Records Commission (NHPRC), a congressionally mandated organization embedded in the National Archives. The NHPRC published the edited papers of Thomas Jefferson, John C. Calhoun, Henry Clay, Andrew Jackson, Ulysses S. Grant, Jefferson Davis, Frederick Douglass, Booker T. Washington, Emma Goldman, Samuel Gompers, and many other prominent historical figures. Additional NHPRC projects included documentary histories of the First Continental Congress, emancipation,

---

[27] DA Journal, 5 July, 12, 29 August 1977; DA draft finding aid for Jedediah Hotchkiss Papers, typescript, ca. September 1977, Office of Presidential Libraries—Training Assignments File; DA to J. Mills Thornton III, 10 October 1977, DA Collection.

[28] DA Journal, 12, 15, 22, 25–29 July, 1 August 1977, DA Collection.

and the US Supreme Court.[29]

Sara Dunlap Jackson's NHPRC staff in Room 200A at the National Archives provided research support for all of these publication projects. When I reported to her on 31 January 1977, she greeted me like we were lifelong friends. I suspected that Allen W. Jones, my former Auburn University professor, had contacted her in my behalf. On many occasions, he asserted that I would not find a better mentor or friend at NARS than Sara Jackson.[30]

Born in South Carolina and orphaned as a child, Sara Jackson was one of the first African Americans hired by the National Archives, beginning her career there in 1944. Over the next twenty-five years, she acquired an encyclopedic knowledge of US military and Freedmen's Bureau records. In 1969, she joined the NHPRC staff. During her NARS career of forty-seven years, she shepherded countless numbers of archivists and historians through the labyrinth of military and African American records.[31] In January 1977, I did not know the details of her prolific, influential career as an archivist, researcher, and educator. But I was aware that she was universally respected and admired throughout the archival and scholarly communities.

On my first day in NHPRC, Sara Jackson sat motionless at her desk, smoking a cigarette while describing my duties. I noticed that she spoke with a slight stammer in her soft voice. She occasionally paused to allow me to ask questions or offer comments. She escorted me deep into the mysterious catacombs of the Old Military Branch stacks, where the captured "Rebel Archives" containers were shelved. She casually asked if I had any ancestors who "wore the grey" and demonstrated how to locate their Compiled Service Records—the first of many memorable archival tutorials. Everything that she did seemed so effortless—without any dramatic

---

[29] Richard A. Jacobs, "Changing Some Contours of History," unidentified clipping, ca. May–June 1990, DA Collection.

[30] DA Journal, 31 January 1977, DA Collection.

[31] "Sara Dunlap Jackson, Service of Worship, Praise, and Celebration," The Church of the Savior, Washington, DC, 27 April 1991; Roger Bruns, "Remembering Sara Jackson: A Memorial Tribute," 1991; Mary Elizabeth Ruwell, "Internship at National Archives, 1977–79, Reminiscences," email typescript, 29 January 2019, DA Collection.

fanfare or wasted motion, but with dexterity and enthusiasm. To me she was an archival wizard—expertly navigating us through the records of the US and Confederate Army and Navy, the Adjutant General's Office, and, of course, the Freedmen's Bureau.[32]

During the next month (February 1977), I located records for the various NHPRC projects. Whenever I retrieved a document that appeared to be of even minimal historical value, Sara Jackson shared my joy of discovery as if I had unearthed the rarest of manuscripts. Under her deft, gentle supervision, I drafted explanatory letters and memos to accompany my findings and spoke directly with the projects' editors. Along with other trainees, I accompanied Ms. Jackson on a field trip to the University of Maryland, where she introduced us to Louis R. Harlan, Raymond Smock, and their staff at the Booker T. Washington Papers Project. She later arranged a delightful lunch for us on Capitol Hill with Dr. Harlan and his wife.[33]

Despite our woeful lack of archival expertise as trainees, Sara Jackson treated us all with deep respect. She affectionately called us her "girls and boys," "biddies," and "angels." She knew about our ordinary joys and sorrows, but not in an intrusive way. She proudly celebrated the progress of our careers long after we left her sheltering arms. She mentored, mothered, spoiled, and scolded us. She also shielded us from the National Archives' treacherous political landmines and quicksand, *agent provocateurs*, charlatans, con-artists, grifters, and chronic malcontents.[34]

For me personally, she not only identified "playground bullies" to avoid. Drawing upon her own life's experiences, she also taught me, by

---

[32] DA Journal, 3 February 1977; Alsobrook, "A Southerner in Washington, DC, 1977," DA Collection. See also Ira Berlin, "In Memory of Sara Dunlap Jackson," *Prologue Magazine*, https://www.archives.gov/publications/prologue/1997/summer/sara-dunlap-jackson.html; "Dr. Sara Dunlap Jackson," https://scafricanamerican.com/honorees/dr-sara-dunlap-jackson/ (both accessed 14 December 2018).

[33] Misc. NHPRC correspondence, memos, and notes, February–March 1977, Office of Presidential Libraries—Training Assignments File; DA Journal, 17 June 1977, DA Collection.

[34] DA to Sara D. Jackson, 22 June 1981, 28 February 1983, 13 May 1987, 20 November 1990, DA Collection.

word and deed, guidelines for survival and success in the National Archives: always treat everyone with courtesy and respect; play nice with others; never lie, cheat, or steal; volunteer for even the most menial, unpleasant, unrewarding tasks; and make yourself indispensable. I never forgot these lessons and everything else that she taught me. For example, in November 1990, I wrote to her: "When I think about my year as a 'trainee' in the Office of Presidential Libraries, I don't remember much about my rotations, *except* for the time I spent with you. I will never forget that experience and your endless patience, great enthusiasm, and wise counsel.... I wouldn't trade that time with you for any of the archival training I've had before or since."[35]

A month later, after learning that she was gravely ill with cancer, I wrote again but with more specificity: "Let me simply say that by being around you, I am today a much better archivist and human being. Beyond all the archival and historical knowledge that you generously imparted to me, you taught me by example how to get along with people."[36] When Scott Parham informed me in April 1991 that she had died at age seventy-one, I felt like my own mother had passed away.[37]

Almost forty-two years ago, as my training class finished our final rotations, I think we implicitly understood Sara Jackson's special importance to us. However, I seriously doubt that we fully grasped the magnitude of her selfless gifts to us until much later in our lives and careers.

In summer and autumn 1977, we all were preoccupied with our future employment prospects. Since our supervisors had invested considerable time and staff resources in our archival training and development, we were confident that they wanted to keep us in the NL/NARS family. Yet, because I had assumed that we all aspired to serve in a presidential library after our training ended, I was quite surprised that many of my colleagues evinced little interest in pursuing careers beyond Washington, DC.[38]

As early as summer 1974, during my internship at the NARS regional

---

[35] DA to Sara D. Jackson, 20 November 1990, DA Collection.

[36] DA to Sara D. Jackson, 11 December 1990, DA Collection.

[37] Byron A. "Scott" Parham to DA, ca. 22 April 1991, DA Collection. Several years afterward, I realized that Sara Jackson and my mother were born a few weeks apart in May 1919.

[38] Alsobrook, "A Southerner in Washington, DC, 1977," DA Collection.

branch in East Point, Georgia, I had dreamed of a future career in one of the presidential libraries. The LBJ Library always was my top choice. Sometime in summer 1977, David Humphrey announced that he soon would depart for the LBJ Library. Only one archivist vacancy existed in Austin, Texas, so I instantaneously had to recalibrate my career plans.[39]

My most promising job opportunities appeared to be limited to NL or the Nixon Presidential Materials Project, neither of which appealed to me. While hopeful of securing a position with promotion potential beyond a GS-11, I primarily was interested in archival processing and reference duties. I surmised that any future NL positions would be administrative—with an emphasis on budgetary and personnel issues. The Nixon Project's top priority was the production of copies of documents and audiotapes for lawsuits. Nixon archivists thus spent much of their time reviewing and copying rather than performing basic processing measures such as preservation, arrangement, and the preparation of finding aids. Furthermore, their staff already was top-heavy with GS-9/11 archivists, and I would rank behind them in the promotion hierarchy.[40]

In August 1977, as I fretted over my future, my fellow trainees also were weighing their career options. Scott Parham selected the Nixon Project as the safest roll of the dice—it offered solid job security because of the seemingly endless litigation related to the former president's materials. The Nixon Project also was one of several choices being considered by our energetic, multilingual colleague, Mary Elizabeth Ruwell, who wanted to finish her PhD in American Civilization at the University of Pennsylvania. Soft-spoken David Van Tassel, who had demonstrated a natural affinity for archival administration, apparently was destined for an NL slot. George Mazuzan, my wise, urbane "Yankee" compatriot from Vermont, was searching for a historian's position in a federal agency.[41]

---

[39] Ibid.; misc. correspondence, ca. 1975–1976, Office of Presidential Libraries File; DA to Edward M. Steel, Jr., 5 November 1979, DA Collection.

[40] Alsobrook, "A Southerner in Washington, DC, 1977," DA Collection.

[41] Ibid.; Mary Elizabeth Ruwell email to DA (with attached vita), 15 January 2019; Mary Elizabeth Ruwell, "Internship at National Archives, 1977–1979, Reminiscences," email typescript, 29 January 2019, DA Collection. Each of these friends went on to productive, distinguished careers after our training in 1977: Parham as an archivist with the Nixon Project, Van Tassel in NL and later with

In the meanwhile, our original supervisor, Trudy Peterson, had ascended to the position of Deputy Archivist of the United States, just a heartbeat away from NARS' pinnacle of leadership on Mahogany Row. Her successor, Maygene Daniels, called me in August 1977 and inquired about my job preferences. I responded that since the LBJ Library was off the table, I was uncertain about my future destination. She said that NL was "staffing up" to review Nixon audiotapes, and I could join that team of archivists. Then, almost as an afterthought, she mentioned that some archival jobs might be available in the White House. She asked me to take some time and think about which venue I preferred. I paused for about a second and chose the White House. She laughed and promised to keep me in mind if anything developed at 1600 Pennsylvania Avenue.[42]

Not long after my conversation with Daniels, I heard persistent rumors that Bert Rhoads had approved Dan Reed's proposal to establish a small liaison office as an NL/NARS "beach head" at the EOB. This office would provide information and guidance on presidential libraries to the White House in early preparation for a future Carter Library. NARS had staffed and operated a similar liaison office during the Nixon era. After President Nixon's resignation, that office was disbanded, and the archivists were reassigned to other government units.[43]

Fearing my imminent assignment to the Nixon Project tapes reviewing team, I sent a memo to Dan Reed on 21 August 1977, volunteering to serve in the new liaison office and promising to transfer later to a Carter Library in Georgia. Daniels attached her own note to my memo: "I've spoken to [David] in general but have no idea how he learned that the staff

the National Security Council records directorate at the White House, Ruwell as an archivist with several corporations and currently at the USAF Academy, and Mazuzan as the chief historian at the Nuclear Regulatory Commission and the National Science Foundation. Our genial, esteemed colleague, David Humphrey, served as an archivist for many years at the LBJ Library and later joined the State Department historical staff.

[42] Alsobrook, "A Southerner in Washington, DC, 1977," DA Collection; "Trudy Huskamp Peterson: Certified Archivist," https://www.trudypeterson.com/resume (accessed 15 January 2019).

[43] Alsobrook, "A Southerner in Washington, DC, 1977," DA Collection; Raymond H. Geselbracht and Daniel J. Reed, "The Presidential Library and the White House Liaison Office," *American Archivist* 46/1 (Winter 1983): 70–71.

had received approval (he may not have understood that it was subject to White House approval). He asks to meet with you to discuss the matter. I recommend that we wait for such a meeting until we know a little bit more about who will be heading the project and what kind of pattern for other archivists will be required."[44] Reed responded, "Pl[ease] tell David we have his preferences in mind, but we'll have to see what develops."[45]

I was somewhat puzzled by Reed's cautiousness about the establishment of a new liaison office. Later revelations indicate that he had several concerns about detailing his archivists to the White House. Because of NL's recent ill-fated experience during the Nixon era, he was particularly adamant about preserving a clear, statutory delineation between federal employees and White House staff. Any archivists detailed to the White House must understand that as federal civil servants they could not engage in any political activities.

Reed insisted that his archivists should never perform any duties that traditionally were the purview of political appointees. He specifically cited the case of Ellen McCathran, one of his detailees in the Nixon White House, who produced the Presidential Daily Diary. He later described the Daily Diary as a "truly superb document, as became evident when the Watergate special prosecutor's office used it to subpoena tape recordings of presidential meetings and telephone calls…, [and] the National Archives was drawn much further into the Watergate controversy than it should have or wanted to be."[46]

Regarding my candidacy for a position in the new liaison office, Reed feared that as a Southerner I might become overly enamored of the Georgians, thus distorting my objectivity and making me vulnerable to their political influence. NL "scuttlebutt" confirmed that he viewed my "Southernness" as a major factor weighing against detailing me to the White House. I thought his concerns were ill founded and shortsighted. Yet today I know that he simply was protecting one of his inexperienced archi-

---

[44] Maygene Daniels's note, ca. 22–23 August 1977, attachment to memo, DA to Daniel J. Reed, 21 August 1977, Office of Presidential Libraries File, DA Collection.

[45] DJR [Daniel J. Reed]'s note, ca. 22–23 August 1977, DA Collection.

[46] Geselbracht and Reed, "The Presidential Library and the White House Liaison Office," 71–72.

vists from a potentially dangerous political environment. I cannot determine precisely when or why Reed changed his mind, but between late October and early December 1977, he and Rhoads approved my assignment to the liaison office.[47]

While these discussions continued behind closed doors on Mahogany Row, I finished my rotations in early November and returned to NL with the other trainees. Maygene Daniels assigned us to temporary archival tasks. Nixon Project archivist Bill Joyner and I spent about a week inventorying and packing 1976 Bicentennial gifts for shipment to the Ford Library. Joyner, a tall, powerful former star football player at South Carolina State University, had moved to the Nixon Project from the LBJ Library several months earlier. Our joint task was tedious and monotonous, like the other temporary chores that had been assigned to NL trainees. We essentially were running out the clock until the Thanksgiving and Christmas holidays. After the New Year, we would be dispersed to our new permanent duty postings. So, for about two months, we dwelled within this artificial bubble at NARS.[48]

Occasionally, outside events dramatically disrupted our lives, as in mid-November 1977, when President Carter invited the Shah of Iran to the White House. Approximately 60,000 Iranian students were living temporarily on educational visas in the United States—a majority of whom ardently opposed the Shah and SAVAK, his barbaric internal security police. A week before the Shah's White House visit, the Iran Student Movement launched massive protest demonstrations in Lafayette Park. In response, the Iranian Embassy mobilized pro-Shah counter demonstrations in the same location, facing the White House. The US Park Service Police and DC Police tactical squads had the unenviable duty of preventing violence between these two angry, antagonistic groups.[49]

On 15 November, my colleague Christopher Beam, a Vietnam War Marine Corps veteran, and I sought a diversion from our debilitating assignments, so we strolled over to the White House. After four decades,

---

[47] DA Journal, 7 December 1977, DA Collection.

[48] DA Journal, 1 November 1977, DA Collection.

[49] Stuart E. Eizenstat, *President Carter: The White House Years* (New York: St. Martin's Press, 2018) 723–25. SAVAK was an anagram formed by the Persian words for Organization of Intelligence and National Security.

two distinct images from that day still remain sharply etched in my memory: the defiant students with upraised, clenched fists and their faces swathed in scarves as protection from tear gas and identification by SAVAK undercover agents; and the mounted US Park Police, frantically attempting to calm their terrified, wild-eyed horses.

Afterward, I scrawled a few notes: "Went w/ a friend to demonstration by Iranian students at White House—Heard on radio of violence this morning—Apparently tear gas used on crowd…. Very energetic display."[50] This nondescript journal entry clearly reveals that I failed to comprehend the significance of what we had personally witnessed. These violent demonstrations were the first stage in a series of tragic, tumultuous events that ultimately engulfed and eviscerated the Carter presidency.[51]

Even during these traumatic days in November 1977, I remained fixated on my job prospects. I was vaguely aware—courtesy of the reliable NARS rumor mill—that "secret" meetings about the EOB liaison office were still underway. On 30 November, Dick Jacobs called me into his office. After swearing me to secrecy, he said that despite any "hard promises," my name was on the list of potential detailees to the EOB.[52]

Freezing rain and snow rolled into the city during the first week of December. Within the cozy warmth of Mahogany Row, Bert Rhoads and Dan Reed selected South Carolinian Marie B. Allen to lead the new liaison office, now officially designated as the "Presidential Papers Staff." Then about thirty years old, Allen had earned an MA in history at Duke University prior to joining the NARS staff in the early 1970s. Most recently, as a GS-13 supervisory archivist, she worked on a diverse array of records declassification issues and coordinated access to the Nixon materials stored at the EOB and the National Archives. Several archivists who previously had served with her described Allen as hardworking, energetic, intelligent, ambitious, and, like Trudy Peterson, definitely on the NARS "career fast-track."[53]

---

[50] DA Journal, 15–16 November 1977, DA Collection.

[51] Eizenstat, *President Carter*, 720–811; Jody Powell exit interview by David E. Alsobrook, 2 December 1980, Oral Histories, Carter Library, https://www.jimmycarterlibrary.gov/research/oral_histories (accessed 3 March 2019).

[52] DA Journal, 1 December 1977, DA Collection.

[53] DA Journal, 7 December 1977, DA Collection.

Although I still had not been assigned officially to the liaison staff, Allen asked me to meet with her at NARS on 7 December. We sat together on a bench in a crowded, noisy hallway. For about an hour, we discussed her vision for the new liaison office. She described its primary function as a communications "conduit or pipeline" between NARS and the White House to ensure an accurate, systematic exchange of information about presidential libraries and tangential issues. Obviously familiar with my vita and SF-171, she asked how I envisioned my role in her office. I said that my training and experience as an archivist and historian had prepared me to perform a wide range of duties, including basic research and oral history interviews.

She told me that her deputy would be Lee Johnson, a GS-12 archivist in the NARS central research unit. Johnson held graduate degrees in history and library science from the University of Minnesota and was enrolled in an American Studies PhD program at that institution. She left me with the impression that Reed had personally recommended Johnson for the deputy's position. Reed actually had offered Johnson a slot in the proposed liaison office several months earlier at the Society of American Archivists' annual meeting in Chicago. Johnson believed that his work on Ford and Nixon materials during the 1976–1977 transition led directly to his selection for the liaison office. From her meetings with Reed and Rhoads, Allen felt "reasonably sure" that I would be the third archivist in the liaison office. She concluded our meeting with a promise to seek Reed's "final blessing" on my selection.[54]

Two days later, on 9 December, Allen notified me that Reed had "signed off" on my detail to the liaison office. Pending the completion of my FBI background investigation, I would work on "Carter issues" in NL for the remainder of the year. That evening, I characterized the past two days in writing simply as "a memorable time in my life!"[55]

I was greatly relieved, after several months of incessant worry, to know where I would land after the New Year. On 12 December, Allen, Johnson, and I surveyed our future "digs"—EOB Room 492. Since Allen

---

[54] Ibid.; DA notes, 31 March 2019, telephone conversation with Lee R. Johnson, DA Collection.

[55] DA Journal, 9 December 1977, DA Collection.

had retained a permanent White House badge (a "hard pass") from her previous EOB detail, she escorted us on a tour of this magnificent old building. I suddenly realized that this venerable Victorian structure would be my home for at least three years. For an archivist/historian, was there any better work site in the entire federal bureaucracy? I did not think so, and future events confirmed this early assessment.[56]

On 14 December, we met with Reed and began drafting a memo to the White House, briefly describing various liaison office duties, such as oral history interviews with departing White House staff and Carter family members. Reed reminded me that I still had to be "run by the Georgians" for their final vetting. He arranged this session with the White House senior staff for the following week, a few days before Christmas. However, at the last minute, the White House cancelled and rescheduled the meeting for early January 1978. Therefore, I had to surmount one remaining bureaucratic hurdle before being permitted to work in the EOB.[57]

Although the White House eventually would determine my fate, I felt cautiously optimistic that I had a future role as an archivist in the liaison office. Several weeks later, I shared my hopes for the New Year and beyond with Allen W. Jones:

> [I]t now appears that I will become a permanent part of a small NARS staff (Office of Presidential Libraries) in the White House complex (Old Executive Office Building)....[We] will assist in planning a future Carter Presidential Library (assuming there will be such a repository). It is likely we will deal with a variety of archival matters, including records disposition, and eventually, even oral history. In short, we are responsible for seeing that the Carter Presidency is documented adequately for future historians. Hopefully, someday I will have the opportunity to work in a Carter

---

[56] DA Journal, 12 December 1977, DA Collection.

[57] DA Journal, 12, 14, 20 December 1977; "Program Proposal for Presidential Papers Staff," ca. December 1977, attached to memo, Richard A. Jacobs to James B. Rhoads, 5 January 1978; DA memo, 14 December 1977, RE: "Meeting with Daniel J. Reed"; draft memo, Hugh Carter, Jr. to White House Staff, ca. January–February 1978, Presidential Papers Staff—Establishment, 1977–1978 File, all in DA Collection. All citations in this footnote, with the exception of the journal entries, are from this file.

Presidential Library in Georgia.[58]

As Ellen and I prepared to drive to Birmingham for the Christmas holidays, we were extremely excited about our future prospects.[59] A year had passed since we left our loved ones, close friends, and the familiar, comfortable surroundings of "hearth and home." Being completely on our own, far from our families' protective safety net, we were forced to rely on personal survival skills. My long, arduous year of training finally was over, and my new adventure as an archivist beckoned to me.

We also eagerly awaited the arrival of our first child, Adam, who was born in June 1978 at Sibley Memorial Hospital in Washington, DC. Adam's birth dramatically transformed every aspect of our lives. Suffering from infantile jaundice, Adam had to remain in the hospital beyond the specified coverage of our medical insurance. Overnight our living expenses virtually doubled, and we accrued a heavy financial indebtedness that burdened us for over five years. More importantly, we began to view everything in our lives from the perspective of how the Carter administration's domestic and foreign policies would shape the world that our son someday would inherit.

---

[58] DA to Allen W. Jones, 19 March 1978, DA Collection.
[59] DA Journal, 23 December 1977; Alsobrook, "A Southerner in Washington, DC, 1977," DA Collection.

Chapter 4

"Eyewitness to History":
An Archivist in the White House

My job has to be one of the most interesting a person in history could have.... I'm very lucky to be where I am, and I intend to keep my eyes and ears open in order to learn all that I can. I think this knowledge will help me in the future library.
—From the author's letter to
his parents, 5 April 1979

Returning from the holidays in January 1978, I was eager to embark on my new duties at the EOB. Unfortunately, White House officials had not yet authorized the establishment of a NARS liaison office. Two Georgians—White House Counsel Robert J. Lipshutz and Hugh Alton Carter, Jr., Special Assistant to the President for Administration—ultimately would make this decision.

The president's cousin, Hugh Carter, Jr., was born in Americus, Georgia, in 1942. After earning his BS in industrial engineering at Georgia Tech and an MBA at the University of Pennsylvania's Wharton School of Business, he was an executive manager for nine years with the John H. Harland Company in Atlanta. In 1976–1977, he served in the Carter Presidential Campaign and transition. Because of his universally unpopular efforts to eliminate chauffeured vehicles and reduce White House Mess access and other traditional staff privileges, Hugh Carter earned the derisive sobriquet "Cousin Cheap" from Press Secretary Jody Powell.[1]

---

[1] "Hugh A. Carter, Jr., biographical information," Records of the White House Office of Administration, p. 55, Carter Library, https://www.jimmy-carterlibrary.gov/assets/documents/findingaids/Office_of_Administration.pdf (accessed 10 March 2019); Eizenstat, *President Carter*, 78, 323–24; Valerio Giannini exit interview by Marie B. Allen, 14 May 1980, Oral Histories, Carter

Atlanta attorney Bob Lipshutz shared Hugh Carter's parsimonious views as fundraiser and treasurer with the 1976 Carter Presidential Campaign and was firmly committed to the President's pledge to shrink the size of the White House staff and various perquisites. Born in 1921, Lipshutz completed his undergraduate and law degrees at the University of Georgia and served as a US Army officer during World War II. He met the future president in 1966 and later contributed his legal expertise as an unpaid volunteer adviser for several Carter gubernatorial initiatives, including reorganization of the state government.[2]

Both Lipshutz and Hugh Carter were meticulously ethical, modest, self-effacing, and ardently devoted to the President and his programs. Although they lacked the authority and influence of Jody Powell and political adviser Hamilton Jordan, both men conscientiously performed their White House duties. They also hired two experienced aides—Deputy Counsel Michael Cardozo and Special Assistant Valerio Giannini—who became two of our principal White House points of contact.[3]

The two White House lawyers, Lipshutz and Cardozo, met frequently with the NL/NARS team—Reed, Jacobs, and GSA attorney Steve Garfinkel—on a range of complex archival, legal, and political issues. I think that Reed was particularly comfortable in his interactions with Lipshutz, his generational peer and a fellow World War II veteran. Furthermore, Reed, Jacobs, and Garfinkel probably were acquainted with Lipshutz and Cardozo from discussions during the Ford-Carter transition about the disposition of the Nixon presidential materials in storage at the EOB.

Reed and his team also had convivial, but more formal relationships with Hugh Carter and Val Giannini, both of whom were trained academically as engineers. Reed once described Giannini as a different type of "engineer": "He's one of those smart, energetic technical guys who likes to

Library, https://www.jimmycarterlibrary.gov/research/oral_histories (accessed 3 March 2019).

[2] Robert J. Lipshutz exit interview by Marie B. Allen, 29 September 1979, Oral Histories, Carter Library, https://www.jimmycarterlibrary.gov/research/oral_histories (accessed 3 March 2019).

[3] Jody Powell and Valerio Giannini exit interviews, Carter Library; Eizenstat, *President Carter*, 26–27, 31–34, 72, 75–76.

line everything up on the tracks and see that they run on time."

Hugh Carter's expansive management portfolio included overall supervision of approximately 240 employees in various "Operating Units"—Correspondence, Accounting, Military Operations, Chief Executive Clerk, Personnel, Travel, Messengers, Telephone Switchboard, and White House Central Files (WHCF). His office also functioned as a liaison with the US Secret Service, the White House Communications Agency (WHCA), and GSA.[4] Since NARS was a unit of GSA, Carter's office was a logical administrative nexus for resolving any remaining issues about the proposed liaison office.

In January 1978, Dan Reed and Dick Jacobs persistently sought to preserve the distinction between career federal employees and White House staff and to protect NARS detailees from any political pressure in performing their duties. While Lipshutz and Carter appreciated these concerns, they countered with a single question—Would the liaison office records be subject to Freedom of Information Act (FOIA) requests?

As these negotiations proceeded, Lee Johnson and I divided our time between the NL office at NARS and the EOB. Since our direct supervisor, Marie Allen, was on maternity leave, we worked independently in January and February 1978. We determined that, regardless of the liaison office's fate, the future Carter Library needed some basic research tools. An experienced librarian, Johnson compiled a rudimentary bibliography of books and periodicals relating to President Carter, his staff, relatives, and various administration programs and ordered copies of these publications. I prepared an alphabetical file of newspaper clippings and other printed material on Carter-centric topics from "A" to "Z." The books, periodicals, and files later were absorbed into the Carter Library's reference collection.[5]

We remained in limbo, awaiting the resolution of the liaison office's FOIA issue. Then, on 13 January 1978, William Alton Carter, the President's uncle and venerable family patriarch, died at age eighty-nine. A week or two afterward, Hugh Carter notified us that the death of "Uncle

---

[4] Valerio Giannini exit interview, Carter Library.

[5] DA Calendar, 21, 27–28 February, 1 March 1978; DA notes, telephone conversation with Lee R. Johnson, 17 April 2019, DA Collection; Geselbracht and Reed, "The Presidential Library and the White House Liaison Office," 72.

Buddy" reminded the President and First Lady of the urgency of preserving their families' history. Reed believed that any effective White House liaison office depended on the first family's unequivocal support. One of our original program proposals was oral histories. Thus, in mid-January 1978, with Jimmy and Rosalynn Carter fully engaged, we acquired two powerful advocates for establishing our office. Hugh Carter gave us a list of twenty-two Carter and Smith relatives whom the President and First Lady personally selected for oral history interviews. Our marching orders were simple—interview these people as soon as possible. We placed everything else on hold in preparation for the "Carter/Smith Family Oral History Project." Since Marie Allen and I were native Southerners, "fluent in the regional dialects," Hugh Carter asked us to conduct the interviews. He also drafted introductory letters to each of the prospective interviewees, urging their cooperation in preserving their families' history.[6]

Douglas Thurman's NL archivists and WHCA provided technical support and equipment for our interviews. We also purchased an audiotape recorder, microphones, and a large supply of audiocassettes. Between 1978 and 1980, Marie Allen and I traveled to Georgia, South Carolina, Florida, and Pennsylvania and interviewed everyone on Hugh Carter's original list, with the notable exceptions of the President's three siblings. Billy Carter, Ruth Carter Stapleton, and Gloria Carter Spann declined to participate in our program. Nevertheless, we recorded lengthy interviews with the mothers of the President and First Lady—Lillian Carter and Allie Smith.[7]

Launching the family oral history program provided us with, in Reed's World War II nautical terminology, a White House "beach head."

---

[6] "William Alton 'Uncle Buddy' Carter," (1888–1978), *Find a Grave*, memorial no. 35275427, https://www.findagrave.com/memorial/35275427 (accessed 2 March 2019); Geselbracht and Reed, "The Presidential Library and the White House Liaison Office," 71; "DA & MBA [Marie B. Allen] Meeting with Hugh Carter, Jr., RE: Family History," DA Calendar, 10 August 1978; Hugh Carter letters to Carter/Smith Families, ca. January–March 1978, Carter Family Oral History Project File, DA Collection.

[7] Misc. correspondence, memos, and notes, ca. 1978–1981, Carter Family Oral History Project File, DA Collection; "Carter/Smith Family Oral History Project," Oral Histories, Carter Library, https://www.jimmycarterlibrary.gov/research/oral_histories (accessed 3 March 2019).

He earlier had detailed NL personnel to the EOB as a "pre-landing" team to inventory and prepare presidential foreign and domestic gifts for storage at NARS. These artifacts would constitute the core of the Carter Library's museum collection. With our beach head firmly secured, we quickly returned to promoting the other archival and historical services that the liaison office could offer to the White House, including taped exit interviews with departing staff.[8]

Before moving forward with exit interviews and our other missions, the FOIA issue had to be resolved. After three months of negotiations, our attorney, Steve Garfinkel, and Deputy Counsel Mike Cardozo finally devised a resolution to this contentious question. The Garfinkel-Cardozo schematic combined a strict adherence to federal records statutes with a dose of common sense. We would segregate our office records into two discrete series of files. Our administrative, personnel, correspondence, and reference files would be maintained as official NARS records, publicly accessible under FOIA regulations and the Federal Records Act. Other files, containing oral history transcripts and confidential guidance to the White House on sensitive records issues and the establishment of the Carter Library, were designated as "Presidential Historical Materials" (PHM) and were temporarily restricted from public access. While this compromise did not fully alleviate White House concerns about FOIA issues, a formal agreement was reached in May 1978.[9]

While Garfinkel and Cardozo waged legalistic jujitsu, we finalized our preparations for exit interviews. We systematically explored Nixon-era exit interviews to glean information about basic formats and procedures. We next drafted fourteen standard questions for interviewees that emphasized White House staffers' duties and their offices' organization and missions. We added supplementary questions to encompass staffers' previous experience, special projects, and a "typical day" in the White House. We

---

[8] "Program Proposal for Presidential Papers Staff," ca. December 1977, attached to memo, Richard A. Jacobs to James B. Rhoads, 5 January 1978; draft memo, Hugh Carter, Jr., to White House Staff, ca. January–February 1978, Presidential Papers Staff—Establishment File, DA Collection.

[9] Misc. Steve Garfinkel memos and notes, ca. February–May 1978, Presidential Papers Staff—Establishment File; DA Calendar, 15–17 February, 9, 24 March, 3, 22, 30 May 1978, DA Collection.

designed these questions to encourage interviewees' spontaneity. We allowed staffers to go off-script from the standard sequence of questions whenever they wished. I discovered that one particular question often produced fulsome, nuanced responses: "What have you been working on today or this week?" This question usually elicited more detailed, substantive information than simply inquiring about a "typical day."[10]

We originally envisioned our exit interviews as preliminary explorations in advance of more comprehensive oral histories at the Carter Library. Consequently, we generally probed for basic background information that revealed interviewees' levels of involvement in significant policies or events during their White House tenure. We also recorded their permanent addresses on the tapes to facilitate future contacts for follow-up interviews and urged them to donate their personal papers and memorabilia to the Carter Library. Allen, Johnson, and I conducted the majority of the interviews in 1978–1979. North Carolinian Emily Williams, a talented young oral historian at the FDR Library, joined our staff in 1980 and injected a high level of expertise and energy into the exit interview program. Her future husband, Thomas Soapes, who previously had logged extensive oral history hours at the Truman and FDR libraries, also recorded several exit interviews in 1980–1981.[11]

In early June 1978, after Hugh Carter added our office to the White House staff check-out list, our exit interview program gained significant momentum. Each block on the check-out form had to be initialed before staffers received their final paychecks. Although we lacked any official enforcement authority, we encouraged outgoing employees to record a permanent historical account of their White House service. Despite often being physically and emotionally depleted from the rigors of their jobs, they

[10] "Exit Interviews—List of Standard Questions," 1978, Exit Interview Program for White House Staff File, DA Collection.

[11] Misc. memos and notes, ca. 1978–1980, DA Collection; "Exit Interview Project," Oral Histories, Carter Library, https://www.jimmycarterlibrary.gov/research/oral_histories (accessed 3 March 2019). We began recruiting Emily Williams in the spring of 1979, and she transferred from the FDR Library to our staff during the following summer. She and Thomas Soapes were married in Greensboro, North Carolina, on 6 September 1980. Ellen, our son Adam (age two), and I attended the ceremony.

patiently answered our questions. Between June 1978 and January 1981, we taped 163 exit interviews. These sessions varied considerably in both historical content and technical quality. In a few instances, we recorded follow-up interviews with staffers after their departure from the White House. Several interviewees provided important historical background about the politics surrounding the Panama Canal treaties, the 1976 and 1980 Carter Presidential Campaigns, civil service reform, speechwriting procedures, and a variety of domestic policy issues and topics.[12]

Our exit interviews admittedly were somewhat limited in coverage of foreign policy subject matter, primarily because the National Security Council (NSC) staff utilized a separate check-out procedure. Although we interviewed the President's National Security Adviser, Zbigniew Brzezinski, we missed many foreign policy specialists such as Robert Pastor. We were quite successful in interviewing staffers like George Moffett, who played hybrid foreign policy and political roles in organizing public support for the Panama Canal, SALT II, and Middle East Peace treaties. One significant derivative of our exit interview program was that it enabled us to solicit personal papers through direct appeals to the staff. For example, we obtained an extraordinary cache of political *wunderkind* Tom Donilon's 1980 campaign files after his interview. Since adequate funding never materialized for a Carter Library oral history program—in the tradition of those at the JFK and LBJ libraries—our exit interviews eventually gained greater importance as invaluable primary sources for researchers.[13]

With our exit interviews and family oral history program fully operational, we also concentrated on gathering historical documentation for Carter foreign and domestic policies and the organization of the White House. After the Middle East Peace Accords signing ceremony in March 1979, we immediately prepared memoranda for relevant White House

---

[12] "Exit Interview Project," Oral Histories, Carter Library; DA Calendar, 30 May, 15, 28–29 June, 1–3, 27, 30, 30–31 August 1978; DA notes, Panel Discussion on Presidential Oral Histories, Presidential Sites and Libraries Conference, University of Virginia, Charlottesville, VA, 22 June 2010, DA Collection.

[13] Keith Shuler email to DA, 25 March 2019, with attached copy of "Carter/Mondale 1980 Re-Election Committee Papers: A Guide to Its Records at the Jimmy Carter Library," DA Collection; "Exit Interview Project," Oral Histories, Carter Library.

staff, underscoring the historical importance of identifying and preserving documents associated with this event.[14] Despite our best intentions, however, these entreaties to the staff irritated WHCF Chief Frank Matthews and the President's personal aide, Susan Clough, who both accused us of aggressively poaching in their respective domains.[15]

This incident taught us an invaluable lesson about survival within the White House bureaucracy—never underestimate how jealously other offices will protect their turf. Our rift with Clough and Matthews never healed. Following one meeting in WHCF with Matthews and two members of his staff, Clarence "Biff" Henley and Terry Good, my colleague Lee Johnson asked, "Did you notice Frank's reaction? His neck turned red whenever Marie spoke." Later, during our records surveys of White House offices, Matthews demanded that one of his staff accompany us. His directive exacerbated the schism between our office and WHCF. Three years after the original dust-up with Susan Clough, she was still annoyed about her first contact with us.[16] Nurturing a positive working relationship with WHCF and White House senior staff obviously was vital to all of our missions. Yet our overall performance in these two instances, by any objective standard, was abysmal and negatively affected the NL-White House relationship for several years.

Although we occasionally blundered and suffered some setbacks, we forged ahead with our programs. We compiled administrative and organizational histories of many White House offices and collected background papers on major events and policies. Although much of our daily work was routine and repetitive, we believed that our efforts were worthwhile in laying a preliminary intellectual foundation for the Carter Library's archival and research components. Everything we did was designed to augment the

---

[14] Memo, Marie B. Allen to Val[erio] Giannini and Hugh Carter, Jr., 26 March 1979, RE: "Historical Documentation of Middle East Treaty Negotiations," with attached clipping, James Reston, "The Uses of History," *New York Times*, ca. 23 March 1979; draft memo, Marie B. Allen to Susan Clough, ca. 23 April 1979, RE: "Preservation of Documentary Materials Relating to the Middle East Peace Treaty," DA Collection.

[15] DA to Emily Williams Soapes, 23 March 1982, DA Collection.

[16] Ibid.

official historical documentation for the Carter presidency.[17]

We painstakingly chronicled the impact of computerization on the White House. In the late 1970s, an IBM Selectric typewriter was considered to be state-of-the-art office equipment. Rudimentary automated data processing (ADP) hardware was confined to the NSC senior staff offices, the Situation Room in the basement catacombs, the US Secret Service Command Center, the White House Military Operations Office, and WHCA.[18]

Forty-two-year-old Val Giannini, Hugh Carter's deputy, studied engineering at Princeton University in the late 1950s, when computerization was in its infancy. Upon his arrival at the White House in January 1977, Giannini found that even those units like the "Correspondence Shop," which produced heavy volumes of paper, lacked any semblance of automation, other than "Robo" memory typewriters. He and his young ADP designer, Ralph Peck, emphasized the "user aspect" of computers—"You can have the best system in the world, but unless the people use it or 'buy it,' ...have you made progress?"[19] Giannini and Peck determined which operations did not require much automation, such as congressional form letters with standard boiler-plate responses. Giannini asserted, "I think one of our biggest contributions was not trying to use computers in applications where all you really needed was an automatic typewriter tape."[20]

Giannini's heaviest computer applications were in the White House Travel Office and the Presidential Correspondence unit. The Travel Office utilized the American Airlines "Sabre" system to produce hundreds of staff tickets and itineraries. A Presidential Correspondence software program tracked pending legislation, foreign and domestic gifts, and "more important mail," designated by the "MI" acronym. An enhanced "C-Track" system eventually evolved after the Carter administration to include a large percentage of the universe of White House records. In Giannini's assessment of their experimental computer innovations, these were "all things that had never been done before or, at best, had been done very,

---

[17] Alsobrook, "A Portrait of the Archivist as a Young Man," 298–99.
[18] Ibid., 289–90.
[19] Ibid., 290; Valerio Giannini exit interview (quote), Carter Library.
[20] Valerio Giannini exit interview, Carter Library.

very primitively, by hand."[21]

We were particularly interested in Giannini's plans for WHCF. Originally created during the Truman era, Central Files systematically archived presidential papers into precise subject categories. Because of limited space in White House offices, the staff routinely retired their papers to WHCF. These materials formed the bulk of presidential libraries' archival collections.[22] In 1980 Giannini characterized WHCF as one of the "old-fashioned," "somewhat institutional" White House offices: "Frank Matthews has been here for thirty-five years, and half of that as chief of files. He's not an ambitious person; he's a very competent person. He runs a good shop."[23] Giannini also enumerated the specific changes he had implemented:

> In Central Files, we created a true records management system. We modernized the physical environment, added up-to-date methodologies, hired new younger people with computer skills as the older ones retired or left. The result is over the years we had a totally new records management environment, where people are doing their work at computer terminals as well as some of the old manual filing. Instead of making five copies of a document and filing it on five different subjects, you catalog and cross index it by computer and then file the document...by serial number.[24]

These changes in WHCF signaled the dawn of a new age in archiving presidential materials. During the Reagan administration, WHCF was reconstituted as the White House Office of Records Management, with the odd, infelicitous acronym, WHORM. In the George H. W. Bush White House, individual records were subject-coded and then optically scanned

---

[21] Ibid. (quote); DA notes, panel discussion, "The Next Library: Prospects and Problems of the Bush Library and the Advent of Electronic Records," American Historical Association Meeting, 30 December 1992, Washington, DC; DA notes, panel discussion, "The Challenge of Documenting the Presidency," Society of American Archivists (SAA) Meeting, 28 October 1989, St. Louis, MO; Marie B. Allen, memo for the record, 17 September 1980, RE: "Computer Applications in White House Office," DA Collection.

[22] Alsobrook, "A Portrait of the Archivist as a Young Man," 290.

[23] Valerio Giannini exit interview, Carter Library.

[24] Ibid.

into a powerful search and retrieval database. For archival dinosaurs like me, this new electronic format was like "C-Track on steroids." WHORM staff and government software contractors methodically upgraded this system through successive presidencies. The optical scanning component liberated presidential libraries' archivists, allowing them to perform preliminary reference and reviewing tasks at their desks instead of manually searching through original hard-copy records. This revolutionary technological concept—with its ancestral roots in the Carter White House—proved to be a boon for archivists and researchers alike in modern presidential libraries.[25]

In EOB 492 we primarily observed and documented computerization's progress in the White House. While Charles Dollar, John T. Fawcett, and other NARS computer advocates occasionally provided their input to the White House, we rarely had an impact on policy decisions. However, we played an active role in furnishing guidance to the West Wing in 1978 during the congressional debate on the Presidential Records Act (PRA), one of several post-Watergate legislative reform measures.

Prior to the introduction of the PRA legislation, American presidents assumed complete ownership of their papers after leaving the White House. The PRA proposed to abolish this traditional practice by legally mandating that all "presidential historical materials" created after 20 January 1981 would become public property, maintained by the Archivist of the United States and NARS.

This bill specifically differentiated between "presidential records" that documented official, constitutional, statutory, and ceremonial duties, from "personal records" associated with the Chief Executive's political, business, and family interests. Five years after an administration ended, presidential records would be subject to FOIA requests. However, six distinct categories of information could be exempt from public access for twelve years.

---

[25] Alsobrook, "A Portrait of the Archivist as a Young Man," 293; David E. Alsobrook, "The Birth of the Tenth Presidential Library: The Bush Presidential Materials Project," *Government Information Quarterly* 12/1 (January 1995): 39; Bohanan, "The Presidential Libraries System Study," 33; Hugh Thomas Taggart, Jr., email to DA, 14 April 2019; James E. Hastings email to DA, 18 April 2019; DA notes, telephone conversation with Lee R. Johnson, 17 April 2019, DA Collection.

These basic PRA components remained intact in the bill's final draft approved by the US House of Representatives on 4 November 1978.[26]

During the months before the PRA's ratification, we had a rare opportunity to participate directly with White House officials (Bob Lipshutz, Mike Cardozo, and Hugh Carter) in crafting the bill's language. Marie Allen joined Reed, Jacobs, and Garfinkel in giving the White House archival and legal guidance on the legislation from the NARS perspective.

By mid-July 1978, the White House and NARS had reached a consensus on the more problematic portions of the PRA bill. A few constitutional issues required further clarification. For example, was a former president's right to notification and appeal of records releases subject to federal judicial review? Our team also voiced specific concerns about protecting law enforcement and other investigative files, prescribed definitions of presidential and personal records, the six records exemption categories, the presidential appointment of the Archivist of the United States for a ten-year term, and the PRA's implementation date.[27]

We found these two latter issues particularly troubling. If President Carter was reelected in 1980, would the PRA also be applicable to his first term's records? While we assumed that the President's "retroactive compliance" with the PRA would remedy this conundrum, nothing to that effect existed in writing. The draft PRA bill also stipulated that the President would appoint the Archivist of the United States for a single ten-year term, subject to removal only for "good cause." Since the GSA Administrator had appointed Archivist Bert Rhoads a decade earlier, NARS officials feared that he would be replaced in 1981. NARS shared the White

---

[26] "Presidential Records Act (PRA) of 1978," *44 USC* §2201-2209, https://www.archives.gov/presidential-libraries/laws/1978-act.html (accessed 3 March 2019). These six categories that are restricted from public access are security-classified information, federal office appointments, exemptions by federal statute, trade secrets, confidential presidential communications, and personnel and medical files.

[27] Memo, Robert Lipshutz and Hugh Carter to Rep. Jack Brooks, 7 July 1978, "Chairman's Notebook on Presidential Records Act," US House of Representatives Government Operations Committee, https://history.house.gov/House Record/Detail/15032450288 (accessed 5 March 2019).

House objection that "sporadic Presidential appointments" definitely "could politicize the office of the Archivist."[28]

After concurring with our argument about the Archivist's appointment, congressional aides expunged this section of the bill. GSA continued to appoint the Archivist of the United States until NARS became an independent federal agency in the mid-1980s. Afterward, subject to senatorial "advice and consent," presidents would appoint the Archivist of the United States. Congress also acceded to most of the other White House demands and edited the bill accordingly. The negotiators hammered out several compromises. The White House sought fifteen years for enforcement of the six records exemption categories; Congress asked for ten years. The two sides finally agreed that twelve years would be satisfactory.

The final bone of contention was the PRA's implementation date of January 1981. Refusing to capitulate, one congressional staff attorney argued, "[I]t would seem most reasonable that the President would voluntarily adopt the access provisions of the legislation for his first term records, assuming re-election."[29] This statement seemed exceedingly bold, bordering on hypocritical, since Congress rejected a White House suggestion that comparable legislation be adopted for congressional records.

Of course, after Ronald Reagan defeated Jimmy Carter in November 1980, this issue became moot. Preparing to depart with the Carter materials for Georgia in 1981, I thought, "Well, at least I won't ever have to worry about the PRA!" I learned otherwise several decades later, struggling with the complexities of this law at the George H. W. Bush and William J. Clinton Presidential Libraries.

In the wake of the PRA negotiations, Hugh Carter and the White House Counsel's Office established a "Presidential Papers Task Force" to explore the new law's impact on records issues. Over the next two years, Marie Allen played a pivotal role in writing the Task Force's preliminary report, released in January 1980. This report most notably featured precise

---

[28] Ibid.

[29] Briefing paper, "Government Information and Individual Rights Subcommittee Staff Analysis of July 14, 1978 Letter from Robert J. Lipshutz and Hugh A. Carter, Jr.," ca. July–August 1978, "Chairman's Notebook on Presidential Records Act," US House of Representatives Government Operations Committee, history.house.gov/HouseRecord/Detail/15032450288 (accessed 5 March 2019).

descriptions and actual examples of presidential and personal records— essential elements in distinguishing between these two types of documents.[30] Since President Carter was not reelected in 1980, the recommendations were never implemented. However, the report, like our earlier guidance on the PRA legislation, validated the potential contribution of a NARS liaison office in the White House.

We fortified our original beach head and extended our outreach throughout the White House—presidential speechwriters, domestic policy staff, the first lady's office, the vice president's staff, and all the administrative Operating Units. We eventually established positive working relationships with many of these offices. Despite our concerted efforts to win the staff's trust, we encountered considerable opposition from the more overtly political offices.

The so-called "Georgia Mafia"—most prominently, Jody Powell and Hamilton Jordan—who had been close to the President for over a decade, tenaciously protected their White House hegemony and instinctively questioned the motives of any "outside interlopers" like us. They generally perceived our proposals as "Trojan horses" deployed to pierce their inner circle. This stubborn defensive posture undoubtedly evolved from the Beltway media's mockingly condescending depictions of President Carter's senior advisers as "bumpkins from Georgia."[31]

---

[30] DA Calendar, 6–7, 13 November, 11 December 1978; 25 January, 8 February, 21 August, 1 October 1979; 21 January, 8 September 1980; Marie Allen Draft Report, 21 January 1980, typescript, Presidential Papers Task Force File; DA to "Dearest Simon and Hattie Belle [Lester]," 4 January 1980, DA Collection.

[31] Eizenstat, *President Carter*, 26–27, 68–73, 85, 112–14, 684; Robert C. McMath, Jr., "Jimmy Carter: A Southerner in the White House?" in *The Adaptable South: Essays in Honor of George Brown Tindall*, ed. Elizabeth Jacoway, Dan T. Carter, Lester C. Lamon, and Robert C. McMath, Jr. (Baton Rouge LA: Louisiana State University Press, 1991) 256; David E. Alsobrook, "Musings of a Recovering Archivist," keynote address, Society of Alabama Archivists Annual Meeting, 30 September 2011, Spanish Fort, AL, DA Collection. The "Georgia Mafia" sobriquet originated among journalists and political pundits in Washington, DC, during the Ford-Carter transition. Others who later wore this disparaging nickname as a badge of honor included banker Bert Lance, public relations executive Gerald Rafshoon, congressional relations adviser Frank Moore,

On 14 August 1978, at 8:45 a.m., we came face to face with this formidable White House barrier during our long-deferred formal introduction to the senior staff. We met in the Cabinet Room in the West Wing. Reed, Allen, Johnson, and I stood before the assembled senior staff. Hugh Carter, with a quavering nervousness in his voice, introduced us and briefly summarized our role in the White House. In his usual low-key, professorial manner, Reed added that the liaison office was "the historian's conscience to the White House." As he spoke, I recognized several familiar faces around the large table—Jordan, Powell, Lipshutz, Congressional Liaison Adviser Frank Moore, and the politically embattled Margaret "Midge" Costanza, who led the Public Liaison staff but soon would resign under pressure. Domestic Policy Adviser Stuart E. Eizenstat, who later became my trusted friend, was not at the meeting. Jordan sat half-turned in his chair at one end of the table, smiled pleasantly at us, and tried to ease the palpable tension in the room. Powell sat on his right, smoking a cigarette and preoccupied with a thick sheaf of papers before him. Like an inscrutable sphinx, Lipshutz rigidly commanded the far end of the table and never uttered a word during the meeting. A thin trace of a smile gradually appeared on his face, which I interpreted as a tacit affirmation. Powell occasionally interrupted his smoking and reading with a decidedly noncommittal glance toward us. After about ten minutes—which seemed more like an hour—Jordan concluded, "Well, thank y'all for coming. I think what we really need are more good-looking young women and fewer ugly old men!" From where I stood, I could not detect if Jordan's awkward attempt at humor embarrassed Marie Allen, but Reed appeared to be visibly annoyed.[32]

Jordan's comment did not bother me—I realized that he was trying to defuse the pressure that permeated the room. Since our meeting had been cancelled twice over the past six months, I had limited expectations about its outcome. Afterward, I described our brief session with the senior

attorneys Bob Lipshutz, Stuart Eizenstat, Charles Kirbo (in absentia), and First Lady Rosalynn Carter. Apparently because of various unspecified personal and political factors, Georgians Hugh Carter, Jr., and Jack Watson never acquired the full "rights and privileges" of membership in this group.

[32] Geselbracht and Reed, "The Presidential Library and the White House Liaison Office," 72; DA Calendar, 7, 14 August 1978, DA Collection.

staff as "an interesting meeting."[33] Our temporary White House credentials soon were upgraded to permanent green "hard passes," so we assumed that the senior staff, regardless of their indifferent reactions, had given their blessings to our presence in the EOB.

During the remaining months of 1978 and well into 1979, we worked on the family oral histories, exit interviews, a deluge of White House and public reference queries, and sporadic special research projects on the PRA and presidential libraries issues. A succession of young archivists, archives technicians, clericals, and "intermittent" (part-time) college students performed the bulk of our office's "grunt" work. They included Rodney Ross, Robb Storm, Keith Colona, Charley Sullivan, Cassandra Costley, Hildy Forman, Lyndon Flood, and Germaine Belton. Since Marie Allen devoted a heavy percentage of her time to the Presidential Papers Task Force, my supervisory duties increased substantially in 1978–1979. At one point, I succinctly summarized our office's tasks as "records management, reference, and public relations," adding about my own job, "[I]t is routine at times, but for the most part, it is interesting and markedly different from the basic archival work…back at the National Archives."[34]

As a thirty-two-year-old GS-11 archivist, with barely two years of NARS experience, regardless of my own personal job satisfaction I was ambivalent about federal employment as a career. In early spring 1979, I was guardedly optimistic that President Carter's civil service reform proposals would improve the quality of the federal workforce. I complained to my friend Paul Pruitt: "It's almost as if laws governing federal workers are designed to protect the worst ones. I doubt if I will spend my entire life with the government; it's just not challenging enough." Seemingly as an afterthought, I also asserted, "My own job is really the exception—the work is interesting and related to history. My colleagues are competent and hard-working."[35] Five months later, in another letter to Pruitt, I wrote, "The best aspect of living in the DC area now is that there are so many other Southerners up here with us. Of course, in my building at work, I hear a lot of friendly accents, and that makes it easier to survive in this

---

[33] DA Calendar, 14 August 1978, DA Collection.
[34] DA to J. Mills Thornton III, 12 June 1980, DA Collection.
[35] DA to Paul M. Pruitt, Jr., 24 March 1979, DA Collection.

world."[36]

With the historians' "PhD glut" still very much in evidence in the late 1970s, I did not take my position for granted, noting in December 1978, "Extremely lucky to be where I am, with a job I like."[37] A year later, I informed two Alabama friends, "I've really enjoyed my job, and I've been very fortunate to have the chance to work here."[38] I likewise told one of my former West Virginia University professors that my current EOB assignment was "challenging and quite unique, ...one that I will never forget."[39] Yet I did not glamorize the work, as revealed in my remarks in October 1979 to historian Tennant McWilliams in Birmingham: "No great earth-shattering news to report. Everything of a job-related nature is typically hectic. Over the past three or four months, we have worked our asses off."[40]

My parents had sacrificed mightily to support my undergraduate and graduate studies. As typical proud parents, they always were indefatigable advocates who reveled in each of my academic and career mileposts, regardless of their actual significance. Whenever possible, I attempted to let my mother and father know about the direct correlation between my academic preparation and archival career. Via telephone calls and letters, I frequently gave them updates on my activities at the EOB. In early April 1979, after attending the Middle East Peace Accords ceremony on the White House North Lawn, I wrote:

> It was really exciting, and I'll always remember it.... I'm also very lucky to have such a secure job during a period when most of my graduate colleagues are unable to find work, especially in history or related fields. My job has to be one of the most interesting that a person in history could have. In short, I'm very lucky to be where I am, and I intend to keep my eyes and ears open in order to learn all that I can. I think this knowledge will help me in the future library.[41]

---

[36] DA to Paul M. Pruitt, Jr., 22 August 1979, DA Collection.

[37] DA to Paul M. Pruitt, Jr., 7 December 1978, DA Collection.

[38] DA to Deborah and Billy Paul Austin, 16 December 1979, DA Collection.

[39] DA to Edward M. Steel, Jr., 5 November 1979, DA Collection.

[40] DA to Tennant S. McWilliams, 11 October 1979, DA Collection.

[41] DA to "Dearest Mother and Daddy [Frances and Thomas Alsobrook]," 5 April 1979, DA Collection.

After I was first detailed to the EOB, several of my Auburn University professors, including Allen W. Jones and Leah Atkins, reminded me of my obligation as an "eyewitness to history" to preserve records of my observations and impressions of this unique experience. Carefully employing their advice, I wrote detailed "memoranda for the record" and journal entries. These contemporaneous records and my voluminous correspondence with relatives, friends, and former professors featured commentary about everything I observed—President Carter's physical appearance as he aged prematurely, the EOB's depressing atmosphere following his infamous "Malaise Speech" in July 1979, the jubilant White House reception for the US Winter Olympics team in February 1980, and the heartbreaking aftermath of the aborted rescue of the American hostages in Tehran in April 1980.[42]

The day after the failed covert Iranian raid, recuperating at home from the flu, I confided to my journal: "[L]ike many Americans, am still sorting out the facts as they've been presented to us. There seems to be a hint from the Admin[istration] that they may try to go in again—soon. I pray the hostages survive, but I'm afraid that some of them will be killed before all of this ends…[and] more US military may forfeit their lives in this thing."[43]

In spring 1980, I was overwhelmed with a nagging fear that the Iranian hostage crisis would escalate into a major military conflict. The first week of April was extremely nerve-wracking after President Carter formally suspended US diplomatic relations with Iran. I saw a "massive Iranian demonstration" led by students on 7 April and the blockading of Massachusetts Avenue the following day by the police and FBI, "so that they can keep an eye on the Iranian diplomats who are preparing to leave by midnight."[44] I personally thought that the heavy security cordon near the Iranian Embassy was to protect the diplomats from "irate Americans." That evening I further reflected:

Tense atmosphere the day after President's announcement that

---

[42] Alsobrook, "A Portrait of the Archivist as a Young Man," 296–96.

[43] DA Journal, 26 April 1980, DA Collection.

[44] DA to "Dearest Hattie Belle & Simon [Lester]," 7 April 1980; DA to Mary S. Miller, 8 April 1980 (quote), DA Collection.

diplomatic relations would be severed w/ Iran. Heard on news to-night that all Iranian diplomats are at Dulles Airport, preparing to fly to London & on to Iran…. It looks as if we are only a short distance away from a blockade or mining of Iranian ports.

And if that comes, how far away can war be? I pray that if war comes again (it would be the 3rd since I was born) that my genera-tion & others who are slightly younger can go ahead & fight it, so [our two-year-old son] Adam will never have to face such a terrible situation….I wonder if my father had similar feelings in 1940–41?[45]

During this tumultuous week in April 1980, Egyptian President Anwar el-Sadat also was meeting with President Carter. On 8 April hun-dreds of curious sightseers milled around the White House and along Pennsylvania Avenue. I watched this scene unfold: "Beautiful spring day in the afternoon—very warm. Most security I've seen in the three years I've worked in the EOB. As usual, DC cops most uptight & rude to pe-destrians trying to cross streets near EOB. Sadat motorcade departed Blair House around 5:10 p.m.—coincided w/ departure of thousands of federal employees for home…."[46]

Sadat's departure reminded me of the triumphant event a year earlier, when he embraced Israeli Prime Minister Menachem Begin and President Carter after signing the Middle East Peace Accords. During the dreary winter and spring of 1980, with the Iranian hostage crisis steadily sapping the lifeblood from the Carter presidency, celebratory occasions were rare. However, one exceptional day still resonates with me.

On 25 February 1980, the young American Olympians who recently had competed in the Winter Games came to the White House. The US hockey team, victorious over the mighty Russians and en route to a gold medal, had acquired a heroic status. Jody Powell was struck by "how young they were. Here these kids were, at least, for those brief few days, probably as idolized as any group of young people, …in the country."[47] I also was in the crowd that day and tried to crystallize that moment:

Today will always be one of the most memorable days of my life.

[45] DA Journal, 8 April 1980, DA Collection.
[46] DA to Mary S. Miller, 8 April 1980; DA Journal, 9 April 1980 (quote), DA Collection.
[47] Jody Powell exit interview, Carter Library.

We were invited to see the arrival of the US Olympics team at the White House. This is the first South Lawn function we've been invited to in about 2 years....From where Keith Colona & I were standing, we could see the team members pass by & wave. I would estimate we were about 15 yards from them when they passed. The only one of the hockey players I recognized was [Jim] Craig, the goalie. The President, Mrs. Carter, & Joan Mondale were waiting on the steps near the Truman Balcony. The President looked very good. His color seemed to be better than it's been for weeks. He gave a very good speech, esp[ecially] during the opening portions in which he commented on the accomplishments of the team. He singled several people out, incl[uding] Beth Heiden, [the speed skater]. He exhibited a great deal of warmth toward her in particular—He hugged and kissed her when she came up the stairs. The hockey players looked a little dazed by all of the attention. They were wide-eyed & smiling. They responded to the crowd's applause by waving & taking pictures. This was an occasion when it was simply wonderful to be an American. I think this is what our nation is all about—a group of young athletes receiving heroes' welcomes during a time of international crisis. Our many foreign & domestic problems somehow seem smaller on a day like this.[48]

I understood that although "my attempt to capture this occasion in words is rather puny," I hoped "to experience another day like this one. If not, at least I will have the satisfaction of having it happen once."[49] Today, thirty-nine years after that magical hour on the South Lawn in 1980, I realize that those "kids" now probably are in their late fifties or early sixties. I wonder how they remember that single day in their lives and if they fully comprehend its importance to the entire nation.

This memorable event was only a brief respite from my two major preoccupations in 1980—the Iranian hostage crisis and the presidential campaign. During the campaign's infancy—long before Democratic Senator Ted Kennedy challenged the President and Ronald Reagan seized the Republican nomination—I observed, "Washington eats, breathes, and sleeps POLITICS. I have never seen such a hyped-up political environ-

---

[48] DA Journal, 25 February 1980, DA Collection.
[49] Ibid.

ment in my entire life."[50] Peering into my political crystal ball in January 1980, I cautiously prophesied, "[I]f the President gets the hostages back and keeps us out of a war in the Near East, while simultaneously giving the impression of dealing with the economy and energy-related problems, ...he will surely win the nomination and will be re-elected. Still these are a lot of 'If's.'"[51] Within the context of the campaign, I optimistically speculated about our future in the EOB:

> I'm still enjoying my job tremendously. Since I was promoted last fall, I've been given more supervisory duties in regard to the younger archivists on our staff, especially in carrying out our office's oral history duties. Now that it looks fairly good that Carter will be re-elected, I think our small office will be given more tasks.... We are in a very unique position—We have a good opportunity to see that the historical documentation for this Administration is accurate and comprehensive. We are breaking a lot of new ground, and each day offers a different challenge.[52]

In spring 1980, my greatest personal challenge was maintaining a historian's objectivity as the situation rapidly deteriorated in Tehran. My wife Ellen and I enthusiastically supported Jimmy Carter in 1976 primarily based on his campaign promise that the US would no longer be the "arms merchant of the world" and would avoid protracted overseas military adventures.[53]

In March 1980, I informed Paul Pruitt, "I'm troubled about the domestic and foreign situations at present, and I don't like equating patriotism with blind support for the Administration." Explaining the fading of "my earlier enthusiasm," I added, "Part of my problem is that I've seen a lot of things at close range, and I've become somewhat cynical about the way the system functions. Even though my job is closely connected with this Administration, the historian in me prevents my blindly supporting all of this President's policies."[54] On the eve of the Democratic and

---

[50] DA to Tennant S. McWilliams, 11 October 1979, DA Collection.
[51] DA to Paul M. Pruitt, Jr., 7 January 1980, DA Collection.
[52] Ibid.
[53] DA to Paul M. Pruitt, Jr., 14 March 1979, 24 January, 12 February 1980; DA to Cassandra "Sandy" Costley, 22 June 1980, DA Collection.
[54] DA to Paul M. Pruitt, Jr., 22 March 1980, DA Collection.

Republican primaries in Wisconsin in early April 1980, I commented darkly in my journal:

> It really seems that domestic politics & re-election campaign are getting inextricably tied w/ Iranian crisis. At least, that's the feeling I have. It's almost as if the Admin[istration] wanted some kind of news or crisis that would give the appearance of forward movement as Wisc. voters went to polls....Carter is beginning to act rather desperate, like a man who is willing to take some risky measures to stay in the WH.[55]

Two weeks later, increasingly bombarded with daily "gloomy and jingoistic" news reports, "I sensed that [the] patience of most Americans is wearing very thin, & I think there will be a clamor for military action.... I hope that Reagan's candidacy will not drive the President further to the right & maybe cause him to react in a militaristic fashion to the crisis."[56] Twelve days later, President Carter dispatched the ill-fated "Desert One" mission to extract the American hostages from Tehran.

Secret planning for the clandestine raid had been underway for about five months. Primarily because of a lack of interservice coordination and ancillary bombing and the collision of a C-130 aircraft with a helicopter, the rescue mission failed spectacularly. In Stuart Eizenstat's compelling personal account of that event from the White House perspective, his close friend Hamilton Jordan, realizing that the Carter presidency "had potentially gone down in flames with the military equipment," ran into the President's bathroom and loudly vomited.[57]

Within the walls of EOB 492, after the aborted rescue mission and Secretary of State Cyrus Vance's resignation in April 1980, we faced a sobering reality—the Carter presidency was in a spiraling "free fall." To prepare for the worst-case scenario, as we inventoried the archival holdings in each White House office, Marie Allen drafted a secret moving plan if the President lost the election.

As we quietly fine-tuned our plan, I heard some disquieting news: "Marie told me today that in meeting yesterday, some talk of need to

---

[55] DA Journal, 1 April 1980, DA Collection.
[56] DA Journal, 13 April 1980, DA Collection.
[57] Eizenstat, *President Carter*, 794–806 (quote on p. 803).

'clean' files by WH staffers before end of Admin[istration] to remove certain embarrassing records." Hugh Carter had shared this comment from the senior staff with her. I thought, "Apparently, this outfit failed to learn a great deal from Watergate," and then concluded, "I have grown increasingly disillusioned with these people and their policies. I guess this attitude will be good for me in maintaining a semblance of objectivity in working on their records (if there are any left...)."[58]

Meanwhile, by mid-August 1980, a new NARS leadership team had assumed control on Mahogany Row. After Rhoads resigned as Archivist of the United States, Robert M. Warner succeeded him. Reed retired after a distinguished career as Assistant Archivist for Presidential Libraries and was replaced by James E. O'Neill. In mid-August, Allen and I briefed O'Neill and Warner on our liaison office programs and the Carter moving plan for several hours.[59]

Shortly afterward, I wrote to my mother, "As you can tell, there is a great deal of interest in Presidential libraries and our office in particular at the moment. I think it's because a lot of people expect a change in Administrations in November." Without sharing my own growing doubts about the President's reelection, I also mentioned that the recent Democratic National Convention was not a salutary experience for him and his supporters: "If you saw any of it, I think you know what I mean.... I don't think [it] did him an awful lot of good."[60]

Several days later, I received an impassioned letter about the campaign from Charles Sullivan, one of our former intermittent student workers, who was enrolled in history graduate studies at Columbia University. I agreed with him that "the President has a lot going for him in terms of character, honesty, etc., and if he can hang onto that image, ...he may make a Trumanesque comeback against the challenger from the West."[61] Yet I did not tell my idealistic young friend that I was uncertain if Presi-

[58] DA Journal, 10 April 1980, DA Collection.
[59] Misc. memos and notes, August–September 1980, briefing for Dr. Bob Warner File; Presidential Papers Staff—Summary of White House Activities, 1978–1980 File, DA Collection.
[60] DA to "Dearest Mother [Frances Alsobrook]," 15 August 1980, DA Collection.
[61] DA to Charles Sullivan, 18 August 1980, DA Collection.

dent Carter's admirable personal traits would be enough for him to win the election. I definitely shared Sullivan's positive aspirations for the President's reelection chances. In mid-October, I told my parents that President Carter hopefully would keep his job because the Republican political juggernaut was losing steam and its candidate lacked "what it took for the long haul."[62]

Once more I exhibited my ineptitude as a political prophet. During the final week of the election, I noticed that the EOB's hallways seemed to be unusually gloomy, devoid of the typical convivial banter among staffers. On election day, I was working in the peaceful solitude of the White House Information Center within the ornate EOB Library. René Dupuy, a young graduate student from Texas, pumped his fist at me and exulted, "We're gonna win!" I quietly replied, "Man, I certainly hope so." Although my tone probably sounded less than convincing to him, a few weeks earlier I had confided to my parents: "[I]t's best for the country that Carter be reelected because Reagan could get us into a lot of trouble abroad."[63] Of course, in the grand scheme of political history, my personal views about Ronald Reagan did not matter much. On 4 November 1980, the American people decisively chose the charismatic Republican over the beleaguered incumbent as their next president.

As a Southerner—despite my opposition to some of his policies—I desperately wanted President Carter to succeed and win a second term in office. Because of my own history with stereotypical preconceptions of Southerners as "bumpkins," I commiserated deeply with the "Georgia Mafia" that they had been treated miserably by the press since the transition.[64] I also selfishly believed that the President's reelection would expand our office's role in the White House. Moreover, at the time I thought that Jimmy Carter was among the most ethical, moral, intelligent presidents in US history. I still adhere to this belief.

Although the long lens of history eventually would vindicate him in many ways, the harsh immediacy of presidential politics is not very for-

---

[62] DA to "Dearest Mother and Daddy [Frances and Thomas Alsobrook]," 18 October 1980, DA Collection.

[63] Ibid.

[64] DA to Sherrod and John West, 9 November 1980; DA to Paul M. Pruitt, Jr., 15 November 1980, DA Collection.

giving. Despite President Carter's herculean efforts in behalf of peace in the Middle East, protection of international human rights, and comprehensive environmental and energy programs, the toxic duality of a stagnant economy and the Iranian hostage crisis was politically insurmountable.

After the election, I joined a small archival contingent in triaging and boxing the surviving remnants of records at the central Carter Presidential Campaign headquarters—perhaps the most personally depressing, debilitating experience of my entire EOB tenure. Situated on an entire floor of an old downtown department store, the campaign offices' interiors resembled a large debris field left in the wake of a catastrophic natural disaster. Another historical image also briefly flashed through my mind—the gutted interior of the German Reich Chancellery in Berlin in 1945. We surveyed the devastation and discovered abandoned records haphazardly crammed in file cabinets and desk drawers and littering the floor. Forlorn twisted coils of telephone and television coaxial cable hung from the ceiling.[65] After bringing a modicum of order and stability to this chaotic scene, we returned to the reality of our greatest challenge back in the White House.

We immediately activated our previously secret moving plan. Since President Carter had not been reelected, we no longer had to worry about the PRA and its possible retroactive applicability to first-term records. At first glance, our mission was intimidating for even the most seasoned archivists among us—inventory, pack, and remove *all* of the Carter presidential materials from the White House, EOB, New Executive Office Building, and NARS and transport everything to Georgia before the Reagan Inauguration on 20 January 1981.

Relocating a president's papers, memorabilia, and other possessions at its most elementary level is similar to moving from a personal residence, but multiplied exponentially many times over. Perhaps a more accurate analogy is that a White House move is like emptying and transporting the contents of an entire residential neighborhood or apartment complex. Although a few discrete series of institutional precedent files would be left behind for the incoming Reagan administration, virtually everything else

---

[65] DA Calendar, 16, 21, 24–25 November 1980; DA to Mary S. Miller, 15 November 1980; DA to Debbie Davis, 15 November 1980, DA Collection.

from the Carter era was bound for Georgia. We ultimately assumed custody of 27 million pages of documents, 1.5 million photographs, and 30 thousand artifacts.[66]

To accomplish our daunting relocation mission, NL allotted twenty archivists, including about a dozen from the Nixon Project. Several fellow former NL trainees participated in the move—Scott Parham, Fred Graboske, Mary Elizabeth Ruwell, and David Van Tassel. James O'Neil selected Van Tassel as the overall coordinator of the NARS archival and logistical portions of the operation. He worked closely with the Defense Department, the Federal Protective Service (FPS), and Roadway Trucking Company. He also ensured that we received our moving equipment (pallet jacks and forklifts) and supplies in a timely manner.[67]

Based on our earlier systematic visits in White House offices, we already had a rough estimate of the volume of materials to be moved. Using these figures, we ordered boxes, wooden pallets, and nylon straps. With our direct input, the White House Counsel's Office sent a memo to all staff with guidance on the final disposition of any papers still in their possession and not previously retired to WHCF. We next conducted fresh surveys of each office to determine specific volumes of papers. We also provided the staff with instructions for preparing itemized folder-title and container lists and scheduled a date to pick up their boxes. In multiple instances, we assigned archivists to individual offices to prepare finding aids and box labels prior to the pickup dates. Approximately 95 percent of the White House staff fully complied with our procedures and instructions. In a few isolated cases, they simply abandoned their files in trash cans or corridors.[68] Our moving team worked an average of twelve to fifteen hours each day. In late November 1980, I briefly described the early stages of the move: "[W]e are not yet into chaos in the EOB, but we are

---

[66] Alsobrook, "A Portrait of the Archivist as a Young Man," 290.

[67] DA to Paul M. Pruitt, Jr., 15 November 1980; DA email to David Van Tassel, 23 March 2019; David Van Tassel email to DA, 25 March 2019, DA Collection.

[68] Draft memos, Lloyd Cutler to White House Staff, ca. November–December 1980, Disposition of White House Staff Papers File; DA notes, "The Move to Georgia," presentation, Georgia Archives Institute, 19 June 1987, Atlanta, GA, DA Collection.

fast approaching it."[69]

Throughout November and December 1980, many White House staffers were in a state of denial over the election's outcome. They were stunned, depressed, and embittered. Some of them were reduced to tears; others brooded alone behind closed doors. On one memorable occasion when I delivered a supply of empty boxes to a West Wing office, the occupant angrily reacted, "Oh, I recognize you—you're the undertaker, and you're here to measure the corpse!" Before taping an exit interview with Jody Powell in early December, I detected that he clearly was very morose and distraught. In a futile effort at brightening his spirits, I said that our staff regretted President Carter's defeat and had hoped to have a second term to continue our work. Pointing toward his cluttered desk, Powell sarcastically snapped, "That's just because y'all want to have more stacks of paper like these."[70]

While we personally empathized with the emotionally devastated, inconsolable staff, time was of the essence in expeditiously moving everything from the White House. Van Tassel later reported, "I remember briefing the NARS office heads in December [1980] that the Carter folks were finally acknowledging that they had lost and were beginning to cooperate in move planning."[71] He also had the daunting task of explaining to White House officials which items could be transported legally by NARS. For example, he told Mike Cardozo "or one of his minions that we couldn't move Amy's treehouse with the archival materials."[72]

Acutely focused on identifying and removing all of the Carter presidential papers and related materials from the White House, we seldom noticed the relentless activity of the Reagan transition around us. However, in late November, I offered an overtly partisan glimpse into the President-elect's impact on life in the city:

---

[69] DA notes, remarks, "Sweet History" Event, History Museum of Mobile, 13 November 2011, Mobile, AL; DA to Charles Sullivan, 27 November 1980 (quote), DA Collection.

[70] DA to Cassandra "Sandy" Costley, 3 December 1980; DA Calendar, 2 December 1980, DA Collection; Jody Powell exit interview, Carter Library.

[71] David Van Tassel email to DA, 25 March 2019, DA Collection.

[72] Ibid. Amy was President Carter's daughter.

[I]t's really interesting to observe how we transfer power in this country. All of the media attention is focused on the Reagan headquarters on M Street, and it seems that Carter has already left town. Almost every day the *Post* or the *Star* carries a story about how Reagan will bring back "pomp and circumstance" to the Presidency. We are really into the Reagan honeymoon period, in which he can do no wrong with the media. Reporters are still raving over the visit he paid to the Hill to woo all of the heavyweights up there.... [W]hen Reagan was in town, he stayed in one of the row houses at Jackson Place, just down from the National Trust [for Historic Preservation] offices. I think the address is 735 Jackson Place. They had the entire block roped off to keep the public out, and there were policemen and Secret Service men all over the place. Reporters were camped outside the door around the clock.... [A]s soon as Reagan becomes President and has to make a few unpopular decisions or makes a few mistakes, the honeymoon with the press in this town will be over.73

My prediction, of course, was completely wrong—President Reagan's press "honeymoon" was very lengthy, and his overall personal popularity with the electorate propelled him into a second term.

As we finished our preparations for the Carter move to Georgia, my thoughts were far removed from what might lie ahead for the new president and his staff. Instead, I was concerned with my own upcoming journey and future archival career. I was the only member of our EOB staff who accompanied the Carter materials to Atlanta. Although Allen probably would have moved to Georgia after a second Carter term, she was reluctant to go in 1981. Emily Williams Soapes's husband, Tom, wanted to remain in Washington, DC, so she also did not volunteer to transfer. Our colleague Lee Johnson had left the EOB for a position at NARS in October 1979. He later returned to the EOB and served with distinction for many years as a WHORM supervisor before retiring in 2000. Several Nixon Project archivists expressed an interest in transferring to Georgia, but only if they were guaranteed promotions.74

---

73 DA to Charles Sullivan, 27 November 1980, DA Collection.

74 DA Calendar, 8 October 1979; DA to Charles Sullivan, 27 November 1980; DA to Cassandra "Sandy" Costley, 3 December 1980; DA notes, telephone conversation with Lee R. Johnson, 31 March 2019, DA Collection.

Between late November 1980 and mid-January 1981, FPS police escorted nineteen truckloads of Carter materials to Andrews Air Force Base, where they were secured. On inauguration eve, we were confident that the first part of our mission was finished. Any materials that were not shipped on the final trucks would be stored temporarily at NARS and transported later to Atlanta.

In the chilly, pre-dawn darkness on 20 January 1981, Ellen delivered me to Andrews Air Force Base. NARS Security Chief Larry Oberg met me at the gate, and we proceeded to an administrative building, where our Roadway truckers and military escort were waiting. Fifteen US Army Airborne military policemen from Fort Bragg, North Carolina, would accompany our truck convoy on the long trek to Atlanta. Armed with loaded pistols and clad in Class-A dark green uniforms, spit-shined paratrooper boots, and maroon berets, these young men from the 101st Airborne Division "took their jobs very seriously," I noted later.[75]

Our convoy of nineteen tractor trailer trucks departed from the base around sunrise at 6:45 a.m. "By the time we got to the first overpass going into Northern Virginia," I recalled, "there were already people gathered to look at the trucks. As we got farther into Virginia, the crowds on the overpasses got bigger.... [B]y about the third or fourth overpass, there must have been 400 to 500 people hanging over the road.... They probably thought we were carrying something dangerous."[76] Upon reaching the North Carolina line via Interstate 95, the Virginia State Troopers who had led us from Andrews Air Force Base were replaced with North Carolina Highway Patrol officers.

Ronald Reagan had become our new president by the time we arrived at the Roadway truck terminal in Kernersville, North Carolina, for a safety

---

[75] Amy Gandy, "Library Commemorates Tenth Anniversary," *The Center-piece* [Carter Center Newsletter] 4/2 (February 1991): 3 (quote); DA to Charles Sullivan, 2 February 1981, DA Collection.

[76] Memo, Donald B. Schewe to NL [Office of Presidential Libraries], 27 May 1982, RE: "Progress of the Carter Presidential Materials Project," DA Collection; DA quoted in Gandy, "Library Commemorates Tenth Anniversary," 3. Over the years, Martin Elzy and I pondered the question of exactly how many trucks were in the convoy—were there seventeen or nineteen? We eventually agreed on the latter figure.

inspection. After a quick bathroom break, I placed a long distance-collect telephone call to the NL office, where the entire staff was watching the inaugural parade on Pennsylvania Avenue. Van Tassel answered my call and passed me on to Jacobs. I gave him a brief update on the convoy's status, which our MP major called a "SITREP," a situation report. After acquiring a fresh group of truck drivers, we continued on to Atlanta.[77]

The trip southward was generally uneventful and monotonous. Our MP major, a Vietnam combat veteran and a West Virginia University graduate, was pleased to learn that I also had earned a degree at his alma mater. To pass the time, we shared mutual memories of our experiences in Morgantown. One of our trucks, accompanied by a couple of MPs, briefly dropped out of the convoy to adjust a tire's pressure. We rotated our state police escort again at the North Carolina-South Carolina line. We paused for dinner just before dark at a sprawling truck stop near Greenville, South Carolina. Wearily sauntering into the restaurant with our armed MPs and state troopers, we were greeted with quizzical stares and dead silence.

The scene reminded me of countless Western movies in which a sheriff enters a saloon and the loud piano music and conversations abruptly cease. I suspected that the diners thought we were desperados being escorted to federal prison. As we prepared to leave, a local television crew was filming the parked trucks. Two MPs asked me if I wanted them "to shoo away" the cameramen and reporters. I told the young paratroopers that would not be necessary unless someone tampered with the trucks' sealed locks.

Back on the highway, our South Carolina state police peeled away from the convoy, and we anticipated the imminent arrival of Georgia troopers to accompany us on the final leg of our journey. However, they never materialized out of the freezing darkness. Several truckers sarcastically proclaimed on their CB radios that this conspicuous absence of the Georgia police vehicles did not reflect well on President Carter's popularity in his home state.

On 21 January 1981, after about twenty-two hours on the road, as freezing rain fell, we finally entered the gates of Fort McPherson around 3:30 a.m. Today, I have distinct memories of that moment: "I'll never

---

[77] DA to Charles Sullivan, 2 February 1981, DA Collection.

forget how tired I was. I hadn't slept for twenty-two hours…. To top it off, it was sleeting, and the weather was terrible."[78] Since our last bathroom visit occurred in South Carolina, and with no idea where the nearest Army latrines were located, we all unashamedly emptied our bladders in the darkness just inside Fort McPherson's main gates. This was an inauspicious "christening" ceremony for the future Carter Library.

Miserably standing in the icy rain at Fort McPherson, I was too exhausted to attach any historical significance to the end of our mission and everything that had transpired over the past three years at the EOB. With the passage of time, however, I gained a sharper perspective and understanding of that time in my life. In January 1981, I assumed that the Carter move would be my only opportunity to participate as an archivist in a presidential transition. But I was assigned to this duty again in 1992–1993 and 2000–2001. I also thought my service in the EOB never would be replicated, but I was detailed to that grand old structure again ten years later. Finally, never in my wildest dreams did I expect to help establish more than one presidential library. Amazingly, that experience occurred two more times during my career.[79]

The Carter transition and relocation established multiple historical landmarks. The 1980–1981 transition proved to be the last time that presidential materials were transported solely by motor vehicles. Afterward, C-5 and C-130 military aircraft (combined with trucks) became the workhorses for White House moves. While I was aware that the Carter Library would the last one in which its archival collections would not be subject to the PRA's statutory regulations, I failed to foresee this law's unprecedented effect on future libraries' processing priorities and researchers' timely access to the records. At some basic level, I also inherently understood that the Carter Library would be the last traditional research facility in the NARS system that was not heavily reliant on computers. Yet I did not comprehend the magnitude of the dawning electronics revolution.[80]

---

[78] DA quoted in Gandy, "Library Commemorates Tenth Anniversary," 3.

[79] Alsobrook, "A Portrait of the Archivist as a Young Man," 289, 292–93, 296.

[80] Ibid., 290, 292–94; David Van Tassel email to DA, 15 April 2019, with attached DVT memo for the record, 28 April 1989, RE: "Transfer of Reagan Presidential Records from Washington to California," DA Collection.

As the Carter era ended, I was ready to proceed with my career, informing Paul Pruitt, "At this point, I just want to put Washington in the past and not look back too much. Maybe one of these days I'll be able to look back at my time here with greater objectivity. Right now I'm just not ready to do that."[81] Yet, despite the debilitating tumult of the Carter transition, I sensed that a liaison office like ours probably would not exist in the future. Allen and Soapes remained behind in the EOB and gallantly tried to defend our beach head by dispensing guidance on the PRA and presidential libraries issues to the Reagan White House staff. However, much of their time was absorbed in stockpiling scattered remnants of Carter materials and in preparing historical research papers "on deadline" on Camp David, the EOB, and the "location of offices used by the Presidents" other than the West Wing oval edifice.[82]

By spring 1982, the NARS liaison role in the EOB had ended. After Soapes transferred to the Nixon Project, she compared her new assignment with working at the EOB: "In many ways, I feel as though I'm doing more to serve the cause of history. The cataloging and review process may not be exciting, even sometimes tedious, but it's a worthy endeavor.... My experience was that I was used like putty to plug up holes, whenever they sprang up. It's not an intellectual job; at least I didn't find it so. I guess it could be, under some conditions."[83]

My communications with Soapes and other former colleagues over the years reinforced my own pride in our accomplishments at the EOB from 1978–1981. With meager staff and budgetary resources, we implemented an extensive oral history program, produced substantial historical background material, identified and preserved federal records for eventual transfer to the Carter Library, and established procedures for the solicitation and acquisition of personal papers and memorabilia. While we failed to reach all of our ambitious goals, I firmly believe that we achieved much of Reed's vision of "the historian's conscience to the White House."[84] As

---

[81] DA to Paul M. Pruitt, Jr., 15 November 1980, DA Collection.

[82] Emily W. Soapes to DA, 11 February, 17 March, 9 April 1981 (quote); DA to Emily W. Soapes, 14 April, 21 October 1981, DA Collection.

[83] Emily W. Soapes to DA, 11 March 1982, DA Collection.

[84] "Federal Records: Record Group 220, Records of Temporary Committees, Commissions, and Boards," Research, Carter Library, https://www.

an "eyewitness to history," I was one of the truly fortunate archivists who contributed to this remarkable adventure, and I will never forget that experience.

jimmycarterlibrary.gov/research/fed_records; "Donated Historical Materials," Research, Carter Library, https://www.jimmycarterlibrary.gov/research/donated (both websites accessed 5 March 2019); Geselbracht and Reed, "The Presidential Library and the White House Liaison Office," 72.

David Alsobrook, age 3, at Gulf Homes, Chickasaw, Alabama, 1949.

Courtesy of David Alsobrook.

My Peace Corps "mugshot," Northern Illinois University,
DeKalb, Illinois, 1967.

Courtesy of David Alsobrook.

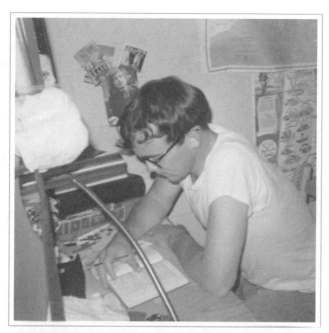

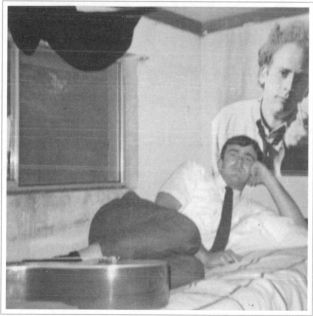

A day in the life during my time at Auburn University, 1967.
Courtesy of David Alsobrook.

David on the phone at the Alabama Department of Archives & History, Montgomery, Alabama, ca. 1975–1976.

Courtesy of David Alsobrook.

David Alsobrook and Ellen Lester, ca. 1975–1976.

Courtesy of David Alsobrook.

My White House identification badge, 1978–1981.

Courtesy of David Alsobrook.

President Jimmy Carter, Rosalynn Carter, and Joan Mondale standing on the Truman balcony at the White House awaiting the arrival of U.S. Winter Olympics Team, 1980.

Courtesy of Jimmy Carter Presidential Library and Museum.

Carter Presidential Materials Project Staff at Carter Library
construction site, Atlanta, Georgia, ca. 1985. *Front row, left to
right:* Donald Schewe, Martin Elzy, Robert Bohanan, James
Yancey, David Alsobrook, and Charles Stokely; *back row, left to
right:* Patrice McDermott, Kathleen Gillespie, MeloDee French,
Roslyn Wright, Evelyn Ward, Faye Jensen, Linda Wyatt, and
Liane Harris.

Courtesy of David Alsobrook.

President Carter's fly-fishing demonstration/tutorial for staff's children, Carter Library, Atlanta, Georgia, ca. 1991.

Courtesy of Jimmy Carter Presidential Library and Museum.

Among the stacks of archives inside the Carter Library. *Front to back:* Director Donald B. Schewe, Assistant Director Martin I. Elzy, and David Alsobrook, 1987.

Courtesy of Nick Arroyo, Atlanta Journal-Constitution.

President George H. W. Bush at his typewriter in the White House, 1989.

Courtesy of George H. W. Bush Presidential Library and Museum.

Inside the Old Executive Office Building during the move of
Bush Presidential materials, 1992. David Alsobrook on the left
speaking with the guard and Terry Good, Director of White
House Office of Records Management, on the right.

Courtesy of George H. W. Bush Presidential Library and Museum.

After President Bush's seventy-fifth birthday parachute jump,
College Station, Texas, 1999. *Left to right:* Frances Alsobrook,
Meredith Alsobrook, President Bush, Ellen Alsobrook, and
David Alsobrook.

Courtesy of George and Barbara Bush Foundation, Chandler Arden.

David Alsobrook with President Bush aboard U.S. Secret Service "Zodiac" boat, Walker's Point, Kennebunkport, Maine, 1999.

Courtesy of Thomas A. Scully.

David Alsobrook with President Bush aboard *Fidelity II*, Walker's Point, Kennebunkport, Maine, 1999.

Courtesy of Thomas A. Scully.

Clinton Presidential Library groundbreaking ceremony, Little Rock, Arkansas, 2001. *Left to right:* Richard Claypoole, David Alsobrook, Alan Sugg, Skip Rutherford, President Clinton, Bruce Moore, Dean Kumpuris, and Bill Clark.

Courtesy of William J. Clinton Foundation.

President Clinton examining artifacts with David Alsobrook, Skip Rutherford, and Bruce Lindsey, at Clinton Presidential Materials Project, Little Rock, Arkansas, 2001.

Courtesy of William J. Clinton Foundation.

Presidents and First Ladies along with Chelsea Clinton at Clinton Presidential Library dedication, 2004.

Courtesy of William J. Clinton Foundation.

Presidents George W. Bush, Bill Clinton, Jimmy Carter, and
George H. W. Bush at Clinton Presidential Library dedication, 2004.
Courtesy of William J. Clinton Foundation.

Standing in the rain at Clinton Presidential Library dedication,
2004. Clinton adviser Bruce Lindsey half-jokingly said, "I'll give
you $300 for your hat."
Courtesy of William J. Clinton Foundation.

David Alsobrook with the self-styled "Bush Boys" at Clinton
Presidential Library dedication, 2004.

Courtesy of George W. Bush Presidential Library and Museum.

David Alsobrook with President George W. Bush in Cabinet
Room exhibit, Clinton Presidential Library dedication, 2004.

Courtesy of William J. Clinton Foundation.

David Alsobrook (right) with Presidents Clinton, "Bush 41,"
and "Bush 43" in Clinton Library exhibit, Clinton Presidential
Library dedication, 2004. President Clinton later inscribed this
photo: "David—You've got three Presidents doing 'research' in
your Library—Not bad!'

Courtesy of William J. Clinton Foundation.

Barbara Bush (at right) speaking with David Alsobrook, Laura Bush (center) and Presidents George W. Bush and Bill Clinton, Clinton Presidential Library dedication, 2004. Barbara Bush exclaimed, "David, where did you find all of these incredible toys?"

Courtesy of William J. Clinton Foundation.

Chapter 5

Building Presidential "Pyramids":
The Carter Presidential Materials Project

A presidential materials project is like an embryonic larva or
chrysalis from which someday will emerge a beautiful butterfly—
a presidential library.
> —Dr. James E. O'Neill, Assistant Archivist
> for Presidential Libraries, ca. April–May 1981

For several decades, critics have disparaged presidential libraries as "pyramids," "shrines," "temples," "mausoleums," and "edifice complexes." In vitriolic books, articles, editorials, television and radio commentaries, and online blogs, journalists and academics have directed a relentless fusillade of invective at the libraries' elaborate architectural and museum designs and exorbitant construction and maintenance costs. Franklin D. Roosevelt's original vision of a presidential library primarily as a research facility has faded considerably as museum and educational programs have acquired greater public support. Moreover, the proliferation of privately endowed foundations, associations, and "centers" affiliated with modern presidential libraries has exacerbated this acrimonious public discourse, often leading to accusations of "the tail wagging the dog."[1]

---

[1] "Ex-presidential monuments," editorial, *Washington Star*, 15 May 1977; Dudley Clendinen, "Ex-Presidents Compete for History's Attention with Libraries," *New York Times*, 13 October 1985; "A palace fit for a pharaoh," editorial, (Harlingen TX) *Valley Morning Star*, 7 January 1994, clippings, DA Collection; Edmund Morris, "A Celebration of Reagan," *New Yorker*, 16 February 1998, 50–57; Richard J. Cox, "America's pyramids: Presidents and their libraries," *Government Information Quarterly* 19/1 (January 2002): 45–75; Robert F. Worth, "HISTORY; Presidential Libraries: Mines or Shrines?" *New York Times*, 24 April 2002, https://www.nytimes.com/2002/04/24/arts/history-presidential-libraries-mines-or-shrines.html (accessed 18 November 2018); Leuchtenburg, "R. D. W. Connor and the Creation of Presidential Libraries," 136–37; "The pyramids we

Despite the media's breathless coverage of these topics, many aspects of presidential libraries remain largely unexplored, such as the National Archives and Records Administration's seminal role in their establishment. Immediately after a president and first lady leave the White House, a small team of archivists and museum specialists assume custody of their presidential materials. This unit, officially designated as a presidential materials project, is staffed by career federal employees from the National Archives. Their traditional missions include preparing all historical materials for research and exhibition in the future library, providing professional guidance to architects and designers, lending archival support for the president's and first lady's research and writing, and a myriad of "other duties as assigned." The following narrative delineates the history of the Carter Presidential Materials Project and its evolution into the Carter Library in Atlanta, Georgia, between 1981 and 1986.

On 21 January 1981, after twenty-two hours in the Carter truck convoy and a brief night of restless sleep, I rode from our hotel in Atlanta with NARS Security Chief Larry Oberg to the Old Post Office Annex at 77 Forsyth Street, Southwest. Originally built by the New Deal's Works Progress Administration in 1931–1933, this monolithic nine-story marble,

---

build our presidents," *THE WEEK*, 2 March 2007, 11; Kenneth Jost, "Presidential Libraries," *CQ Researcher* 17/11 (16 March 2007): 243–54; Jackie Craven, "The Architecture of Presidential Library Buildings," *ThoughtCo*, 3 July 2019, see https://www.thoughtco.com/presidential-library-buildings-178464 (accessed 5 March 2020); Benjamin Hufbauer, *Presidential Temples: How Memorials and Libraries Shape Public Memory* (Lawrence, KS: University Press of Kansas, 2005), 124; Benjamin Hufbauer, "Billion-Dollar Boondoggle?" *Inside Higher Ed*, 4 June 2013, https://www.insidehighered.com/views/2013/06/04/essay-questions-push-put-presidential-libraries-campuses (accessed 5 March 2020); Benjamin Hufbauer, "Turning Presidents Into Pharaohs," *POLITICO* Magazine, 1 May 2015, http://www.politico.com/magazine/story/2015/05/obama-presidential-library-116695_full.html (accessed 4 May 2015); Jonathan Zimmerman, "Does every president need a separate library?" *Washington Post*, 9 January 2015, https://www.washingtonpost.com/opinions/does-every-president-need-a-separate-library/2015/01/09/344dfa52-966e-11e4-927a-4fa2638cd1b0_story.html (accessed 15 December 2018); Wendy R. Ginsberg, Erika K. Lunder, and Daniel J. Richardson, "The Presidential Libraries Act and the Establishment of Presidential Libraries," CRS Report, 6 February 2015 (Washington DC: Congressional Research Service), 3–4, 16–23.

granite, and limestone structure would serve as the Carter Presidential Materials Project's home for the next five years. Distinguished Atlanta architect A. Ten Eyck Brown designed the Post Office Annex in "stylized flattened or starved classicism," with art deco ornamentation. Sited in close proximity to urban Atlanta's railroad network, the Post Office Annex became the central mail-processing facility for the entire Southeastern region.[2]

During the presidential transition in 1980–1981, NARS and NL searched for a suitable location for the Carter Project. Tom Hudson, director of the NARS Federal Archives and Records Center (FARC) in East Point, conducted a systematic reconnaissance of potential sites in Atlanta and elsewhere, including the US Marine Corps Depot in Albany, Georgia. David Van Tassel from NL and Ford Library Assistant Director William J. Stewart winnowed down Hudson's list of possible sites to two Atlanta venues—a vacant portion of Rich's department store and the Post Office Annex. They finally chose the latter location because it required fewer security and storage modifications. The post office's historical connection with the federal government also would simplify GSA's acquisition of the Annex. Moreover, President Carter already had selected office space across the street in the Richard B. Russell Federal Building.[3]

---

[2] "Martin Luther King, Jr. Federal Building, Atlanta, GA," GSA, US General Services Administration, http://www.gsa.gov/historic-buildings/martin-luther-king-jr-federal-building-atlanta-ga; Jim Nicolow and Susan Turner, "GSA Rehabilitates Historic King Federal Building in Atlanta," *FacilitiesNet Newsletter*, October 2012, https://www.facilitiesnet.com/green/article/-GSA-Rehabilitates-Historic-King-Federal-Building-in-Atlanta--13583 (both websites accessed 7 May 2019); Gandy, "Library Commemorates Tenth Anniversary," 3. A plaque mounted on the building's exterior indicates that President Franklin D. Roosevelt officially dedicated the Post Office Annex during his first term in office. In 1988 the structure was renamed the Martin Luther King, Jr. Federal Building. GSA initiated extensive renovations in 2012 and incorporated energy-efficient "green" features. Listed on the National Register of Historic Places, it is included among GSA's 250 "most significantly historic" buildings.

[3] David Van Tassel email to DA, 22 April 2019; memo, Donald B. Schewe to NL (Office of Presidential Libraries), 27 May 1982, RE: "Progress of the Carter Presidential Materials Project," DA Collection; Gandy, "Library Com-

Only two months after the 1980 presidential election, carpenters, electricians, painters, and security technicians (all GSA subcontractors) miraculously had carved out the Carter Project's basic layout for offices and storage on the Annex's second-floor mezzanine level, which once housed the post office's mail sorting and distribution operations. In December 1980, when I toured the Annex with my new colleagues, Martin Elzy and Roslyn Wright, despite our initial shock over the unfinished renovations, we happily noted that our spacious quarters featured a loading dock, a reliable service elevator, a security-classified vault, vast records and artifacts storage areas, four offices, and a "bull pen" for archival processing.[4]

Elzy, Wright, and I were reunited at the Post Office Annex on 21 January 1981. Elzy was the only one of us with any previous presidential libraries experience—he had served as an archivist for seven years at the LBJ Library in Austin, Texas. He and I were then in our mid-thirties. Twenty-six-year-old Roslyn Wright, a native Floridian, had earned a BA in history at Lincoln University in Pennsylvania in 1975. Prior to the Carter move, she had gained considerable expertise in dealing with presidential materials as a member of Doug Thurman's NL team. She was an impressive young archivist—articulate, well read, witty, and insatiably curious. I immediately thought that she had a bright future with the Carter Library or elsewhere in NARS.[5]

In January 1981, we optimistically assumed that other archivists soon would join us in Atlanta. We also thought that NL's appointment of a Carter Project director was imminent. However, neither of our assumptions came to pass. Over five months elapsed before any new personnel arrived, and we worked on our own without a director until August 1981.

With nineteen trucks to unload, we had little time to speculate about

---

memorates Tenth Anniversary," 3; Donald B. Schewe, "Establishing a Presidential Library: The Jimmy Carter Experience," *Prologue* 21/2 (Summer 1989): 127.

[4] Martin Elzy oral history interview, Carter Library.

[5] Ibid.; Ginny Dunaway Young misc. text messages to DA, 7 May 2019 (with biographical information about Roslyn Wright), DA Collection; Roslyn Wright's obituary, *Austin (TX) American-Statesman*, 1 July 1990, 28. Around 1984 Roslyn Wright relocated to Austin, Texas. She earned a law degree and in 1987 married Rudolph H. Green. Their son, Andrew, was born in January 1989. She succumbed to cancer at age thirty-six in June 1990.

future staff accretions. Tom Hudson loaned several of his FARC staff to us, and for two days we emptied the trucks and moved boxes into our storage areas. Before we unloaded the last truck, several former White House staffers, including Susan Clough and Jane Simpson, began rummaging through the boxes in search of their office files. Since our steel shelving had not been erected, we tightly packed the pallets of boxes into long rows. Using pallet and container inventories prepared during the transition, we recorded the locations of boxes from each White House office. While this situation was far from ideal, we established rudimentary control over our archival holdings. We were not open to the public for research, which was fortuitous given our limited knowledge of the unprocessed archival collections. The bulk of our earliest reference requests originated in President Carter's offices in the Russell Building and in Plains, Georgia. We also responded to sporadic queries for information and documents from NL, the White House, GSA, and other federal agencies. We seldom dealt directly with press inquiries—GSA, NARS, NL, and the Carter staff wrangled the national and local media.[6]

For the first eight months of the Carter Project's existence, we were like a "frontier outpost," loosely tethered by an 800-mile-long supervisory umbilical cord to NL in Washington. Van Tassel monitored our daily progress by telephone. James E. O'Neill, Assistant Archivist for Presidential Libraries, also frequently inquired about any problems we had encountered. From January through February 1981, at O'Neill's behest, Bill Stewart visited with us for several days at a time and then returned to the Ford Library in Michigan. One day when I asked Stewart if he was "our boss," he coyly grinned and said, "We'll see."[7]

As the "senior archivist" in Stewart's absence, Elzy coordinated our official communications with NL, including any written reports. Since he

[6] Schewe, "Establishing a Presidential Library," 127; Martin Elzy oral history interview, Carter Library; memo, Donald B. Schewe to NL, 27 May 1982, RE: "Progress of the Carter Presidential Materials Project"; DA FAX message to Sherrie Fletcher, 29 August 1989; DA notes, Archives Institute Remarks, 19 June 1987, Georgia Archives Institute File; DA to Diane S. Nixon, 9 June 1988. With exception of the first two citations, all in DA Collection.

[7] DA to Charles Sullivan, 2 February 1981, DA Collection; Martin Elzy oral history interview, Carter Library.

and I were both GS-12 archivists and Roslyn Wright was a GS-11, this situation was quite awkward at times, particularly after Stewart informed us, "This is the organizational and supervisory structure" that O'Neill personally preferred. Regardless of this directive, Elzy, to his credit, wielded a gentle supervisory touch. Later, he laughingly reflected, "So things were not as well organized as we might have liked down here, but we got along. We got along."[8]

An informal division of labor for our reference duties quickly evolved—Elzy and I responded to requests for textual documents; Wright answered queries about foreign and domestic gifts and audiovisual items. Since the audiovisual collection was in Thurman's NL custody in 1981, she simply called his office after receiving requests for photographs, videotapes, and audio recordings. Whenever our reference load was relatively light, we surveyed various boxes to enhance our growing knowledge of the archival holdings.[9]

Performing our archival duties was generally simple. As a federal outpost, however, we faced some early logistical difficulties with acquisitions of office equipment and supplies. Several pallets in storage contained boxes of NARS letterhead paper and franked envelopes, scissors, staplers, stainless-steel staples, acid-free folders, and other standard archival supplies and tools of our trade. Thurman, Emily Soapes, Jacque Wood, and other NL colleagues periodically replenished our depleted stockpiles of supplies. We also had a government credit card for purchasing cleaning supplies, plastic garbage bags, work gloves, etc., from the local GSA self-service store.

GSA's overall building maintenance was adequate but not exceptional. They provided us with contract security guards and cleaning personnel. However, we did not have our own facility manager or custodian. Elzy objectively assessed our parent agency's performance:

GSA was running our building. I remember we told them we couldn't stand fire...[or] water. We never did have a fire. We did

---

[8] Martin Elzy oral history interview, Carter Library.

[9] DA notes, Archives Institute Remarks, 19 June 1987, Georgia Archives Institute File; memo, Donald B. Schewe to NL, 27 May 1982, RE: "Progress of the Carter Presidential Materials Project," DA Collection.

have a leak, however, in one of our storage areas, where we had some of the museum items, but fortunately they were in big wooden crates, and so far as I know, there was no damage done there....We had a terrible time just getting anyone to pick up the trash, and so for weeks we would load up our plastic bags with trash at the end of the day and take them down and put them in the trash receptacles on the street because we couldn't get GSA to come clean up.10

A post office skeleton crew remained after we moved into the Annex. Postal inspectors, for example, regularly used the enclosed soundproofed firing range several floors above our space. A custodian who was skilled in carpentry, plumbing, and electrical repairs also had an office in the Annex. No problem appeared to be insurmountable to this genial jack-of-all-trades, who probably was well into his late fifties or early sixties. We frequently shared the elevator with him—he always was heavily laden with lumber, Sheetrock, pipes, conduits, electrical wiring, and a large toolbox. After my "close encounter" with a ferocious, menacing rat on another floor of our building, I alerted the custodian. The following day, he entered the Annex—unburdened of his usual tools and construction supplies—with a large cat tucked under his arm. After this formidable "mouser" joined us in the Annex, we never had another rodent sighting during our residency. This resourceful, indomitable custodian became our unsung hero in the Annex.

Although we occasionally expressed our displeasure with GSA's uneven performance in cleaning and maintaining the Annex, a more serious problem also arose during our occupancy. Possibly seeking to upgrade the building's future marketability, GSA scheduled the removal of asbestos insulation that was embedded in the walls and around the plumbing fixtures. When we vehemently objected to this plan, one senior GSA official casually assured us that he had "rolled around in asbestos for many years" without suffering any ill effects from his exposure. GSA ignored our complaint and proceeded with the asbestos removal.

Robert Bohanan and I requested and received temporary assignments at the Georgia Department of Archives and History (GDAH), but several of our colleagues remained in the Annex for about a month while the

---

[10] Martin Elzy oral history interview, Carter Library.

asbestos was extracted. Although we definitely should have filed a formal complaint about GSA's reckless, potentially dangerous procedure, we lacked the political leverage to do so. Today, after over forty years of documented scientific evidence of the long-term health hazards associated with asbestos exposure, the federal government strictly prohibits employees from occupying buildings that contain even a slight trace of this carcinogen.

Beyond our troubled relationship with GSA, we faced additional problems in dealing with the federal bureaucracy. The Reagan administration implemented draconian freezes on hiring new personnel and purchasing office equipment and furniture. As a result, for about two months we sat on the floor. As a stopgap measure, GSA, FARC, and GDAH loaned us some surplus furniture and equipment.[11] In mid-February 1981, I described our working environment:

> We have learned that our office furniture is supposed to arrive this week. It's beginning to get a little difficult to do our job without a place to sit down and write. At present we have one rather broken-down typewriter, a fiche reader that doesn't work, two work tables, and several chairs. We have to go to the Russell Building to do any Xeroxing. However, we do have several nice offices with many windows, and that makes up for the lack of adequate office equipment. I guess this is the way all new Presidential libraries begin.[12]

Since none of us had worked in a presidential materials project, we really did not know if our current plight was typical of earlier libraries. During one of Bill Stewart's brief visits with us, I sought his guidance as we forged ahead with our archival duties. I figured that Stewart was familiar with spartan working conditions from his service at the Ford Project and could offer some words of wisdom. When I approached him, Stewart was gnawing on his ever-present unlit cigar. Before I spoke, he asked, "How long do you think someone should be a GS-14? Are ten years enough?" He obviously was pondering whether to remain in Ann Arbor

---

[11] Ibid.; DA to Charles Sullivan, 18 March 1981; DA FAX message to Sherrie Fletcher, 29 August 1989, DA Collection; Gandy, "Library Commemorates Tenth Anniversary," 3.

[12] DA to Emily & Tom Soapes, 15 February 1981, DA Collection.

or join our staff in Atlanta.

Such questions were beyond my pay grade and familiarity with the federal government's bureaucratic mysteries. So I just silently shrugged with a palms-up gesture and asked him two questions: "How can we gain greater intellectual control over our archival collections?" "Can you help us get a photocopier?" He angrily pivoted his head toward me, pursed his lips, and sputtered, "Jesus H. Christ—you have to *process* all of that crap! And why in the hell do you need a goddamned photocopier?" This particular moment seemingly validated what I had heard about him from others: "Beneath that gruff, crusty exterior lurks a gruffer, crustier interior." However, as I learned in the future, Stewart was a consummate professional archivist with a great deal of wisdom and common sense. We subsequently became good friends in the years to come.

After this distasteful episode, I refrained from asking any archival questions whenever Stewart appeared. Like a captain without a ship, he gloomily paced around the office, chewed on his cigar, and silently kept his own counsel. By early February 1981, his weekly trips to Atlanta abruptly ended without any explanation. We never fully understood why Stewart repeatedly visited the Carter Project—was he monitoring our progress on behalf of O'Neill or simply weighing his own career options? Elzy asserts that Stewart "helped us get started." Stewart already had survived the rigors of the evolution of a project into a library and perhaps did not wish to repeat that arduous process and uproot his family in Ann Arbor.[13]

As the Stewart saga concluded, we prepared for President and Mrs. Carter's first visit to the Annex. On 12 February 1981, at 4:30 p.m., the Carter entourage arrived at our front door: the former President and First Lady, their son James Earl "Chip" Carter III, aides Phil Wise, Bob Dunn, and Susan Clough, and a trio of GSA officials—Wesley Johnson, Leeman Baxter, and an unidentified photographer.[14]

We pointed out the boxes on pallets and explained our current system of control and access to the papers and artifacts. We were puzzled to learn

---

[13] Martin Elzy oral history interview (quote), Carter Library; Martin Elzy email to DA, 11 May 2019; Donald B. Schewe email to DA, 20 May 2019; Dennis A. Daellenbach email to DA, 30 May 2019, DA Collection.

[14] DA memo for the record, 12 February 1981, DA Collection.

that Rosalynn Carter and Susan Clough thought that archival processing already was underway. After we mentioned that steel shelving was scheduled to be erected, President Carter inquired if it was the same type that would be in the library. We responded, "It's very similar." He also was interested in the foreign gifts collection and indicated that they wanted to exhibit some head of state artifacts in his office. Inside the security-classified vault, Susan Clough asked if we had a current list of our staff and everyone in the President's office with Top Secret/Codeword clearances. We told her that we all had the requisite clearances but did not know about their staff. After about an hour, as the tour ended, Chip Carter said, "Well, Dad, I think you have enough records to work on."[15]

We interpreted this comment and Clough's question about clearances as obvious indications that the President was preparing to write his memoirs. For well over the next year or so, we provided copies of documents to him as he wrote *Keeping Faith* at his home in Plains. We were excited that President Carter understood our role in supporting his research and writing. In May 1981, I apprised my friend Paul Pruitt, "The former President has indeed taken a keen interest in our work.... Almost daily we are asked to locate specific documents that [he] needs in writing his memoirs. It's very interesting to be involved in the early stages of a Presidential library."[16]

Nevertheless, throughout spring 1981, our expanding research duties exacted a heavy toll on our small archival team. I bluntly confided to a former colleague in New York, "There are still only three archivists on the staff, including me. We have no idea when they will name an acting project director. [Because of] the freeze on federal hiring, ...we have been forced to do the work of about eight people."[17]

Back in the nation's capital, O'Neill was acutely aware of the hiring freeze's effect on our morale and visited us several times that spring. I vividly remember his addressing an Atlanta audience of historians and archivists and describing a presidential library's evolution with an analogy from nature: "A presidential materials project is like an embryonic larva or

---

[15] Ibid. In addition to Clough, Wise, and Dunn, other members of President Carter's staff included Daniel J. Lee, Nancy Konigsmark, Bernstine Wright Hollis, Tom Donilon, Jane Simpson, Madeline McBean, and Faye Dill.

[16] DA to Paul M. Pruitt, Jr., 28 May 1981, DA Collection.

[17] DA to Charles Sullivan, 18 March 1981, DA Collection.

chrysalis from which someday will emerge as a beautiful butterfly—a presidential library." His comments undoubtedly were intended for us as much as his audience. We were heartened by his message and eagerly anticipated the day when our efforts produced "a beautiful butterfly."

Meanwhile, in late May 1981, the federal hiring freeze still prevented our adding any new archivists from outside the government. Hudson graciously detailed a receptionist from his staff to handle our office phones and greet visitors via intercom at the front door. Although this additional person freed us from two onerous burdens, we desperately needed more archivists, as I briefly observed: "Unless we get some relief very soon, I don't see how we can process the records."[18]

Fortunately, the hiring freeze was not applicable to GSA's labor contract for erecting shelving in our storage areas. As the shelving went up, Elzy and I removed boxes from pallets and arranged them in precise series and subseries. Having everything shelved with a location register immeasurably expedited our intellectual control over the materials and the response time for reference requests.[19]

As summer approached amid threatening rumors of a federal RIF (Reduction in Force), we realized that any new staff recruits would be available only through transfers within NARS and the other libraries. In June 1981, Robert Bohanan, an experienced GS-11 archivist at the Eisenhower Library, relocated to the Carter Project. With his diverse background in archives and librarianship, Bohanan was an invaluable asset to us.

On 10 August 1981, O'Neill officially selected our director, Donald B. Schewe, who was currently serving as the FDR Library's assistant director. Elzy and I had met him in the 1970s when our NL training classes were on their annual spring field trips. After eight months without a permanent supervisor, we enthusiastically welcomed Schewe and his family to Atlanta. In September he interviewed and hired two GS-5 archives technicians from the NARS Declassification Division—James Albert

---

[18] DA to Paul M. Pruitt, Jr., 28 May 1981, DA Collection.

[19] Ibid.; DA FAX message to Sherrie Fletcher, 29 August 1989; memo, Donald B. Schewe to NL, 27 May 1982, RE: "Progress of the Carter Presidential Materials Project," DA Collection.

Yancey, Jr., and Charles "Chuck" Stokely. Both young men held Top Secret/Codeword clearances and had Atlanta roots—Yancey was a Morehouse University alumnus; Stokely grew up in the suburbs outside the city, where his parents still resided. By October 1981, our archivists' ranks had grown to seven, solidifying our core staff framework for the future library.[20]

In a strange twist of fate, the hiring freeze, which initially impeded our efforts, ultimately became a source of strength. Several years later, I characterized this situation as a "mixed blessing": "Obviously, during our formative period of development as a project, we could have used some additional staff…, especially in light of the heavy load of manual labor….We also needed a museum specialist and audiovisual person during those early months. However, since we were unable to hire permanent employees from the outside…, this allowed us to be more selective in recruitment."[21]

The disastrous Reagan RIF, which decimated NARS, ironically also was advantageous for our staff's morale and professional development. Yancey and Stokely—facing the brutal reality of being displaced by federal employees with greater seniority—were enthusiastic about joining our staff. They began working immediately and did not require a lengthy indoctrination and training in NARS procedures.

None of us at the Carter Project seriously worried about losing our jobs during the RIF in 1981–1982. However, NL took twenty three of our unfilled vacancies that were allotted for the future library to offset the RIF's impact. Don Schewe viewed this decision as only a temporary setback that would earn us "good will" among our NARS colleagues whose careers would be saved by these vacant personnel positions.

Since so many of our friends suffered personally from the RIF, we

[20] DA FAX message to Sherrie Fletcher, 29 August 1989; DA to Douglas Clare Purcell, 4 October 1981; DA to "Dearest Mother and Daddy [Frances and Thomas Alsobrook]," 18 October 1981; DA to Mary Elizabeth Ruwell, 26 October 1981; memo, Donald B. Schewe to NL, 27 May 1982, RE: "Progress of the Carter Presidential Materials Project"; Martin Elzy email to DA, 10 May 2019; Donald B. Schewe email to DA, 22 May 2019. All in DA Collection. See also Gandy, "Library Commemorates Tenth Anniversary," 3–4; Martin Elzy oral history interview, Carter Library.

[21] DA FAX message to Sherrie Fletcher, 29 August 1989, DA Collection.

never complained publicly about losing our vacancies. A week before Christmas 1981, 208 NARS employees received official RIF notices. While they all would not be terminated, many were "bumped" from their jobs by more senior employees at other federal agencies. The Nixon Project lost fifteen of its archivists and technicians to the RIF. My friend and former EOB colleague, Emily Soapes, was bumped by a GS-12 GSA Federal Supply Service clerk. As a "career-conditional" employee, she lacked any bumping privileges. She subsequently found a position as a NARS educational specialist, but as a result, NL lost an outstanding archivist and oral historian.[22]

As the RIF dominoes relentlessly fell, and archivists vacated their jobs or transferred to other federal agencies, my former supervisor Dick Jacobs sardonically remarked, "At the National Archives, we kill our young." He was not overly dramatizing this episode. The RIF eviscerated an entire generation of archivists. "It's a lamentable situation," I bitterly told a friend. "NARS is so small and so highly specialized that it's very tough for us to sustain such wholesale cuts." "I hope you don't consider me to be a 'cry-baby' or just another bitching federal worker," I added, "[but] it doesn't help us when we lose our highly-trained archivists...and receive people who know nothing of the archival profession.... Most of the people who will lose their jobs in 1982 are young career archivists who don't make a lot of money anyway."[23]

While the RIF obliterated any semblance of job security for our friends, we focused in Atlanta on archival processing. As a seasoned presidential library veteran, Don Schewe brought a wealth of practical experience and knowledge of researchers' needs to our formulation of processing goals and priorities. After spirited staff discussions in autumn 1981, we

---

[22] DA to Charles Sullivan, 22 December 1981; DA to Paul M. Pruitt, Jr., 27 December 1981, DA Collection.

[23] DA to Paul M. Pruitt, Jr., 27 December 1981, DA Collection. Through a strange bureaucratic anomaly, NL's budget actually increased to cover the larger salaries of employees transferring to NARS from other federal agencies. Yet, even with an enhanced annual budget, NL lacked enough funding to pay for security clearances for new staff. Consequently, many of these new Nixon Project archivists could not process security-classified materials, which were scattered throughout the White House files.

concentrated on the archival series that did not contain a large volume of security-classified materials. Therefore, instead of processing the National Security Council records, we worked on the voluminous WHCF Subject File, the White House Press Office and Speechwriter series, and the papers generated by senior advisers like Jody Powell, Hamilton Jordan, and Stuart Eizenstat.[24]

As we established processing priorities, Elzy was our most vocal champion for assigning the WHCF Subject File to the top of the list. We soon understood the wisdom of his advocacy. The Subject File documented a wide swath of domestic and foreign policy topics. Although lacking the depth of senior staff papers, the Subject File included something of interest to the majority of our future library patrons. Moreover, organized into multiple discrete series and subseries, it was ideal for archival training assignments. When we officially opened our research room in January 1987, the Carter Library became the first presidential library in which the entire WHCF Subject File was available so early to scholars.[25]

Those formative years at the Carter Project before 1987 became our processing honeymoon. Freed from extraneous bureaucratic and political pressures, we devoted much of our time to basic archival processing, preparation of finding aids, and staff training and development. After finishing the WHCF Subject File and selected senior staff papers, we moved on to other archival treasures, most notably the presidential "Handwriting File," the contents of Mr. Carter's in- and out-boxes.

Meticulously arranged in chronological order, the Handwriting File contained each document that the President read, annotated, and initialed between 1977 and 1981. The White House Staff Secretary, who controlled the flow of papers to and from the President, stamped each item in red ink: "The President Has Seen." Processing this collection, we immediately recognized its extraordinary historical and intrinsic importance,

---

[24] Schewe, "Establishing a Presidential Library," 127–28; Martin Elzy oral history interview, Carter Library; DA notes, "Processing Priorities," Archives Institute Remarks, 19 June 1987, Georgia Archives Institute File; memo, Donald B. Schewe to NL, 27 May 1982, RE: "Progress of the Carter Presidential Materials Project"; DA to Diane S. Nixon, 9 June 1988, DA Collection.

[25] DA notes, "Processing Priorities," Archives Institute Remarks, 19 June 1987, Georgia Archives Institute File, DA Collection.

particularly in documenting specific presidential decisions and directives. Among the Carter Library's twenty-seven million pages, two collections are uniquely irreplaceable primary sources—the Presidential Handwriting File and the President's Daily Brief (PDB), prepared by the various intelligence agencies. Of course, the sensitive, highly classified PDB will only be opened in its entirety for research after rigorous declassification procedures that typically require many years of reviewing and vetting. Elzy and I occasionally discussed which Carter papers we would rescue first in case of fire, flood, or swarming termites. The Presidential Handwriting File and the PDB invariably were our top candidates for emergency removal.[26]

During our processing honeymoon and afterward, we performed four standard archival procedures: preservation, arrangement, review, and description. In completing all of our processing tasks, we strictly practiced the Greek physician Hippocrates' maxim, *Primum non nocere*—"First, do no harm." I always instructed our archivists to leave a collection in better condition than they found it. As a demonstrably hands-on supervisor, in training our younger archivists who lacked processing experience I usually sat at their desks during each stage of work. We first surveyed the entire collection and its series and subseries. Adherence to provenance and *respect pour des fonds* (maintenance of original order) ruled our arrangement decisions.[27] Whenever feasibly possible, we kept the files and individual papers in their original arrangement schemes, such as alphabetical or chronological. If a collection was haphazardly arranged or completely unorganized, we imposed our own arrangement plan.

With twenty-seven million pages of documents in our custody, of

---

[26] Ibid., Keith Shuler email to DA, 17 May 2019, DA Collection; Douglas Brinkley, *The Unfinished Presidency: Jimmy Carter's Journey Beyond the White House* (New York: Viking, 1998) 76, 88–89, 217.

[27] Ernst Posner, "Some Aspects of Archival Development Since the French Revolution," in *A Modern Archives Reader: Basic Readings in Archival Theory and Practice*, ed. Maygene Daniels and Timothy Walch (Washington DC: National Archives and Records Administration, corr. repr. 2002) 10–12; Timothy Walch email to DA, 27 May 2019, DA Collection. Walch adds a revisionist corollary to this standard archival principle: "More important than original order is for the archivist to be transparent and clear in establishing an order that allows easy access to the collection."

necessity, our preservation techniques were rudimentary. We replaced any existing paper clips and other rust-prone metallic fasteners with stainless-steel staples. All documents were placed in acid-free folders. We photo-copied highly acidic newspaper clippings and torn, deteriorating docu-ments. The original documents were removed ("retired") from the open files, and we discarded clippings and identical, unannotated photocopies of textual records.

These routine preservation measures could be completed quickly by a novice archivist. We concentrated our preservation efforts on identifying "high-value" documents—those with presidential or "VIP" handwriting or of exceptional historical and intrinsic significance. To minimize the threat of theft, we photocopied these items and removed the originals. Such safe-guards, however, would not protect our archival holdings from the more crazed, obsessive autograph collectors who might steal photocopies.

Reviewing was our most demanding, labor-intensive archival task. At this crucial stage of processing, our archivists reviewed *each* document in accordance with national security regulations, federal laws, and the specific terms of President Carter's deed of gift, by which he donated his historical materials to the National Archives in January 1981. We closed and re-moved any documents that contained security-classified information, sen-sitive personal data, and anything that potentially could be used to "libel, defame, or harass" any individual. In discussing the specific restrictions and applications of his deed of gift with Don Schewe, President Carter surprisingly replied, "My staff must have put them in—I think they should all be open, except for the classified material."[28] However, he did not re-quest that Schewe draft a new version of his deed of gift that reflected this rather extraordinary opinion.

The Carter Library was the last of the so-called "deed of gift" presi-dential depositories administered by the National Archives. Our archivists were spared the unprecedented pressures generated by an onslaught of FOIA requests mandated by the 1978 Presidential Records Act (PRA). I firmly believe that we processed and opened a much greater volume of materials at the Carter Library than the PRA would have allowed. By early

---

[28] Carter Deed of Gift (January 1981) File; DA to Estelle Owens, 9 June 1983; Donald B. Schewe email to DA, 23 May 2019, DA Collection.

summer 1988, we had processed seven million of the twenty-seven million pages of Carter presidential papers.[29]

More than twenty years after we launched the Carter Project's processing, Elzy expressed his concerns about the PRA's impact:

> The libraries that follow the Carter Library are under the Presidential Records Act. I've not worked in one of those. My impression is it's very difficult to deal with. I'm glad that my experience was at the Johnson and Carter Libraries, where we were dealing with the Presidents' deed of gift. Processing entire collections, I think that we serve researchers better than just waiting for researchers to come in, make requests and then…find individual documents. To me, it seems that the Presidential Records Act is sort of like if you have a public library that didn't buy any books until a member of the public came in and said, "I want this book." Well, you wouldn't end up with a coherent collection, and you wouldn't be serving subsequent readers who came into your library, and I fear that the Presidential Records Act may have that same effect.[30]

My experience at the Carter Library and later at two "PRA Libraries" (Bush 41 and Clinton) mirrored Elzy's assessment of the law's far-reaching impact on researchers and archivists. Although archivists at the Bush and Clinton Projects initiated systematic processing of entire collections and series, five years after these presidents left office and their records were subject to the terms of the PRA, we diverted most of our archival resources to FOIA requests. The PRA originally was designed to facilitate public access to presidential records. However, because of its cumbersome restriction categories and the proliferation of legal applications that have arisen since 1978, this law has impeded rather than expedited the efforts of archivists and researchers.[31]

The preparation of finding aids—known simply as description—was our final "station of the cross" in processing. During that era, prior to extensive White House records scanning and retrieval programs, our finding

---

[29] DA to Diane S. Nixon, 9 June 1988, DA Collection.

[30] Martin Elzy oral history interview, Carter Library.

[31] DA email to Lynn Scott "Scottie" Cochrane, 16 April 2002; DA email to Leah Atkins, 11 November 2008, DA Collection; Alsobrook, "The Birth of the Tenth Presidential Library," 40.

aids' hierarchal descriptions seldom probed deeper than the folder level. During the description phase, I emphasized to our archivists the importance of including *everything* that they had learned about a collection during processing—its provenance, missions and organizational structure of a particular White House staff office, and the files' specific contents. I expected our archivists to share this information with researchers through clearly written scope and content notes that highlighted the collection's contents at the series, subseries, and folder levels. The dissemination of knowledge from archivists to researchers in a usable format became our processing goals' top priority.[32]

Rudimentary word-processing equipment alleviated some of the more repetitive, debilitating chores, such as retyping multiple drafts of edited finding aids. Yet the introduction of new technology did not mitigate our need for additional archival personnel. Between 1981 and 1986, we hired several outstanding local students as part-time employees, including Ralph Peters and Keith Shuler, Georgia State University; Faye Lind Jensen, Emory University; and Charlaine Burgess McCauley, Oglethorpe University. Only permanent federal employees with security clearances were authorized to process collections containing any classified documents or other sensitive materials. However, these young students preserved and arranged large series of papers, and, with close supervisory guidance, they conducted routine reference and nonsensitive reviewing tasks.[33]

In addition to recruiting students from Atlanta's colleges and universities, we also actively utilized interns who were preparing for careers as archivists and librarians. For example, in September 1981 we initiated discussions with Allen W. Jones at Auburn University about his archival students serving as interns in Atlanta. Over the next decade, at least eight Auburn graduate students interned at the Carter Project and Library; they all had productive archival careers, and three became archivists in

---

[32] DA to Estelle Owens, 9 June 1983; Timothy Walch email to DA, 27 May 2019, DA Collection; Bohanan, "The Presidential Libraries System Study," 32–35.

[33] Bohanan, "The Presidential Libraries System Study," 38; DA to Allen W. Jones, 31 July 1985; Keith Shuler emails to DA, 25 April, 17 May 2019, DA Collection.

presidential libraries.[34]

Since Emory University had an outstanding graduate program in librarianship, we also employed several talented MLS students as interns, including Patrice McDermott, Tony Coursey, and Anne Johnson. The Library of Congress's automated cataloging service produced preprinted cards for many recently published books. Since our presidential gifts collection contained several thousand books, Don Schewe investigated how we could tap into the online Library of Congress (LOC) system. After consulting with the LOC's officials, he ordered an "electronic typewriter with enhancements," which featured a special platen for catalogue cards. Utilizing this equipment, intern Anne Johnson made remarkable progress that exceeded Schewe's expectations:

> Our student got busy, and within six months had catalogued the three or four thousand volumes we wanted to keep. We had projected that as a full-time librarian's job for five to seven years....The next time Jim O'Neill came to Atlanta, I showed him the completed card catalog. He was amazed. "How was that done so quickly?" he asked. So I showed him our electronic typewriter. "That's a computer!" he exclaimed. "No, that's the electronic typewriter with enhancements you authorized me to buy." ...I understand Joe Marshall, the librarian at NLR [FDR Library] was able to get an "electronic typewriter with enhancements" from the Library of Congress the following week.[35]

This episode underscores one of Schewe's most significant contributions as director of the Carter Project and Library—his innovative introduction of computerization into our work. By his own account, in the late

---

[34] Allen W. Jones, "Grad Students at AU Who Completed Archival Training Program," August 1983, handwritten list; Allen W. Jones to DA, 3 September 1981, 22 July 1985; DA to Allen W. Jones, 10 September 1981, 31 July 1985; memo, DA to Donald B. Schewe, 5 August 1985, RE: "Pendleton, Gatlin, & Stanhope"; DA email to Allen W. Jones and Jeff Jakeman, 13 May 2019; Jimmie Purvis emails to DA, 13, 16 May 2019. All in Auburn University Archives—Interns File, DA Collection. These students included Robert J. Jakeman, Debbie Pendleton, MeloDee Loebrick French, Jim Gatlin, Jimmie Purvis, David Stanhope, Susan Fraysur Ament, and Mary Kloser Finch.

[35] Donald B. Schewe email to DA, 22 May 2019, DA Collection.

1970s, NARS "looked into" electronic technology and "determined computers could do nothing for archives. I think the general opinion on Mahogany Row was that archivists wanted…computers so they could play Pong."[36] Elzy asserts that "two great things" Schewe achieved as director were "getting us into a permanent building and also his interest in computers, …and we were often ahead of the National Archives'…use of computers."[37]

Within a few months of his selection as Carter Project director, Schewe also had unified our small staff. In October 1981, I notified Emily Soapes: "I love working for Don, and I really wonder how we got along before he arrived. He has knitted us together into a well-organized, efficient unit, and with a little help from NL, …there's no limit to what we can accomplish. We just don't have enough people to do the job that we want to do, and with Reagan's budget cuts, I don't see how we'll get additional staff."[38] Soon afterward, I told another friend, "Needless to say, this is not an opportune time to start a new Presidential library."[39]

In March 1982, Kathleen Gillespie, our first administrative employee, joined the staff. She immediately became an essential member of our team. However, Elzy argues, "[O]ne big mistake that was made in staffing was we didn't get a museum curator until much later."[40] Without a curator, we were unable to respond expeditiously to the museum designers' requests about artifacts that were available for exhibition.[41]

James R. Kratsas, a resourceful, innovative curator from the Kansas Museum of History in Topeka, finally came on board in April 1985—a year before the scheduled Carter Library dedication. Over three decades after he was hired, Kratsas recounted the monumental tasks that awaited him:

> I remember Don telling me the museum and the care of the objects [were] in my hands, and all I saw were the huge crates back in the storage area, some with lids pried off and packing material laying

---

[36] Ibid. (quote); Martin Elzy oral history interview, Carter Library.

[37] Martin Elzy oral history interview, Carter Library.

[38] DA to Emily W. Soapes, 21 October 1981, DA Collection.

[39] DA to Mary Elizabeth Ruwell, 26 October 1981, DA Collection.

[40] Martin Elzy oral history interview, Carter Library.

[41] Ibid.

around. The only thing[s] I had to begin my job were the cursory little pink and yellow pieces of paper to go on [from the White House Gift Unit]. It was a bit daunting, even more so because we would be moving into the new building in just a year. There were still objects to select for the exhibits, cataloging all of the artifacts, hiring of staff, proofing the labels, buying artifact storage and art racks, etc. While it was a bit much, it was also exciting—having to basically create a museum and its operations from the beginning.[42]

Over the next year, Kratsas hired Museum Craftsman James Doherty, Registrar Nancy Hassett, Education Coordinator Sylvia Naguib, and Tyrell Lumpkin, our museum store manager.[43]

In 1985–1986, our newly minted curator's presence dramatically altered our lives at the Carter Project. Although we continued to provide archival and administrative assistance for our museum missions, Kratsas immediately began planning an exhibits schematic in coordination with the designers hired by President Carter. Kratsas carefully orchestrated the entire exhibits development process, from the drawing board to installation in fall 1986. As we watched the museum become a reality, our only regret was that a curator and other exhibits professionals had not been hired earlier. But, of course, the Reagan budget cuts had blocked those personnel actions. For future projects, hiring a curator or a registrar became an early staffing priority.

By spring 1986, we were all fully engaged in our transition from a project into O'Neill's "beautiful butterfly." We temporarily halted our archival processing in preparation for the move into the new building. Based on shelving construction diagrams, Elzy devised a precise location register for each box of Carter materials. As the shelving was built, he continually updated his register to ensure its accuracy. He also drafted a comprehensive procedures manual for our research room. I revised our notebook on

---

[42] James R. Kratsas email to DA, 29 April 2019; James R. Kratsas text message to DA, 26 May 2019, DA Collection. Born in Pittsburgh, Pennsylvania, in 1954, Kratsas earned his BA and MA in history at West Virginia University and an MA in public history at Duquesne University. In June 1989, he was appointed Supervisory Curator of the Gerald Ford Museum in Grand Rapids, Michigan. Sylvia Naguib succeeded him as the Carter Library Curator.

[43] James R. Kratsas text message to DA, 26 May 2019, DA Collection.

processing guidelines and techniques.[44]

Elzy and I thus gradually were transitioning into the roles we would play in the Carter Library—respectively, as assistant director and supervisory archivist. Since he excelled in his administrative duties and was well versed in federal laws and regulations, Elzy was ideally suited to be the library's first assistant director. I personally envisioned spending the rest of my career teaching and mentoring young archivists; the supervisory archivist's position would allow me to pursue this goal. Looking back on that time, although we both were quite ambitious and eager to advance, this division of supervisory responsibilities worked well for us.

Elzy would be in charge of the library's overall administrative functions and supervision of the entire staff below the director, including contract security and housekeeping personnel. He also oversaw the research room operations and reference services. As supervisory archivist, my main duty was coordinating the library's systematic processing and preparation of finding aids. I also responded to numerous reference requests.[45]

By 1988, two years after the Carter Library opened, I was supervising two archivists, five archives technicians, and an archives aide. That summer I compared my current duties with those of the Carter Project:

> During the "early days" of our existence (ca. 1981-83), I did a substantial amount of processing myself…. [I]t enabled me to identify some of the potential processing problems that might arise later. Now that we have a larger staff, I devote much of my time to training my people and planning processing assignments…. [O]ne of the most dramatic changes in my job since the opening of the Library has been the daily flood of reference calls. Prior to the move to the new building, we were well isolated from journalists, scholars, curiosity-seekers, etc. Now it's quite different. Quite frankly, the reference load makes it more difficult to maintain a consistent level of processing like we accomplished in the old building.[46]

Although Curator James Kratsas's supervisory role differed significantly from mine, his transition from the Post Office Annex to the Carter

---

[44] DA to Diane S. Nixon, 9 June 1988, DA Collection.
[45] Ibid.; Martin Elzy oral history interview, Carter Library.
[46] DA to Diane S. Nixon, 9 June 1988, DA Collection.

Library also was memorable. "Once the Library and Museum were opened," he wrote, "we had the pressure of the public we had to serve, the exhibits to maintain, the building to keep clean, publicity, sales operations, public events, and the usual litany of personnel matters."[47] In contrast, he spoke nostalgically about our project days: "While our lodgings were spartan, the building was old, the Annex also had a great sense of collegiality. The atmosphere was better to encourage the closeness of the staff than when we were at the Carter Center. Maybe because we had a smaller staff or…we were crammed into spaces, but I will say it was fun."[48]

We spent many long hours in the Annex, including one unforgettable overnight "pajama party" when Schewe, Elzy, and I served as "babysitters" during the security-classified vault door replacement. Perhaps the most epochal unplanned Annex "sleepover" occurred in January 1982. Elzy, Roslyn Wright, Robert Bohanan, and I were all at work. Early in the morning, Schewe drove Robert Warner and James O'Neill down to Plains for a meeting with President Carter. Hamilton Jordan, who lived in rural Gwinnett County, joined us in the Annex for research in his personal papers. Everything proceeded normally—then snow began to fall in the early afternoon.

Since our director was on the road, Elzy was in charge. As snow grew heavier, we suggested to him that early departures would be wise. Elzy responded that since our bosses had not authorized us to close the office early, someone had to remain on duty. We then mentioned that all three of our supervisors were en route to Plains. Jordan overheard our discussion, quickly packed up his briefcase, and drove to his home. In commuting to the Annex, we were all dependent in some degree on MARTA (Metropolitan Atlanta Rapid Transit Authority) trains and buses. If the blizzard incapacitated MARTA, we would be snowbound in the Annex.

Wright, Bohanan, and I finally departed in the late afternoon, but Elzy stayed behind. Although MARTA's rail lines were operational, the buses stopped running. Elzy was unable to reach his vehicle in a bus parking lot for his long commute to Riverdale, near Atlanta's Hartsfield Airport. He spent the night alone in the Annex without any food—the

---

[47] James R. Kratsas email to DA, 29 April 2019, DA Collection.
[48] Ibid.

downtown restaurants were all closed. The next day, a postal worker in the Annex, whose car was equipped with snow tires and chains, gave Elzy a ride to his vehicle, and he safely reached his home.[49]

Although this incident was not humorous, particularly for Elzy, it became enshrined in the Annex's "legend and lore." Afterward, whenever threatening, inclement weather approached, Elzy became our human "early warning system" that we carefully heeded. We no longer relied on weather radar. If the local forecasts predicted a wintry mix of ice, sleet, or snow, and Elzy headed toward the door, we immediately secured the office and left with him.

Episodes like the famous "Elzy sleepover" in 1982 solidified our staff's unity and dedication. We probably spent more time together as a staff than we did with our families—extracting Carter records and memorabilia from the peanut warehouse in Plains, unloading trucks, attending Atlanta Braves games, the Six Flags Over Georgia amusement park, birthday parties, and picnics. We were serious about our archival and museum assignments, but we also enjoyed socializing together. Each day at the Annex was enlivened by casual banter, laughter, and practical jokes. We had less time for after-hours frivolity when the library opened and evening events dominated our schedules.

This spirit of light-hearted camaraderie somehow survived our relocation to the Carter Library. I think our shared experiences in the Annex's primitive close quarters made us more appreciative of the library's palatial offices and other amenities. After a difficult day at work in the library, with an evening special event looming, Schewe often jokingly hearkened back to our pioneer days in the Annex: "Guys, it appears that we're left with only one option in dealing with this problem—we'll have to drink our way out of it!" Regardless of how many times he delivered that line, it never failed to elicit laughter.

Fortunately for us, our boss had a healthy sense of humor and patiently tolerated some of our more outrageous adolescent shenanigans. Archivist Keith Shuler, whose satirical wit became legendary, was our

---

[49] DA email to Martin Elzy, 10 May 2019; Martin Elzy email to DA, 10 May 2019; Donald B. Schewe email to DA, 21 May 2019; DA email to Donald B. Schewe and Robert Bohanan, 21 May 2019, DA Collection.

anointed "King of Comedy." In 1986–1987 when we organized an elaborate picnic featuring chicken dinners "with all the fixin's" from a local "Po-Folks" restaurant and a tour of historic Oakland Cemetery, Shuler quickly dubbed this event "The First Annual Carter Library PoFolks/Dead Folks Picnic."[50]

Yet, on the eve of the Carter Library's dedication on 1 October 1986, Shuler delivered perhaps his most celebrated comedic performance. Our entire staff gathered in the conference room for a briefing by the director on the dedication's logistics and security. Gesturing expansively through the window toward the hillside overlooking the Japanese Garden, Schewe said, "The Secret Service will bring the Presidents in on the sidewalk to the podium, and the photographers will be up there with us on the grassy knoll where they'll get their best shots." Without any pause, Shuler quipped, "Don, never say *Secret Service*, *Presidents*, *grassy knoll*, and *shots* in one breath."[51]

The dedication ceremony in October 1986 officially commemorated our successful evolution from a project to a full-fledged presidential library. Eagerly anticipating opening our research room and launching various public and educational programs, we did not dwell too much on the past five years. Immersed in the Carter Library's fresh "new car smell," we had little incentive to revisit our days in the Annex as a "frontier outpost." Therefore, in 1986 and in successive years, nobody wrote a postmortem analysis or a study of lessons learned at the Carter Project.

I think each of us was very proud of everything we had achieved as a team during the previous five years. We had trained a small, relatively inexperienced cadre of archivists who became highly proficient in our profession's basic trade craft. They processed a substantive representative sample of presidential papers that would appeal to many different researchers. Although none of these young archivists previously had served in a research room, Elzy patiently and masterfully prepared them for that duty. Despite massive federal budget restrictions, we built the future Carter Library's core archival staff.

---

[50] Keith Shuler email to DA, 28 May 2019, DA Collection.

[51] Keith Shuler email to DA, 22 April 2019; DA email to Donald B. Schewe, Martin Elzy, Robert Bohanan, and Keith Shuler, 20 April 2019, DA Collection.

The Carter Project's experience also revealed the advisability of hiring a museum curator early in the staffing process—this particular lesson benefitted three succeeding projects. Later as director of the Bush 41 and Clinton Projects and Libraries, I relied heavily on everything that I learned during my ten years in Atlanta, such as the importance of nurturing supportive relationships with the former president and the local academic community.

Although the FARC and GDAH archivists warmly welcomed us to Atlanta and were our earliest, most ardent supporters, we realized that establishing professional and personal relationships with local academics was essential to the Carter Library's future development. In pursuit of this goal, we joined the Society of Georgia Archivists (SGA) and the Georgia Association of Historians (GAH). Elzy played an active SGA and GAH leadership role and later invited the annual Georgia Archives Institute to the Carter Library. Our staff participated in the Archives Institute sessions and also served as judges for GAH's Georgia History Day presentations. Schewe taught an Emory University history seminar on President Carter. Kratsas and I served as adjunct US history instructors at DeKalb Community College for several years. Dan Carter, Linda Matthews, and Virginia J. H. Cain (Emory University); Les Hough and Gary Fink (Georgia State University); Robert C. McMath, Jr., and Mel Kranzberg (Georgia Tech); and Bradley Rice (Clayton State Junior College) were among our staunchest academic boosters.[52]

We were much less successful in garnering President Carter's allegiance. When he was writing *Keeping Faith* in 1981–1982, the President appeared to be interested in our archival and research activities. But he soon directed his attention to the Carter Presidential Center's programs. In September 1986, he announced, "We wanted to make something different of our library, our museum. We wanted it be a teaching center rather

---

[52] Misc. correspondence and memos, ca. 1982–1991, Carter Library—University System of Georgia File; Georgia Association of Historians (GAH) File; Society of Georgia Archivists (SGA) Business File; Georgia Archives Institute File; Donald B. Schewe email to DA, 21 May 2019, all in DA Collection. See also Martin Elzy oral history interview, Carter Library.

than a monument to me."[53] Schewe emphasizes that Carter "did not view his Presidential Library as a way to polish his image, put his own twist on history, or push his own point of view."[54]

Closely affiliated with Emory University, the Carter Center organized programs that specifically reflected the President's own interests: arms control, international diplomacy, human rights advocacy, conflict resolution, and multiple initiatives relating to poverty, hunger, and health. Several former White House advisers characterized the Carter Center's ambitious public policy agenda as an integral element of the "rehabilitative process" after the President's defeat in 1980.[55] Not surprisingly, given President Carter's personal work ethic and energy, he literally toiled day and night in behalf of these programs. In his "spare time," he championed Habitat for Humanity, which builds homes for the poor all over the globe. Carter not only personally participated in Habitat's construction projects; he spearheaded several fundraising campaigns.[56]

Nevertheless, the Carter Center was his primary focus and headquarters for his activities after 1986. By any measurement standards, the Carter Center's accomplishments have been impressive. In Africa alone, the center's programs achieved remarkable results in eradicating famine, hunger, and the parasitic Guinea worm scourge that once killed thousands of humans and animals. In recognition of his tireless advocacy for disarmament, human rights, international election reforms, and other humanitarian causes, President Carter was awarded the Nobel Peace Prize in 2002.[57]

The Carter Presidential Library and Museum had the potential to be

---

[53] William E. Schmidt, "Reshaped Carter Image Tied to Library Opening," *New York Times*, 21 September 1986, https://www.nytimes.com/1986/09/21/us/reshaped-carter-image-tied-to-library-opening.html (accessed 6 May 2019); Brinkley, *The Unfinished Presidency*, 210–18.

[54] Donald B. Schewe email to DA, 1 June 2019, DA Collection.

[55] Schmidt, "Reshaped Carter Image Tied to Library Opening."

[56] Brinkley, *The Unfinished Presidency*, 143–60, 254–62, 347-51, 358, 441, 456, 477.

[57] "The Carter Center: 20 Years Later"; Moni Basu, "Reflections of the Man," both articles in *Atlanta Journal-Constitution*, 20 March 2002, A1, E1–E3; "2002 Nobel Peace Prize Awarded to President Carter," press release, 10 October 2002, Carter Presidential Center, https://www.cartercenter.org/news/documents/doc1235.html (accessed 29 May 2019).

another "jewel in the crown" of "The Man from Plains." Yet, despite O'Neill's persistent lobbying campaign between 1981 and 1987 to win the President's support for the library, he was continually rebuffed. When O'Neill and Warner personally asked Carter in January 1982 to become a public voice for presidential libraries and NARS' independence from GSA, he adamantly rejected their invitation. O'Neill believed that Carter "paid less attention to his library than any other President."[58] Until his death in 1987, O'Neill never wavered in his quest to convince President Carter that his support was vital for programs that the federal government did not fund—oral histories, museum exhibits, researchers' grants, publicity, and educational outreach.[59]

From Schewe's perspective, the President's reluctance to champion funding for his own library's programs had a deleterious impact: "[W]e didn't get a large endowment to do the sorts of things other libraries had."[60] He also noted, "I got a lot of heat about not having any Foundation money, from NL after O'Neill, several other Library Directors…, and Don Wilson as Archivist [of the United States]. But considering the heat other Directors got from their President (and staff and family), I think I got the better end of the deal."[61] Other than O'Neill, nobody from Mahogany Row ever courageously volunteered to speak with President Carter about this sensitive issue.

Seeking to ameliorate the President's position on an endowment, Schewe solicited assistance from influential former White House advisers Hamilton Jordan and Jody Powell. They both responded, "He'll never go for it. It's against his Christian understanding."[62] Schewe's interpretation of the President's "Christian understanding" is illuminating: "I think his own faith told him not to brag, or try to justify what he and his administration had done. His interests had moved on to the Carter Center and

---

[58] Donald B. Schewe email to DA, 23 May 2019, DA Collection.

[59] Ibid.; "James O'Neill, Archivist, Dies at Age of 58," obituary, *Washington Post*, 8 March 1987, clipping, DA Collection.

[60] Donald B. Schewe email to DA, 23 May 2019, DA Collection.

[61] Ibid.

[62] Donald B. Schewe email to Jay E. Hakes and DA, 25 May 2019, DA Collection.

what it was doing, and that's where he wanted to put his time and effort."[63]

According to an old Christian homily, "Charity begins at home." Since NARS was the Carter Library's bureaucratic home, perhaps from President Carter's perspective, the federal government was responsible for these extraneous expenses. Elzy cites the earlier example of President Lyndon B. Johnson, who concentrated on his library rather than the public policy school at the University of Texas that bore his name: "Jimmy Carter was the opposite….He put his time and attention into the Carter Center and thought the federal government would take care of the museum and archives."[64] Additionally, by the early 1980s, the President had grown weary of fundraising. He already had amassed over $25 million in private donations for the construction of the Carter Library and Museum.

With the passage of time, every presidential library experiences evolving "life cycles"—alterations in its staffing needs, processing and research priorities, public programs, and museum exhibits.[65] When Jay E. Hakes succeeded Schewe as director in 2000, almost twenty years had elapsed since President Carter had left the White House. Both in its historical content and technology, the museum needed extensive renovations. In 2009, Hakes coordinated "a total redo" of the museum's exhibits, with the President's generous support and guidance: "He raised about $10 million (including a $1 million check from him and Rosalynn), provided numerous insights to the consultants working on the project, and sat for special film interviews."[66]

The "new" museum's interactive exhibits covered Carter's post-presidential career and humanitarian contributions. Although the President continued to focus on his Carter Center initiatives, he also participated in numerous special book events for his publications at the library.[67] During Hakes's innovative shepherding of the Carter Library into the twenty-first

---

[63] Donald B. Schewe email to DA, 1 June 2019, DA Collection.

[64] Martin Elzy email to DA, 29 May 2019, DA Collection.

[65] Memo, Donald B. Schewe to the Director [William Emerson], FDR Library, 10 July 1978, RE: "Staffing Patterns and Archivist Ratios," DA Collection.

[66] Jay E. Hakes email to DA, Martin Elzy, and Donald B. Schewe, 25 May 2019, DA Collection.

[67] Ibid.; Jay E. Hakes email to DA, 30 June 2019, DA Collection; Martin Elzy oral history interview, Carter Library.

century, he also initiated discussions with the President about establishing an endowment. However, when Hakes retired in 2013, the Carter Library still did not have an endowment.[68]

Presidential libraries' directors, like many college head football coaches, seldom receive adequate credit for their accomplishments. Directors serve many masters—former presidents, first ladies, and their families; White House aides and assorted political advisors; multiple National Archives officials and others—each of whom often has competing agendas. Directors' careers also are subject to the turbulent political winds generated by the White House, Congress, state legislatures, and local governmental entities. Together, over a span of about four decades, Schewe and Hakes presided over the transformation of a frontier outpost, the Carter Project, into a mature presidential library—one of the last of its genre that was built primarily around its archival and museum collections and research and educational missions.

I spent ten years at the Carter Project and Library—one-third of my career with the federal government. As the Carter Library's first supervisory archivist, my job was a perfect combination of purely archival work, administrative and personnel responsibilities, and training younger staff members. Many years afterward, I realized that my decade in Atlanta was the most professionally productive, intellectually creative, and personally fulfilling of my entire archival career. I also gradually understood that I preferred the primitive, formative stages of presidential libraries over the mature finished products.[69]

By spring 1991, I had become increasingly restless—my daily routine no longer was exciting or challenging. When Archivist of the United States Don Wilson dropped by the Carter Library, in the solitude of our stacks I confided to him that I was weary of "massaging" Carter presidential papers. I wanted new archival challenges and problems to solve. He listened attentively to my request for a transfer if any job possibilities developed in Washington, specifically in preparation for the next presidential

---

[68] Jay E. Hakes emails to DA, 2, 30 June 2019, DA Collection; Ginsberg et al., "The Presidential Libraries Act and the Establishment of Presidential Libraries," 21n.3.

[69] Alsobrook, "A Portrait of the Archivist as a Young Man," 290–91.

library. Within a week, John Fawcett, Assistant Archivist for Presidential Libraries, telephoned and informed me that he might have a vacancy for me in the EOB in a liaison role. He cautioned that my spending "some time" at the Nixon Project could be a prerequisite for this position. Several follow-up telephone conversations ensued throughout the spring.

Meanwhile, preparing to return to the nation's capital, I realized that much had changed over the past decade. After its successful struggle for independence from GSA, NARS was now a separate federal agency, renamed the National Archives and Records Administration (NARA) and led by a presidential appointee as Archivist of the United States. I inherently understood that these changes were far more significant than merely switching our name from NARS to NARA and ordering new letterhead supplies for each office.

By July 1991, I was again at the EOB, officially detailed and designated as the National Archives White House liaison person. This new assignment was vastly different from my previous stint as an EOB detailee. I was stationed in WHORM, then headed by Terry Good and his deputy Lee Johnson, my former colleague. Returning to the EOB after ten years, I immediately experienced a "Rip Van Winkle" moment upon seeing the impact of the computer revolution. I discovered that the White House staff now relied almost exclusively on computers for their written communications and document production. Typewriters were virtually obsolete. The entire White House complex, including the Oval Office, was wired for email transmissions.[70]

Although President George H. W. Bush loved his IBM Selectric (like I did) and pecked out countless "self-typed" notes to family members, friends, and advisers, on 1 May 1991, he transmitted his first "computer-letter" to a confidant. He stubbornly preferred "self-typed" and handwritten messages over emails in his personal communications—a habitual vestige of his days as a US congressman. He thus reminded me of President Woodrow Wilson, who personally typed letters and speeches seventy-five years earlier in the Oval Office. Recalling my own awkward transition from typewriters to computers, I doubted that any of President Bush's staff

---

[70] Ibid., 292–93.

called him a "Neo-Luddite."[71]

My daily duties in WHORM were relatively routine. Since WHORM's records scanning and retrieval system was completely alien to me, I essentially became an archival intern for the third time in my career. Luckily for me, a forty-five-year-old neophyte, I received comprehensive instruction from Terry Good, Lee Johnson, Thomas Taggart, William Roberts, and their other comrades. My "other duties as assigned" included document retrieval and photocopying for White House staff, picking up records in the West and East Wings, coordinating the delivery of retired boxes from the National Archives via Doug Thurman's office, and occasional exit interviews.

In striking contrast to my job during the Carter era, I had no supervisory responsibilities, and my daily marching orders came from Terry Good and Lee Johnson rather than a boss located back in NL. I assumed that my current EOB assignment would last for about six years, and I tried to acquire any archival and historical knowledge that would be useful at the future Bush Presidential Library.[72]

However, as in 1980, the unpredictable outcome of a presidential election altered the trajectory of my life and archival career. When William J. Clinton exiled President Bush back to Texas in November 1992, what followed was, to me, familiar territory. Over the next two months, a combined team of NL archivists and WHORM staff surveyed the records holdings of each White House office and scheduled pickup dates for boxes. Between November 1992 and January 1993, we secured and packed 36 million pages of textual records, 1 million photographs, and 40 thousand museum artifacts. We also acquired all White House electronic records (including thousands of email messages) and the entire WHORM database of scanned documents. My most unique task during the move was accompanying a small team of archivists to Camp David. We photographed the precise arrangement of everything within President Bush's office. We then inventoried and packed the office's entire contents. These

---

[71] Ibid., 293; George Bush, *All the Best, George Bush: My Life in Letters and Other Writings* (New York: Scribner, 1999) 518.

[72] DA to Allen W. Jones, 28 December 1991; DA to Paul M. Pruitt, Jr., 30 December 1991; DA to Stanly Godbold, 9 January 1992; DA to Eugene Current-Garcia, 14 January 1992. All in DA Collection.

items became essential in our re-creation of his Camp David office at the Bush Library.[73]

The Bush Presidential Materials Project's temporary site—an abandoned bowling alley in College Station, Texas—was refurbished and prepared for our arrival in January 1993. As during the Reagan move, the first stage of shipments was by C-5 military transport aircraft from Andrews Air Force Base to Fort Hood, Texas, followed by a truck convoy to College Station. Once again, as in 1981, NL initially assigned three archivists to the Bush Project: Warren and Mary Finch, a young married couple, and myself. I was selected as the Bush Project's acting director.[74]

As preparations for the Bush move to Texas steadily progressed in November 1992, I was discussing my departure plans with several friends at NL. Our boss, John Fawcett, and Harry Middleton, the legendary LBJ Library director and "dean of presidential libraries," walked into the office. Fawcett casually pointed toward me: "Harry, you know Dave—he worked on Carter materials in the EOB, went to Georgia with the Carter Library and returned to work on Bush materials. Now he's on the way to Texas." Grimacing slightly as if he had a sudden attack of dyspepsia, Middleton drolly intoned in his flat Midwestern accent that bespoke his Kansas and Iowa roots, "For God's sake, don't let him work on Clinton's."[75]

---

[73] Alsobrook, "A Portrait of the Archivist as a Young Man," 293; Alsobrook, "The Birth of the Tenth Presidential Library," 36–39; DA notes, "The Next Library: Prospects and Problems of the Bush Library and the Advent of Electronic Records," panel discussion, American Historical Association Meeting, Washington, DC, 30 December 1992, DA Collection.

[74] Alsobrook, "A Portrait of the Archivist as a Young Man," 285; David Van Tassel, memo for the record, 28 April 1989, RE: "Transfer of the Reagan Presidential Records from Washington to California"; Michael Precker, "The Trip Down Bush's Memory Lane Starts Humbly in Old Bowling Alley," *Dallas Morning News*, reprinted in *Washington Post*, 30 August 1993, A-17; "Three Alabamians to Serve at Future George Bush Presidential Library," draft press release, 3 January 1993; "A Presidential Task," *Auburn Alumnews*, undated clipping, ca. June 1993; DA to Martin Elzy, 13 November 1992. With exception of first citation, all in DA Collection.

[75] DA notes, RE: "Harry and Dave Show," DA discussion with Harry Middleton on future Bush Library and Bush-LBJ friendship, LBJ Library, Austin, TX, 18 February 1997; DA to Martin Elzy, 13 November 1992, DA Collection.

By that time I had gained some infamous notoriety as a harbinger of bad political fortune for a first-term president, as evidenced by my service to Carter and Bush, who both failed in their reelection bids. In an ironic turn of events, eight years later, Bill Clinton became the third and final president I served during my career.

Sifting through the disparate elements of my life as a "presidential archivist" always seems to bring me back full circle to the Carter Project. For about forty years, I often have thought about that experience's impact on our staff, the Carter Library, and future projects. My "micro" perspective on such matters obviously was forged by working at these projects. Conversely, my colleague David Van Tassel had a unique opportunity from his NL supervisory position to observe several projects throughout their respective life cycles. He offers the NL insider's view of the overall project concept:

> [I]t provide[s] a cooling off period between the frenzy of the last days in the White House, the hurried move of sensitive materials, and the relocation of those with continuing involvement. It may not cool things off too much, but it at least slows them down and gives the professional archival staff a chance to tutor the former Pres[ident] and his staff about historical evidence, preservation, and perhaps teach them to take the longer historical view of the worth of the materials. Both O'Neill and Reed saw the project stage as…[the time] to find competent staff, get a grasp on the extent and organization of the materials, and get to know the most effective ways to work with the former P[resident] and his people…. [T]he project period also gives the time for necessary planning—institutional, architectural, design, [and] programming.[76]

In his incisive "macro" analysis, Van Tassel astutely summarizes the essence of our efforts as a project team in Atlanta, and also in College Station and Little Rock. Because of my personal investments in each project, I have a biased view of the results of our labor. Nevertheless, I think each modern presidential library is a unique, remarkable success story and illustrates the long-term value of a project's contributions.

---

[76] David Van Tassel email to DA, 21 May 2019, DA Collection.

Chapter 6

"National Treasures":
My Presidents and First Ladies

For those who think they have nothing to share. Who fear in their hearts there is no hero there. Know each quiet act of dignity is that which fortifies the soul of a nation that never dies.... What shall be our legacy; what will our children say? Let them say of me, I was one who believed in sharing the blessings I received.... Let me know in my heart when my days are through—America, America, I gave my best to you....

—Gene Scheer, "American Anthem," as
performed by Norah Jones in 2007 on the
soundtrack for Ken Burns's *The War*

During my National Archives career, I had the unique privilege of knowing several presidents and first ladies: Jimmy and Rosalynn Carter, George H. W. and Barbara Bush, George W. and Laura Bush, and William J. and Hillary Clinton. Such opportunities are rare for typical federal employees; therefore, I savored each of these relationships, however casual. It will not come as a surprise that, like any archivist, I systematically preserved records of my observations of these remarkable men and women who have given so much to our country.

Of this entire group, my most substantive interactions were with the elder Bushes and the Clintons. However, I never aspired to join their inner circles of advisers, friends, and other confidants. I merely sought to serve them to the best of my ability. In "speaking truth to power," I always tried to provide honest, unembellished guidance and advice whenever they asked for it. In dealing with former first families, I silently repeated this mantra: "You are first and foremost an apolitical federal civil servant; never behave otherwise." I also often delivered this admonition to my staff. These presidents and first ladies never inquired if I was a Democrat or a

Republican—a fact that clearly revealed their understanding of my status as a federal employee. My abiding respect and admiration for the Carters, Bushes, and Clintons superseded any personal and political perspectives. Today I am still in awe of their substantial sacrifices in faithfully serving our nation. To me, they all are "national treasures," and I believe that history will remember them as such.

Our founding fathers abhorred any vestige of the oppressive monarchism from which they had escaped by virtue of the American Revolution. Still, over the past two centuries, our presidents and first ladies—while not kings and queens—have evolved into a distinctively American royalty, characterized by an amalgamation of ceremonial "pomp and circumstance" and egalitarianism. We traditionally bestow upon our current and former presidents and first ladies varying degrees of respect, deference, and adoration. Yet their public appearances, magnified exponentially by the power of television, the press, and electronic social media, suggest that they are similar to our own families and friends. In other words, while endowing our first families with a special brand of celebrity status, we also assume that they are like other Americans.

Our presidents and first ladies are neither royal sovereigns nor ordinary citizens. As with all of us, their lives are fraught with tumultuous highs and lows—lofty aspirations, dreams, bitter disappointments, scandals, and tragedies. We need look no further for examples than the Kennedy family saga. At their core, our first families, like their fellow Americans, love our nation with the same fierce devotion and pride. However, they also have relinquished their constitutional rights to personal privacy and to live in "peace and tranquility." Very few American citizens would be willing to sacrifice these basic freedoms, regardless of guarantees of fame and fortune.

I want to share some personal observations about the presidents and first ladies whom I have known over the past four decades. This journey begins with Jimmy and Rosalynn Carter, whom I first met on 9 August 1978 at a concert on the White House South Lawn. The Carters, accompanied by Phil Wise and a few other aides, emerged unexpectedly from the White House Rose Garden and plunged into the large crowd. The Carters appeared to be energized yet slightly intimidated by the surging throng. The First Lady firmly shook my hand and then silently navigated through the sea of eager outstretched arms that awaited her. Although President Carter flashed his usual wide grin, he looked exhausted. Carter's grip was strong, and his shirtsleeves were rolled up above the elbows. His sinewy forearms were deeply tanned, as if he had just finished a long day in the peanut fields. He spoke directly to me—"Lots of hands out here today"—perhaps a weary realization that his interrupted perusal of the stacks of documents on his Oval Office desk would have to wait for at least another hour.[1]

Although the Carters both were famously portrayed by the press as excruciatingly shy, private people, they also could be ebulliently charming, conversational, and engaging in a social setting, like on that warm summer day in 1978 on the South Lawn. Despite the First Lady's reputation for supposedly being painfully introverted and diffident, I always regarded her as quiet, soft-spoken, and gentle but also undergirded with fearlessness. She spoke forcefully about her chosen causes, such as mental health reforms, educational issues, and Habitat for Humanity. In 1980 she appealed to our nation's "better angels" by unabashedly charging that Ronald Reagan "makes us more comfortable with our prejudices." The media labeled her the "Steel Magnolia," which I think was grossly simplistic. Like her mother, Allie Smith, and the rest of her family, the First Lady politely eschewed bombastic tirades, but she was a sensitive, articulate, and energetic champion of issues that were vitally important to her and the President.[2]

Prior to meeting President Carter, I had read and heard about his penchant for punctuality and the judicious use of his time. One day at the Carter Presidential Center sometime in the early 1990s, Faye Dill, one of his aides, and I were laughing boisterously in her office. I became aware of another presence in the room and slowly pivoted to see President Carter standing silently, his "icy blue stare" focused on me. "Excuse me," he softly said, which was my signal to leave. Without uttering another word, he had expressed his displeasure over our jocularity that had interrupted his

---

[1] DA Calendar, 9 August 1978, DA Collection.

[2] Misc. notes, ca. 1978–1980, Carter Family Oral History Project File, DA Collection; transcripts, "Carter/Smith Oral History Project," Oral Histories, Carter Library.

concentration.[3]

Anne Edwards, who served in the 1976 Carter Presidential Campaign and in the White House Press Advance Office, knew personally about his "icy blue stare": "Oh yeah. Cold blue glare, yes, it's there. It's real good, ...sets your knees knocking, hands sweating. Sure, it works."[4] She elaborated further on Carter's personal demeanor and other defining qualities:

> He is one of the most honest men I've ever met in my life. One of the most disciplined—...not in the sense of being a Spartan liver....[H]e has a tremendous intellect, a tremendous capability, and even going back through his life, he has been determined. Sometimes hard on other people, I know, but determined that he's got to figure out what his capabilities are and apply himself. Develop what he's got and shore up what he doesn't have. [H]e didn't have a knowledge of economics. Well, ...he'd read and read and read to give it to himself or find somebody who did.... He grasps everything real fast.... But I like the guy. I really do. I even like him when he'd get mad. He'd get mad a lot, not angry, ...he does get tight. He gets quiet, and he is in no mood for small talk. It would be because someone hadn't delivered something he needed they should have done, for which there are no excuses. The President...can handle a rational reason for something not happening, but it better be a real good reason.... And he's great when he's mad, as long as he's not mad at me.[5]

Echoing Edwards's assessment, journalists and scholars have wrestled with the nuances of Carter's disciplined work ethic. Historian Arthur S. Link, Woodrow Wilson's biographer, in comparing these two Southern presidents, portrays them as "Christian idealists, both 'good men,' decent, with great personal integrity...very intelligent, with disciplined, organized

---

[3] In conducting exit interviews with departing White House officials in 1978–1981, I frequently heard President Carter's withering gaze described as the "icy blue stare," or the "cold blue glare." See, for example, Anne Edwards exit interview by David E. Alsobrook, 5 September 1980, Oral Histories, Carter Library.

[4] Anne Edwards exit interview, Carter Library.

[5] Ibid.

brains."[6] Yet Link also characterizes Carter as "a managerial type," lacking Wilson's deep academic grounding in history, political science, literature, and other humanities: "He believes that all problems can be solved by intelligence. He was educated as an engineer, and he clearly believes...when a difficult problem arises, you sit down and solve it."[7]

Jimmy Carter also applied a rational approach to his post-presidential career, perhaps best exemplified by his leadership of the Carter Center's diverse programs. He seemingly viewed every endeavor with seriousness and discipline—mastering the latest word-processing technology; writing *Keeping Faith*, historical fiction, poetry, and other published works; building furniture; and designing fly-fishing lures. Wasting time was anathema to him. Carter Center meetings began and ended punctually as scheduled, without any extraneous chit-chat or *bonhomie*. This tightly structured format may work well in the White House or federal agencies; it deadens creativity and spontaneity in other settings, such as a presidential library.

Around 1990 at the Carter Library, I proposed a series of informal taped debriefings with the President on his latest initiatives and activities. Since we lacked funding for an oral history program, I hoped that these recorded sessions would help fill that gap. After President Carter approved my request, I began preparations for our interviews. One afternoon Faye Dill telephoned and said, "The President wants to know long these interviews will last." I replied that it would be entirely up to him. I knew instantaneously that my proposal was dead on arrival; the Carter debriefings never materialized.

In mid-summer 1991, I prepared to leave the Carter Library for my new assignment at the EOB in Washington, DC. As a gracious gesture to my unfulfilled proposal to interview the President, Don Schewe arranged a perfunctory taped session at the Carter Center prior to my scheduled departure date. For about forty-five minutes, President Carter spoke passionately with me about his current and future projects and his cordial relationship with President George H. W. Bush. I thought that this interview possibly could form the basis for future taped conversations with the

---

[6] Arthur S. Link, "A Wilson-Watcher Measures Carter," *Washington Post*, 7 April 1979, clipping, DA Collection.

[7] Ibid.

President. After returning to my office, I was horrified to discover that my audio equipment had malfunctioned; the tape contained only static. President Carter subsequently rejected my request for another interview, which came as no surprise to me.

He was not mean or ugly in vetoing a "do-over" interview. Although deeply embarrassed by my failure to record our interview, I fully understood President Carter's rules of engagement, as elucidated by Anne Edwards. I was personally responsible for the performance of my audio equipment, and I had not fulfilled that duty. The President undoubtedly learned this lesson of assuming responsibility as a young naval officer under the exacting command of Admiral Hyman Rickover. My colleagues and I were not US Navy sailors on board a nuclear submarine, but we deeply respected President Carter and always sought to meet or exceed his expectations for our work. We did not consistently achieve this goal. However, I also believe that President Carter failed to utilize the library staff's full range of archival, museum, and historical expertise.

I also doubt that President Carter grasped the intimidating impact of his full-bore didactical "preacher mode" on his staff and ours. During one Christmas season at the Carter Project, he invited us to join his staff for an office party at the Russell Building. It was a delightful, festive event, featuring bountiful hors d'oeuvres, non-alcoholic beverages, and spirited fellowship. Archives Technician Chuck Stokely aggressively attacked the shrimp bowl and dipping sauce and accidentally "body-checked" President Carter, almost knocking him to the floor. While stifling our laughter over this awkward moment, we cautiously eyed the alarmed Secret Service agents.[8]

President Carter appeared to be unfazed by Stokely's "assault" on him and the shrimp. We presented the President with a necktie emblazoned with the Christian "fish" symbol, which apparently prompted him to unveil a "Bible quiz," fashioned after the then-popular Trivial Pursuits game. He asked a series of questions about Jesus and the twelve disciples. Whenever someone eagerly responded with an incorrect answer, he curtly said, "No, that's wrong; anyone else want to try?" The room became uncom-

---

[8] James R. Kratsas email to DA, 30 June 2019; DA notes, telephone conversation with James R. Kratsas, 30 June 2019, DA Collection.

fortably silent; we all were afraid to disappoint the President with another wrong answer. Don Schewe offers some additional historical and biblical context to this episode:

> [I]t was on Friday afternoon, and I found out later that when Carter was in Atlanta on Fridays, he reserved the afternoon…for preparing his Sunday School lesson…. The lesson he was working on was from the Gospel of John, when Jesus appeared to some of the disciples after his crucifixion. The disciples had been fishing and had caught nothing. Jesus…said "Cast your net on the other side" and they caught a large number of fish. Carter's question…was "What did the disciples do when they got ashore?" As I recall, no one knew the answer. Carter said…(with his grin very large on his face) "They were fishermen—they counted their catch."[9]

The day after the party, Schewe thought of the perfect answer to Carter's question about the disciples: "They were fisherman. They *lied* about their catch." Many years later, he finally had a chance to use this line when his Episcopalian priest asked an identical question about the disciples. Although Schewe's quip elicited much laughter at his church, he was glad that he originally was unable to respond in this fashion at "that long ago Christmas party": "I don't know if Carter's sense of humor would have stretched far enough back then."[10] I concur completely with Schewe— President Carter probably would not have appreciated our injecting levity into the serious context of his Bible quiz.

As the Carter Library director, Schewe met frequently with the President and discovered that he often unveiled a keen sense of humor in private and enjoyed hearing jokes from his close friends and associates.[11] According to Anne Edwards, the President "has a tremendous sense of humor. It's extremely dry. It is not a backslapping sense of humor. But he's more of a wisecracker, …than anything else, and very sharp, very quick, and very funny because he's primarily a quiet man."[12]

As an archivist who spent many hours reading Carter's papers rather than meeting privately with him, I unearthed multiple examples of his

---

[9] Donald B. Schewe email to DA, 30 June 2019, DA Collection.
[10] Ibid.
[11] Ibid.
[12] Anne Edwards exit interview, Carter Library.

humor, which could be sarcastic, satirical, or "salty." His neatly inscribed marginalia were legendary in the White House. In response to a particularly egregious typographical error in a staff briefing paper, citing the "Attorney *Genetal*," Carter helpfully corrected, "That's *Genital*." He annotated virtually any item that appeared on his desk, including newspaper clippings. In late July 1977, Jody Powell highlighted an article about Filbert Maestes, who, after his conviction in Denver for the theft of 1,200 beef rectums, blurted out in court, "If I go to jail for stealing beef assholes, I'm really going to be mad." Powell scrawled on the clipping, "Mr. Pres., Thought you might like to see that everyone makes mistakes now and then." Carter retorted, "Jody—I ran for *two* years—& Sometimes feel like Mr. Maestes—Don't laugh—J.C."[13] Although any direct analogy between a hapless convicted felon's frustration and the President's own campaign experiences is a bit obscure, Carter's deadpan written reaction to the story resonated with Powell, Hamilton Jordan, and their comrades who had soldiered together in the bitterly contested political wars since 1975. In this instance, Carter's droll commentary also belied journalists' assertions that he was completely devoid of humor.

The public rarely saw this side of Carter during his presidency. Historian Robert C. McMath, Jr., who has closely examined the Georgian's career in the White House and afterward, argues persuasively that Carter relaxed considerably in public after freeing himself from the crushing burdens of the Oval Office.[14] Carter's evolving comfort level eventually allowed him to insert his own comedic style into the cauldron of contentious political discourse. McMath cites the example of Carter's appearance about a decade after leaving the White House at the annual Organization of American Historians meeting in Atlanta. Toward the end of the "Q&A" session, "An eager young historian stood up and asked, 'Mr. President, do you think the country is ready for a woman President, an African American President, or a gay or lesbian President?' Carter let that sink in

---

[13] Memo, Rick Hutcheson to Jody Powell and Hamilton Jordan, 3 August 1977, with attached annotated newspaper clipping, "Court upholds officer's right to laugh at hapless beef thief," (Denver CO) *Rocky Mountain News*, 21 January 1977, Presidential Handwriting File, Staff Secretary's Office, Carter Presidential Papers, Carter Library.

[14] Robert C. McMath, Jr., email to DA, 13 June 2019, DA Collection.

for a few seconds and then replied, 'Well, probably not all at one time.' That brought down the house."[15]

Carter had several memorable "performance opportunities" that evening, as witnessed by Schewe. Another historian dusted off the threadbare old chestnut about the President's sighting of a UFO in the late 1960s. Carter affirmed that "he and several others had seen something strange in the sky over South Georgia," and a published report had been issued. He briefly paused and glanced at Schewe, who silently mouthed, "We have it," and Carter then indicated that the library had a copy. To a follow-up question about whether he regretted filing the UFO report, the President replied, "No, I saw something." In response to a query about where he expected historians to rank him among US presidents, Carter dryly said, "Between Washington and the bottom," which elicited more laughter and applause from his audience.[16]

Perhaps another personal aspect of President Carter that has gone unnoticed is his ease in communicating with children. While adults often aroused his ire, children emotionally touched his familial instincts. In late April 1991, he invited the Carter Library staff's children to the Japanese Garden for a fly-fishing tutorial. Martin Elzy, Sylvia Naguib, James Yancey, and I all were there with our spouses and a combined total of seven children. The media coverage for this low-key event was sparse. The celebrated *New York Times* author Howell Raines, who had known the President for many years and shared his enthusiasm for the sport, was present with a photographer. Although his young students at first were apprehensive, Carter quickly put them at ease, speaking in a soft tone reminiscent of Fred Rogers on his popular daily television program. We watched mutely in the background as the President patiently guided each child through the intricate mechanics of fly fishing.[17] Our son Adam was twelve at the time; his sister Meredith was four years younger. Ellen and I were certain that they always would remember their private "face-time" with the

---

[15] Robert C. McMath, Jr., email to DA, 14 June 2019, DA Collection.

[16] Donald B. Schewe email to DA, 28 July 2019, DA Collection; "Governor Jimmy Carter's UFO Sighting Report," 18 September 1973, vertical file, Carter Library.

[17] Howell Raines, "In Fly Fishing; Carter's Record Can't Be Assailed," *New York Times*, 4 May 1991, "Lifestyle," 32.

President. After Meredith demonstrated her fly-fishing prowess, a beaming Jimmy Carter whispered, "You're much better at this than your brother." His words of adulation became a competitive bone of contention between our children for many years to come.[18]

I think one quantifiable measure of the extent of my direct involvement with presidents and first ladies is how many letters they wrote to me. Although Jimmy and Rosalynn Carter personally inscribed several photographs for me, I received only a single letter from the President—a typed thank-you message for my participation in the White House move to Georgia in 1981. This letter expressed his appreciation for my "continued hard work and friendship": "You and your colleagues did an excellent job in advising my staff on archival matters and in collecting, documenting and protecting my records during the transition period."[19] This document is not a unique piece of presidential memorabilia; identical "boiler-plate" versions probably went to everyone who was involved in the move. For that matter, Carter's personal assistant, Susan Clough, who was adept at "forging" his signature, may have signed this letter. However, as an archivist, I am especially proud of this item because it accurately recognizes the tasks that I performed in 1981. Furthermore, like his mentor, Admiral Rickover, President Carter was not known for penning effusive commendations.

My personal remembrances of Jimmy Carter are not extraordinarily revelatory. Like Anne Edwards and many of her White House friends, I found the President to be an exacting taskmaster who demanded an exhausting level of productivity from himself and others. Frequently stubborn and impatient, he "never suffered fools gladly."

Moreover, communications between Carter and the National Archives brass were uneven at best. He failed to understand our traditional missions and potential contributions as his federal partners. I also doubt that archives officials ever completely fathomed how Carter's Baptist faith and "Southern ethos" shaped and informed his personal perspectives.

---

[18] Adam Alsobrook text messages to DA, 2, 4 July 2019, DA Collection. Our son Adam vehemently claims today that he has no detailed recollection of President Carter's words of praise for Meredith's fly-fishing expertise.

[19] President Jimmy Carter to DA, 24 April 1981, in author's possession (framed and mounted on the wall of our home).

Despite their best motives, they rigidly applied their standard bureaucratic template in dealing with President Carter that was implemented with varying degrees of success with his predecessors. This approach was doomed from the outset—Carter was obviously different in multiple ways from LBJ, Nixon, and Ford—and not merely because he was the first Southern president since Woodrow Wilson. However, library directors Schewe and Hakes both adamantly assert that Carter's Southern heritage did not significantly affect their relationships or communications with him.[20]

Historian Robert McMath offers another perspective of the President's "Southernness": "Many Americans who didn't care for Carter at the time [1981] have come to admire him as an ex-President. What's not to like? I think part of that appeal in recent decades stems from the fact that Carter has become more comfortable in his own skin and less defensive about his Southern heritage. His own burden of Southern history was to try to explain his region and himself to people who started out with some big misconceptions and couldn't be bothered to reconsider them."[21]

Native Minnesotan David Van Tassel, who served in the NL office during the Carter Library's formative era, suggests that any communications obstacles vis-à-vis the former President primarily resulted from conflicting "individual approaches to problems" in those early years.[22] He also argues further:

> Carter's "Southernness" never occurred to me as a condition, in and of itself, as a quality that could be considered apart, let alone as having an effect on communications with NL....Obviously, his religion, his naiveté, even his accent had a "hometown" quality about them that "Southern" alone doesn't quite define. Heck, if anyone had Southern qualities that made communications difficult, it was LBJ (Maybe those were just traditional Texan). Carter seemed too considerate to be as demanding and difficult as Johnson in his post-Presidency. So, any obstacle to effective communication probably arose from his being a former President which always entails at least

---

[20] Donald B. Schewe email to DA, 30 June 2019; Jay E. Hakes email to DA, 30 June 2019, DA Collection.

[21] Robert C. McMath, Jr., email to DA, 13 June 2019, DA Collection.

[22] David Van Tassel email to DA, 6 July 2019, DA Collection.

a few protective former hangers-on.[23]

Fortunately, political "strap-hangers" who traditionally attach them-selves to former presidents were virtually nonexistent in Jimmy Carter's life after the White House. He later acquired a few academic sycophants as the Carter Center's programs expanded, but many of his senior White House advisers, such as Powell, Jordan, and Eizenstat, immediately em-barked upon independent careers in 1981.

Originating with his enlightened racial views as a "New South" gov-ernor in Georgia in the 1970s, I always have respected and admired Jimmy Carter. My personal esteem for him and Rosalynn Carter has grown after observing their exemplary lives of unselfish public service to our nation. My enduring impressions of President Carter are of his intellectual bril-liance, indefatigable work ethic, honesty, morality, and decency—the same traits embodied in his wife. They always will be two of our "national treas-ures."

Although the Carters and Bushes (George H. W. and Barbara) all were born in the 1920s, and thus were members of the "Greatest Genera-tion," my relationships with them were considerably different. My inter-actions with the Carters most accurately can be described as respectfully formal, primarily because I served as the Carter Library's supervisory ar-chivist rather than as the director. The Carters always treated me and my entire family with thoughtfulness and respect. However, the Bushes went a step further—they warmly welcomed us into their large extended family and essentially became our surrogate parents.

Our introduction to the Bushes was at a White House Christmas party in December 1992. After Ellen and I had our "grip and grin" pho-tograph taken with the Bushes, I briefly mentioned that we were moving to College Station, Texas, my assigned duty station as an archivist with the Bush Project. Since President Bush had served in a succession of po-sitions in the federal government for over twenty-five years, he and the First Lady immediately understood how I fit into the transition's organi-zational schematic.

In mid-December 1992, I also met their son, George W. Bush, for the first time. In preparation for moving the Bush presidential materials

---

[23] Ibid.

to Texas, I flew down to College Station (the site of the Bush Library) with my boss, John Fawcett, and archivist Warren Finch, my future colleague at the Bush Project. We huddled with a large cadre of "Aggies"— Texas A&M University (TAMU) officials, alumni, and boosters, including Perry Adkisson, William "Billy Mac" McKenzie, and Michel Halbouty. Attorney James W. Cicconi, currently serving in the White House Counsel's Office, and James Oberwetter, a Bush family friend and Texas political consultant, also attended the meetings. Outgoing Archivist of the United States Don Wilson had sent Bill Stewart to College Station as his official envoy.[24]

George W. Bush, who soon would launch his first Texas gubernatorial bid, appeared during a break in our TAMU meetings. Self-confident and garrulous, he greeted each of us with "Howdy, George Bush," and a prolonged handshake. He appeared to be saying, "This is how Texans corral strangers and take their measure—eyeball to eyeball." While I found him to be charmingly likable, I wondered what my "Yankee" associates, John Fawcett and Bill Stewart, thought about George W. Bush's flamboyant, Texas-sized entrée.[25]

He obviously had given considerable thought to the Bush Library and tangential issues. He told us that the future library should commemorate his father's life and achievements without excessively "glorifying" him. He also was deeply concerned about how the Bush Library would be perceived fifty years in the future. To protect his father from campus dissent by hostile students and faculty who opposed his policies, Bush informed us he only needed a "nanosecond" to reject the Yale University president's site proposal. Vigorously animated, he concluded that the first order of business was the selection of a "bright, young conservative scholar" to lead TAMU's Bush School of Presidential Studies, ideally by March 1993.[26] After listening patiently to our brief explanation of NARA's role in establishing the Bush Library and in supporting his parents' future endeavors, he nodded approvingly, seized our hands again, and quickly departed.[27]

---

[24] DA notes, meeting at Texas A&M University, College Station, TX, 15 December 1992, DA Collection.

[25] Ibid.

[26] Ibid.

[27] Ibid.; DA to George W. Bush, 17 December 1992, DA Collection.

In October 1994, George W. and Laura Bush accompanied the senior Bush on an extensive tour of the Bush Project in College Station. Don Wilson, by then the Bush Library Foundation Executive Director, and Don Evans, a loyal Bush *factotum*, also joined the tour. We showed them our entire operation. The two self-styled "Bush Boys" were fascinated with the security-classified vault and wanted to know who worked in there. We explained that only our staff and the former President's designees with the requisite security clearances could access the vault and its records. We pointed out weapons and artifacts from the Gulf War, including the bullet-riddled paper target of George H. W. Bush's image that had been captured in the possession of Iraqi prisoners. That day—with the former and future presidents and a future first lady in our midst—was uniquely historical, but we failed to capture it on film.[28]

About five years later, Ellen and I were at an evening event sponsored by the Bush Library Foundation. She subtly gestured with a glance to my left, and I turned almost nose to nose with George W. Bush. Clasping my shoulder, he said, "David, on behalf of all the Bushes, I want to thank you for what you did in building the library!" He sharply snapped his head like a punctuation mark and was gone. This episode probably lasted about two minutes and was typical of our conversations—casual, friendly, and brief.

I recall only chatting with Laura Bush a couple of times. In both instances we discussed the library's educational programs. Since we all were baby boomers of approximately the same age, Ellen and I felt comfortable around George and Laura Bush. We undoubtedly were miles apart politically, but partisan issues never factored into our conversations about the George H. W. Bush Library.

In all of my dealings with the younger Bushes, they were disarmingly approachable and unpretentious. Moreover, like his parents, George W. Bush valued the contributions of federal employees, revealed in his words to me in June 2007: "Our Nation is deeply indebted to the men and women who devote their lives to public service. You have preserved Presidential history for the last three decades, and your good work has helped to honor and secure the legacies of President Carter, President Clinton, and my

---

[28] DA memo for the record, 17 October 1994, RE: "President's Visit to NLBP [Bush Presidential Materials Project]," DA Collection.

father."[29]

While he vehemently hated the "L-word" ("legacy"), the nobility of public service was President George H. W. Bush's personal creed—he honored this cherished principle by his own example in war and peace. This notion that serving our nation is honorable, righteous, and patriotic formed the basis for my relationship with the two elder Bushes—as members of my parents' "Greatest Generation," I held them in high esteem; they in turn enfolded Ellen and me in their loving arms like their own children.

They always were there for us during some of the more difficult times in our lives. Both unfailingly knew exactly what to say, even when words seemed inadequate. After my father passed away in September 1996, President Bush wrote, "When my Dad died I hurt for a long, long time. I am sorry that you've lost your father, and I just want you to know you have my most sincere condolences, Barbara's too."[30]

His wife also gently sheltered us with her loving words when we desperately needed some serious mothering. In 1999 our sixteen-year-old daughter, Meredith, was in a terrifying automobile accident in College Station with two of her high school classmates. Although Meredith miraculously survived the crash (along with her friends), several months of excruciatingly painful oral surgery followed to replace four of her upper front teeth. She also suffered a compound fracture to her right arm. Several months later, she fell victim to an adult sexual predator, disguised as a TAMU student. "I have been reeling since I got David's email," Mrs. Bush told us, adding, "Our hearts are truly troubled over Meredith's awful experience. We know she'll be fine, but this was so ugly and unfair. She will certainly need a lot of loving and support and is lucky to have you two. George and I send you both our love—".[31]

The Bushes treated everyone in their orbit with kindness, dignity, and generosity, including the permanent White House domestic workers who serve all of our first families. President Bush was exceedingly gracious,

[29] President George W. Bush to DA, 20 June 2007, DA Collection.

[30] President George H. W. Bush to DA, 5 October 1996, DA Collection.

[31] Barbara Bush to DA and EA (Ellen Alsobrook), 4 November 1999, DA Collection.

diplomatic, inclusive, modest, and self-effacing. In any social setting, he ensured that everyone had been properly introduced and included in conversations. He assiduously followed the rules of etiquette and good manners his parents had taught him. In other words, he was the consummate gentleman. He could be irritable and impatient at times, but not very often.

Barbara Bush also exhibited many of the same social graces as her husband and was thoughtful of others' personal feelings and sensitivities. However, she was much more direct in expressing herself whenever she was exasperated or upset. This striking difference in the Bushes' personalities became readily apparent to me during the years that I knew them.

In early December 1996, the Bushes toured the library construction site. They were interested in virtually every architectural detail of the building and how archival and museum materials would be utilized. When I mentioned that her records were included in our archival collections, Mrs. Bush loudly guffawed, "Well, that wouldn't be very much!"[32] I tried to assure her otherwise, but she responded with skepticism. At the rear of the building bordered by a thick grove of trees, she asked Don Wilson where "the Bushes were going to be laid out" after they died. As we all looked toward the future grave site, the President weighed in on her question, "Bar—It's a secret!" "No, it's not, George; it's been in the press," she quickly interjected.[33]

Mrs. Bush seldom seemed reluctant to contradict her husband. On 6 December 1993, President Bush and I were discussing our acquisition of his personal papers and memorabilia for inclusion in the library's holdings. He asked, "Do you want my boat?" He then explained that he hosted several foreign leaders aboard the *Fidelity*, and they had spoken to other heads of state via secure satellite phone. I agreed with him that *Fidelity* had unique historical significance, and we would welcome her donation for exhibit in the museum. He responded, "Well, someone will have to move the damned thing down here."[34] I told him that would not be a problem.

---

[32] DA notes, 2 December 1996, RE: "President & Mrs. Bush's Visit to the Library Construction Site," DA Collection.

[33] Ibid.

[34] DA notes, telephone conversation with President George H. W. Bush, 6 December 1993, DA Collection.

We immediately initiated plans to move *Fidelity* from Kennebunkport, Maine, to College Station.

A few weeks later, Barbara Bush was in the museum and asked me if her husband had offered to donate *Fidelity* to the library, and in doing so, did he emphasize the boat's historical importance? I answered, "Yes, ma'am," to both questions. She chuckled and said, "All of that may be true, but George also wants a new boat!"[35]

Mrs. Bush did not always laugh when we spoke together. For example, while visiting the museum during President Clinton's Monica Lewinsky scandal, she disgustedly said to me, "Do you think he'll manage to wiggle out of this mess? He's awfully slippery." In fall 1997, upon my customary greeting to her as "Mrs. Bush" as she arrived in College Station, she delivered this ultimatum: "Now, David, let me get something straight with you. If we're to keep going along like this as friends, I want you to call me 'Barbara' or 'Bar,' but not 'Mrs. Bush,' and I want you to stop saying 'ma'am' to me. Do you understand?" I instinctively replied, "Yes, ma'am." Seeing that she was displeased by my reply, I explained that my language simply was a reflection of my respectful "Southern upbringing," but I would try to conform to her wishes.[36] Despite Mrs. Bush's insistence on my informally addressing her, I never felt comfortable doing so. We eventually reached an unspoken compromise: In my letters I addressed her as "Barbara," but not when we spoke in person or on the phone. In return she allowed me to use "ma'am" whenever I wished.[37]

This episode is one of many sharply etched memories I have of Barbara Bush. I always will associate her with *Guarding Tess*, the 1994 film starring Shirley MacLaine and Nicolas Cage, which poignantly depicts the mutual bond between an irascible, free-spirited former First Lady and her

[35] DA email to Patricia Reilly Koch, 10 May 2005; DA, "Call Me Bar: Remembering Former First Lady Barbara Bush," transcript, author's interview with Stan Ingold, Alabama Public Radio, 19 April 2018, http://apr.org/post/call-me-bar-remembering-former-first-lady-barbara-bush#stream/0 (accessed 21 April 2018).

[36] DA to President George H. W. Bush, 18 November 1997, DA Collection.

[37] DA to Barbara Bush, 3 February, 30 March (unmailed draft) 1998, DA Collection.

Secret Service protective detail. Mrs. Bush reportedly liked this film so much that she accompanied her entire staff to view it in a Houston theater.[38]

Barbara Bush, like Shirley MacLaine's "Tess," was very independent and occasionally escaped from the constraints imposed on her by the Secret Service. Mrs. Bush loved driving her own vehicle without any protective escort. Once, while driving alone, she rear-ended a TAMU student's car on the campus. There were no injuries, and the damage to both vehicles was minimal. Although the young student became almost apoplectic when she recognized the other driver, Mrs. Bush soothingly calmed her down, and they both went on their way.[39]

Around 1998, in an episode eerily similar to scenes from *Guarding Tess*, Mrs. Bush, driving from Houston to College Station, somehow lost her Secret Service escort vehicles. That day I was in my usual position at the Bush Library's entrance, awaiting her scheduled arrival. A frantic, sweat-soaked young Secret Service agent suddenly emerged on the run from behind the building and breathlessly exclaimed, "Have you seen Mrs. Bush?" I answered, "Isn't that your job?" Needless to say, he was not amused by my awkward attempt at levity. Mrs. Bush drove up a few minutes later—blissfully unaware of the pandemonium she had unleashed during her "great escape."[40]

I cannot recall any attempts by President Bush to jettison his Secret Service detail. However, he sometimes ignored efforts by his handlers to restrict his mingling with the public. During a public event at the library, one of our volunteers approached the President and introduced himself as the former State Forester of Texas. As the two men chatted amiably, a Bush aide angrily asked me, "Who is that guy and why is he talking to the President?" I answered that he was one of our best volunteers and that he had known him when Bush was a Texas Congressman in the 1960s. I added that the President appeared to be enjoying himself with our volunteer.

---

[38] David E. Alsobrook, "Eyewitness to History: Four Presidents and their First Ladies," September 2018, unpub. paper, DA Collection.

[39] Ibid.

[40] Ibid.

I think he relished these informal times at his library. One night when his special guest, actor Chuck Norris, attracted a sizable gathering of excited fans, he jokingly waved and said, "Remember me—George Bush, forty-first President of the United States?" I once saw a very different reaction from him toward a boisterous crowd of Aggies in the library. He nervously whispered behind his hand, "Who are these people? I don't know their names." He worried that his memory was fading like President Reagan's during his declining years when he struggled with Alzheimer's. I told President Bush, "But they all know *your* name." He smiled crookedly at me and said, "Well, you're right—there's that."

Through our face-to-face conversations, phone calls, and voluminous letters and notes, President Bush became completely immersed in all of the library's programs and issues. If he liked or disliked our museum exhibits, he usually told me. In November 1998, when I shared our computer-generated model for exhibiting his boat in the museum, he wrote, "I have no suggestions regarding the *Fidelity* display. It looks perfect to me."[41] In 1999, when we walked together through "The Longest Winter," our exhibit on the Cold War, he asked, "Why do you have so much about the Vietnam War?" I already was aware that the conflict's negative legacies deeply disturbed him. So I explained that we incorporated the Vietnam experience into the exhibit as an example of proxy wars waged by Russia, China, and other countries during the Cold War. Although not completely satisfied with my answer, he said, "Okay, I understand."[42]

He also praised our staff's efforts in behalf of his library. In September 1997, he wrote, "The archives will be the very best in the world. Your people seem fired up. And we are lucky to have you at the archival helm."[43] He described the Bush Library's dedication in November 1997 as "one of the happiest days of my life. That building is fabulous, Dave, and thanks

---

[41] "GB" [President George H. W. Bush] to DA, 16 November 1998, DA Collection.

[42] Exhibit brochure, Bush Library—Museum Exhibit, "The Longest Winter: Berlin & The Cold War" File, DA Collection; Kelly Brown, "Bush Library to Explore Cold War," (Bryan-College Station TX) *Eagle*, 13 November 1999, A1, A8.

[43] President George H. W. Bush to DA, 15 September 1997, DA Collection.

to you it will be for a long, long time. Please know that Barbara and I are so appreciative of you and the commitment you made on our behalf."[44] While deeply humbled by his personal accolades, I was extremely proud that he commended our entire team. In June 1999, after Bush celebrated his seventy-fifth birthday by parachuting onto the library grounds, he sent this handwritten note: "You and your troops did it again—with perfection."[45]

Unfortunately, all of my communications with President Bush were not lovely bouquets. In spring 1999, I had the distasteful task of informing him that some former White House officials or Bush family friends apparently were selling his personal letters and notes via various online presidential memorabilia websites. I was particularly concerned about this situation because the Carter Library's staff had been suspected (without any tangible evidence) of selling original presidential letters and speech drafts. Secret Service agents questioned us about our knowledge of this matter. Although one of President Carter's aides proved to be the guilty party, we did not receive any apology for this false accusation.

Determined to avoid any repetition of what happened at the Carter Library, I updated President Bush as his original documents appeared for sale. He was infuriated: "It really burns me up that friends will sell letters that I have written, and it burns me up more to think that inside memos find their way into the hands of autograph sellers." However, he refrained from shooting the messenger (*me*): "Keep us posted. Thanks for calling this to our attention."[46] As in the previous Carter episode, one of President Bush's former staff members later confessed and apologized profusely for his actions. I think their reactions to these incidents illustrate the two presidents' starkly different levels of trust in federal employees. Carter quickly added us to the suspects' list; Bush did not.

President Bush publicly avoided commenting on foreign and domestic issues that arose after his term ended. Privately, however, he carefully scrutinized any topic in the media that was at odds with his public service

---

[44] President George H. W. Bush to DA, 17 November 1997, DA Collection.

[45] President George H. W. Bush to DA, ca. 18 June 1999, DA Collection.

[46] "GB" to DA, 16 April 1999, DA Collection.

creed. In spring and summer 1996, an avalanche of press accounts revealed that Clinton White House officials had requested access to sensitive FBI background investigative files of 339 current and former career federal employees and political appointees. My name was on this list, along with at least four of my NARA colleagues. The press dubbed this scandal "Filegate."[47]

In mid-summer 1996, I spoke several times by phone about "Filegate" with Jean Becker, President Bush's chief of staff. She previously had served on the First Lady's staff during the Bush era. She was living in Kennebunkport near Walker's Point as she did each summer. Since Becker's name also appeared on the list, she shared my personal outrage about this matter. In one of our conversations, we discussed the possibility of a published response to "Filegate." I suggested that a former Bush speechwriter or a senior White House adviser should write this article. She abruptly interjected, "David, you're not listening to me—President Bush wants you to do it."[48]

Since Becker always spoke for the President, I immediately began drafting an opinion piece that eventually appeared in the *Dallas Morning News* in August 1996. I focused on how presidential libraries preserved and protected FBI investigative files and other sensitive personnel records from unauthorized access. I concluded that if a NARA or other federal employee "negligently mishandled one sensitive document from one FBI file, he or she would be fired."[49] My piece touched a chord with President Bush: "Your article on the abuse of FBI files was excellent—outstanding. I hope it is widely printed and reprinted; but knowing the media I have my doubts. In any event, you have made a fine contribution to the truth—."[50]

---

[47] David E. Alsobrook, "Mishandling FBI files no excuse for clamping down on archives," *Mobile* (AL) *Press-Register*, 1 September 1996, 1D, 4D. The original version of this article appeared in the *Dallas Morning News*, 4 August 1996.

[48] DA misc. memos and notes, ca. June-October 1996, "Filegate"—DA Communications with Bush Staff File, DA Collection.

[49] Memo, DA to Jean Becker, 5 August 1996, RE: "FBI Files Article," DA Collection; Alsobrook, "Mishandling FBI files," *Mobile Press-Register*, 1 September 1996, 4D (quote).

[50] George H. W. Bush to DA, 20 July 1996, DA Collection.

The President penned this note in his cramped office at Walker's Point. He had spent every summer at Kennebunkport since his birth in 1924, except when he was serving as a US Navy aviator during World War II. Fishing, boating, swimming, playing tennis, and communing with the vast Atlantic Ocean all were beloved elements of his life at Walker's Point. Bush was always at peace with the world and himself whenever he escaped to this special refuge.[51] When I think about President Bush and everything that he meant to our nation, I do not associate him in my memory with Houston, College Station, and Fredericksburg, Texas; Little Rock; or Berlin—all places where our lives briefly intersected. Instead, I am continually drawn back to a memorable day at Kennebunkport in late August 1999.

I flew up to Maine for meetings of the Bush Library Advisory Council, which included several former presidential advisers—Andrew Card, Boyden Gray, Kathy Super, Phillip Brady, Marlin Fitzwater, Tom Scully, and Ronald Kaufman. On the second day of my visit, President Bush invited me to accompany him aboard *Fidelity II* on a cruise to a newly commissioned US Navy nuclear frigate, the USS *O'Kane*, anchored off the Atlantic coast. He was scheduled to participate in a sailor's reenlistment ceremony on the *O'Kane*.[52]

The weather was pleasantly cool, and the skies were a leaden grey color that day. As we strapped on our life preservers aboard *Fidelity II*, President Bush proudly pointed out his new GNS (Global Navigational System) equipment that would steer us back safely to Walker's Point. After clearing the shallow, buoyed inlet, the President opened up the throttle, and we bounced over the choppy waves. Barbara Bush's earlier words echoed in my mind: "George also wants a new boat." *Fidelity II* was that sleeker, more powerful craft. His armed Secret Service detail skimmed alongside us in a sturdy rubber "Zodiac" boat. Bush occasionally gave the helm to a Secret Service agent so that he could troll the waters for bluefish.[53]

---

[51] Jon Meacham, *Destiny and Power: The American Odyssey of George Herbert Walker Bush* (New York: Random House, 2015) 26–27, 540, 600–601; Herbert S. Parmet, *George Bush: The Life of a Lone Star Yankee* (New York: Scribner, 1997) 14, 34–35, 332–33.

[52] DA email to Patricia Reilly Koch, 12 April 2005, DA Collection.

[53] Ibid.

After about fifteen or twenty minutes, we were rapidly approaching the *O'Kane*, silhouetted against the distant Atlantic horizon. As we reached her massive hull, this giant warship dwarfed *Fidelity II*. A steep, precarious staircase extended down the length of *O'Kane*'s burnished steel hull to the waterline. Both vessels hove up and down in the waves. We each had to time our leaps from *Fidelity II* to the bottom landing of the suspended stairs. A young naval officer, resplendently attired in his starched white dress uniform, saluted the President at the top of the stairs and led us through a winding maze of compartments and electronic circuitry. The assembled crew loudly greeted President Bush with cheers and applause. It was a very emotional moment for him; he choked back tears several times in administering the sailor's reenlistment oath.[54] Our brief stay aboard the *O'Kane* was unforgettable.

The return trip to Walker's Point proved to be equally memorable. Despite *Fidelity II*'s sophisticated GNS system, we became hopelessly lost in heavy fog, forcing the frustrated President to gear down to idling speed. A Secret Service agent—his billed cap turned backward and binoculars glued to his eyes—lay prone on the bow to guide us through a minefield of bobbing lobster pot markers and buoys. President Bush wearied of our snail's pace and coasted *Fidelity II* into a secluded cove where numerous small fishing boats were safely anchored and snugged closely together in advance of nightfall. He cheerfully hailed one boat, "George Bush, here—can you give me directions to Walker's Point?" The startled crew, all broadly grinning, provided simple instructions for the final leg of our journey.[55] Those genial Maine fishermen probably are still talking about the day that the forty-first President of the United States with his intrepid Secret Service detail suddenly materialized from the fog and asked for directions to his home. It was a tale worthy of passing down to their children and grandchildren.

Upon our safe return to Walker's Point, Jean Becker eagerly inquired, "So, how was our trip in the fog? Tell the truth! ...I hear you had quite an

---

[54] Ibid.; Alsobrook, "Eyewitness to History"; DA email to Jean Becker, 30 August 1999; DA to Tom Scully, 20 September 1999, DA Collection.
[55] Alsobrook, "Eyewitness to History," DA Collection.

adventure. Do tell all."[56] I told her that when we embarked on "a little ride in *Fidelity II*, I envisioned GB taking a few of us down to the nearest buoy/bell off The Point and then back to the dock. I never dreamed [of] a trip to the USS *O'Kane*, ...one of those defining moments in life..., and I'll never forget it."[57]

Today I have another vivid mental image from my visit to Kennebunkport in 1999. One evening after a splendid lobster feast, at President Bush's invitation, we all adjourned with our drinks to their spacious living room. He sat in a large comfortable chair, with Andrew Card, Phillip Brady, and the rest of the Bush Library Advisory Council entourage all seated or kneeling on the floor around him. The President's face was red and wind-burned, and his damp, tousled hair was standing on end.

For about two hours, they all talked and laughed together, and shared their serious concerns about federal governance, the body politic, and the world at large. President Bush was acutely attuned to all they said, seldom speaking but often slowly nodding in agreement with something that caught his attention. The surf crashing on the rugged shoreline just outside the windows punctuated the lively banter. From my perspective off to the side of everyone, President Bush seemed to be as happy and contented as I ever saw him. Barbara Bush had retired for bed long before this meeting ended.[58] This scene of the Bushes at home in one of their most beloved places will stay with me for the rest of my life.

The Bushes and the Clintons essentially "inherited" me during their respective transitions from the White House. Since the Bushes first saw me at the White House in December 1992, they perhaps subconsciously categorized me along with other federal employees who would assist in their passage back to their private lives in Texas and Maine. In contrast, in 2000 I was assigned to the Clinton Presidential Materials Project in Little Rock and did not meet the Clintons while they were living in the White House. At some level they were aware that their records and memorabilia were destined to be delivered to a renovated Oldsmobile dealership in Little Rock. However, unlike the Bushes, I doubt that the Clintons

---

[56] Jean Becker email to DA, 30 August 1999, DA Collection.
[57] DA email to Jean Becker, 30 August 1999, DA Collection.
[58] DA Journal, 17 December 2000, DA Collection.

knew much, if anything, about my role with the Clinton Project.

When John Carlin, Archivist of the United States, announced my selection as the Clinton Project director in August 2000, he cited my previous experience at the Carter and Bush Libraries. President Clinton noted my archival background with a heavy slash of his pen on the NARA press release and a question for his adviser Bruce Lindsey, "[I]s this okay?"[59]

Fortunately, I had two influential advocates who championed my appointment—James L. "Skip" Rutherford and Stuart Eizenstat. Eizenstat, whom I had known from my years at the Carter Library, was serving then as President Clinton's Deputy Secretary of the Treasury. As Executive Director of the Clinton Foundation, Rutherford coordinated the planning, fundraising, and construction of the future Clinton Presidential Center and Park in Little Rock. Between 1997 and 2000, I provided him and his associates with extensive background information about presidential libraries that they utilized in publicizing the Clinton Library's potential impact on Little Rock's economic growth and development.[60]

A "Distinguished Alumnus" who majored in journalism at the University of Arkansas at Fayetteville, Rutherford had amassed a sizable portfolio of experience in private-sector communications, public service, and humanitarian endeavors. He also was a seasoned veteran of many local, state, and federal political campaigns.[61] He facilitated the Clinton Project's

---

[59] "Alsobrook Named Director of Clinton Presidential Materials Project," press release (with WJC annotations), 16 August 2000, Case No. 401258, PU001-07, WHORM: Subject File, Clinton Presidential Records, William J. Clinton Presidential Library and Museum, Little Rock, AR (hereafter cited as Clinton Library).

[60] Stuart E. Eizenstat to DA, 10 July, 18 December 2000; Stuart E. Eizenstat to President Bill Clinton, 5 August 2003; Skip Rutherford to President Bill Clinton, 24 April 1998; misc. correspondence, memos, and notes, ca. 1997–2000, Clinton Library/Skip Rutherford Files, DA Collection; Kelly Brown, "Alsobrook named to project," (Bryan-College Station TX) Eagle, 17 August 2000, A1-A2; Suzi Parker, "Archivist to lead search through millions of Clinton items for presidential library," Dallas Morning News, 23 August 2000, http://dallasnews. com/texas_southwest/152889_arlibrary_23te.html (accessed 23 August 2000); C. S. Murphy, "Bush library finalists seek out Rutherford," (Little Rock AR) Arkansas Democrat Gazette, 18 May 2006, 1A, 13A.

[61] Skip Rutherford email to DA (with vita), 20 July 2019, DA Collection.

entrée with Little Rock's commercial and professional leaders, elected municipal and county officials, and academics.[62] His personal association with the Clintons and their advisers such as Bruce Lindsey also proved to be vital to our small staff.

On 5 November 2000, in response to Skip Rutherford's recommendation, President Clinton visited the Clinton Project for the first time. He was about thirty minutes behind schedule following a political event when he appeared at our front door. As he and Rutherford stepped inside, the door slammed shut, briefly barring several Secret Service agents from entry. They stood with their hands flattened against the glass. Clinton looked somewhat haggard after his long day of campaigning for Arkansas Congressman Mike Ross. In a raspy voice, the President told Rutherford that his "drop-by" with us would last only a few minutes. He turned and greeted me as if we were lifelong friends.

As Clinton toured our building, he became increasingly animated and interested in everything we discussed. I explained that since we were awaiting the first shipment of his materials by military aircraft to Little Rock Air Force Base, he would have to visualize how each part of our building would be utilized, including the storage areas for records and artifacts. He said, "I've been told that my presidential records and memorabilia will be the largest collection so far in US history. Is this true?" "Yes," I responded and cited the estimated volume—77 million pages of records, 1.85 million photographs, and 75 thousand artifacts. I added that because of the entire collection's unprecedented size, we usually described it by weight—625 tons.

His mouth hung open slightly and he rubbed his chin as he pondered these figures. He had seen electronically scanned records in the White House and was fascinated to discover that we also could access his documents on our computers. He sheepishly confessed that he kept a few autographed pieces of baseball memorabilia from Willie Mays and Willie McCovey. A brief "drop-by" originally scheduled for ten or fifteen minutes stretched out into almost an hour. We later learned that the President was impressed with our preparations for receiving his materials and planned to

---

[62] Phyllis D. Brandon, "High Profile: David Ernest Alsobrook," *Arkansas Democrat-Gazette*, 21 November 2004, 1D, 6D.

return for another visit in a few weeks.[63]

President Clinton visited us often over the next several months. He once said to me, "I'd like to come over and rummage through all those boxes and especially all those books that were given me. What do you think of that?" I replied, "That's fine, if you want to, come do it."[64] After examining an array of books in our collection, Clinton asked if he could "check out two or three," as in a lending library. One volume about the history of Oxford University especially piqued his interest. "Since Chelsea is going to Oxford, I want to share it with her," he said. Insatiably curious about the books, records, photographs, and artifacts in our holdings, he asked detailed questions about how our staff would preserve and organize everything. Yet, as a serious bibliophile, he was particularly intrigued with the books, especially historical and biographical titles.

In June 2001, Clinton briefly dropped by the project on his way to a U2 concert in New Jersey. He ducked into my office to change his clothes. As I closed the door to leave, he gestured toward my bookshelves and asked, "Have you read all of these books?" "Most of them—for my research and pleasure," I told him. Bruce Lindsey was waiting outside with an urgent warning: "Whatever you do, don't let him borrow any of your books; you'll never see them again!" When Clinton emerged from my office, he asked if I recently had read any interesting presidential biographies, and I cited Geoffrey Perrett's lengthy monograph on Eisenhower. Clinton said, "Well, I'm currently reading William McFeeley's Grant biography and several other titles, but based on your recommendation, I'll add Perrett's book to my stack."[65]

Earlier that day, I had another rather interesting exchange with the President. He listened attentively as our architects unveiled a model of the proposed Clinton Library and presented a detailed briefing on the entire structure. The model's current layout indicated that our staff's offices and

---

[63] DA Journal, 5 November 2000; Stephen Hannestad email to Michelle Cobb, 1 February 2001, RE: "Clinton Stats (for Move)," DA Collection; James Jefferson, "Presidential Items Due in State Next Month," (Fayetteville AR) *Morning News*, 22 September 2000, 5A.

[64] DA email to Angie Lowry, 8 April 2004, DA Collection; Brandon, "High Profile," 6D.

[65] DA Journal, 22 June 2001, DA Collection.

work spaces would be located on the ground level of the building. Looking directly at me, Clinton asked, "What do you think?" He was concerned that we would feel too confined within the lower portion of the library. He lifted this segment of the model in his hands and proposed, "How would you like it if we put this right up here? Don't you think your staff would like that better? They'll have a better view of the river and downtown Little Rock." I answered, "Mr. President, look at this building; it has no windows—our staff will be overjoyed to move down the street to a glass building with plenty of green outside."[66] The next version of the architects' model incorporated President Clinton's changes—our offices would be located on the second floor. This was truly a remarkable moment for me; I previously had never heard a former president express any interest in the staff's office space and working conditions.

This episode in June 2001 typified my conversations with President Clinton. He usually punctuated his comments with "What do you think?" I assumed that he expected candid, unadorned responses to his questions and remarks, and that is precisely what I tried to give him. In return, he did not leave me in doubt or confused about his feelings on any topic that we discussed.

Regardless of whether he was pleased or dissatisfied about something, he let me know without any obfuscation or delay. For example, in September 2003, he called me regarding the disposition of his Arkansas gubernatorial papers that were stored in a suburban warehouse: "I'm just frustrated as hell in trying to write my memoirs because these bastards out there can't get my stuff to me!"[67] Although he did not specify who "these bastards" were, I was relieved that he clearly was not referring to our staff. He wanted to know if we could assume temporary custody of his records prior to their permanent transfer to Executive Director Bobby Roberts at the Central Arkansas Library System (CALS). I told him we would be pleased to take care of his records. Over the next ten minutes, we casually discussed our upcoming exhibit which featured Elvis Presley-themed artifacts, such as a whimsical "Blue Suede Shoe" created by a North Carolina craftsman. Before hanging up, he congratulated the entire staff on our

---

[66] Ibid.; Brandon, "High Profile," 1D.
[67] DA Journal, 2 September 2003, DA Collection.

performance and reaffirmed his trust and confidence in us.[68]

Our telephone discussions covered many disparate topics—the Clinton Library's solar-powered lighting, the logistics and public optics of auctioning his personal book collection, the location of his phonograph records, our exhibiting the Emancipation Proclamation in Little Rock, caring for aging parents and in-laws, and Hurricane Katrina relief efforts.[69] He moved easily between topics, with acrobatic mental acuity. Yet I did not feel like our conversations were scripted or that he was working his way through a laundry list of issues. These random topics had occurred to him, and he simply was seeking our input and guidance. We seldom spoke for more than ten minutes, but he gave me the impression that our time was limitless and without any strictures.

Whenever we conversed, I always marveled at his logical, analytical approach to any issue or problem. Moreover, I was struck by his intellectual curiosity about everything we discussed. I once attempted to describe this trait to a journalist:

> Even though I haven't known President Clinton very long, I'm extremely impressed with his intellect. It sounds a little trite, ...but it's like a laser beam. You know he has a powerful intellect and it's all-encompassing especially when he starts listing different things....
>
> Yet, like Bush 41, he has this way of really putting you at ease, like the day he asked me what I thought about putting this building up on top. He said, "What do you think about that?" He really wants to know what you think about *that*, whatever it is.[70]

When I watched President Clinton in museum design meetings or in delivering public remarks, he was very aware of everyone around him—their reactions were important to his evolving discussion and remarks. I once saw him deliver a lengthy, detailed address to the graduates of the Clinton School of Public Service. He sounded as if he was speaking from

---

[68] Ibid.

[69] DA notes, 18 December 2005, 14 May 2007, telephone conversations with President Bill Clinton; DA Journal, 2 September 2003, 18 December 2005; DA to President Bill Clinton, 22 April, 1 December 2005, 3 January 2006; President Bill Clinton to DA, 5 April 2005, DA Collection.

[70] Brandon, "High Profile," 6D.

an intricate outline with multiple subheadings. I noticed afterward that the single page of "notes" in his hand was completely blank.

This memory has resonated with me, and I asked Skip Rutherford and Bobby Roberts about President Clinton's "notes" for that particular speech. Rutherford answered, "I don't remember that…. I have seen him in the past—jot down notes/names on a piece of paper, but not to have it as a prop."[71] Roberts agreed that while he did not recall "anything like that going on when he was governor…, he would jot down a few notes like on the back of an old envelope."[72] Roberts elaborated further on this topic:

> [H]is image makers may have gotten to his handlers and persuaded them that actually being able to make a speech with no or minimal notes did not look like he was taking things seriously. Presto, the President is now carrying a blank piece of paper as a prop thus making him look more thoughtful…. I was and remain impressed about how clear he can be with no real notes to speak of…. I happened to be in the audience at the White House when he…produce[d] one of these little two-minute radio blurbs. Someone handed him the text—he read it once, then proceeded to deliver a flawless little message…. All done in one take with no notes. He makes it look easy.[73]

Speaking with or without notes, from my perspective, President Clinton usually appeared to be "the smartest person in the room." On those occasions when I personally observed Hillary Clinton, she exhibited a similar attentiveness, "laser-beam" focus, facile intellect, and a wry, ironic sense of humor.

I first met Hillary Clinton, then a US Senator, on 15 June 2002, at a museum design meeting in New York City. She and her husband sat side by side, surrounded by former White House aides. Senior adviser John Podesta, political pollster Mark Penn, and several former domestic policy aides dominated the discussion during this lengthy session. Although the Clintons periodically commented or asked questions, they primarily listened to the other participants.[74]

After the meeting concluded, Senator Clinton patted the empty chair

---

[71] Skip Rutherford email to DA, 18 July 2019, DA Collection.

[72] Bobby Roberts email to DA, 18 July 2019, DA Collection.

[73] Ibid.

[74] DA Journal, 15 June 2002, DA Collection.

beside her and asked me to join her. She asked if Ellen and I enjoyed living in Little Rock and where our house was located. Since the Clintons once had lived in the Heights neighborhood, she recognized our address on Blair Street. She also was familiar with my vita: "Is your job primarily to build new presidential libraries and then move on?" I told her that Little Rock hopefully would be my final career destination. She laughed and said, "I assume Bill and Bruce [Lindsey] were doing something about that."[75]

Shifting to a more serious tone, she then asked, "What's wrong with NARA? Isn't the Archivist of the United States one of our appointees?" She was not pleased about Carlin's recent aggressive efforts to lobby her about appointing the Clinton Library director, bypassing her husband. I briefly summarized the chain of events that had precipitated Carlin's actions. I recounted how several of my colleagues and I had supported Carlin's appointment as Archivist, but soon after his confirmation, he became an unabashed opponent of presidential libraries.

She looked puzzled and said, "That makes no sense; surely there's more to it." "There's one additional explanation for his inexplicable change in behavior," I replied. I pointed out that Carlin had divorced his wife, Diana, and then married Lynn Bellardo, who formerly was married to the Deputy Archivist of the United States. Ellen and I continued to be close friends with Diana Carlin afterward. Senator Clinton grimaced and said, "Oh, that's a bad situation." Although claiming that she lacked "a lot of influence" as a US Senator and former First Lady, she said, "They'll see what they can do."[76] I assumed by "they," she meant the former President, Bruce Lindsey, and herself.

I was not privy to what "They" did in my behalf, but on 5 May 2004, I was appointed by Carlin as the Clinton Library director.[77] Within several months, Allen Weinstein succeeded him as Archivist of the United States. President Clinton issued his official statement in support of my selection:

---

[75] Ibid.

[76] DA email to Allen W. Jones, 20 July 2002; DA email to Skip Rutherford, 28 February 2002; DA emails to Diana Carlin, 24 July, 29 September, 2 October 2001; misc. correspondence, ca. 1995–2000, DA Correspondence with Diana Carlin File; DA Journal, 11 May, 15 June 2002, DA Collection.

[77] "Alsobrook named director of Clinton Library," *NARA Staff Bulletin* 529 (May 2004): 6.

"Dr. Alsobrook has the experience, the credentials and temperament to guide and direct this library. We share the common goal of making history available and accessible."[78] He later added a more personalized endorsement that included my wife: "David is an experienced historian and archivist. His work at both the Carter and Bush Libraries is a big asset, and we are fortunate to have David and his wife, Ellen, in Little Rock."[79]

Two months later, in July 2004, Ellen and I attended a book-signing for President Clinton at hosted by Bobby Roberts at the Central Arkansas Library. We queued up with several hundred "Friends of Bill" ("FOB") to have the President inscribe his new memoir, *My Life*, for our daughter Meredith. When we finally reached him, I leaned down and quietly thanked him for my appointment as director. He wearily looked over his reading glasses and replied, "We finally won." As we were leaving, I congratulated him on delivering a "hellacious" speech at the recent Democratic National Convention, and he said, "You're a good man."[80]

In December 2004, several weeks after the Clinton Library's dedication, he signed my copy of his memoir: "With thanks for making the library a living thing—."[81] Three years later, in May 2007, I retired after completing thirty years with the National Archives. I notified President Clinton that my "post-retirement" job would be with the Museum of Mobile in my hometown. He sent a handwritten note to me: "I just learned that you've decided to leave the library and go home to Mobile. I can't thank you enough for working with us through the early hard times and launches. We all want to go home on many levels. You've earned it and I wish you well."[82]

On 14 May 2007, he called me at home, and we talked for about ten minutes. He said that I would be missed but that he was glad Ellen and I had this opportunity to return to Alabama and care for our mothers. He

---

[78] Andrew DeMillo, "Seasoned hand chosen to direct Clinton Library," *Arkansas Democrat-Gazette*, 6 May 2004, 1B, 6B.

[79] Brandon, "High Profile," 6D.

[80] DA Journal, 30 July 2004, DA Collection.

[81] Bill Clinton, *My Life* (New York: Alfred A. Knopf, 2004), limited ed., No. 409/450, with WJC's inscription, in author's possession.

[82] DA to President Bill Clinton, 10 May 2007; President Bill Clinton to DA, 15 May 2007, DA Collection.

mentioned that his own elderly mother-in-law, Dorothy Rodham, lived in their home in Georgetown. He also thanked me for my efforts during the Clinton Project era when "they didn't know anything" and "didn't have a pot to piss in."[83] While his syntax was less than elegant, as a fellow Southerner I fully understood and appreciated his sentiment.

After Ellen and I left Little Rock in 2007, the Clintons did not expunge us from their lives. The President and I corresponded from time to time, and he kept up with my professional activities. When we encountered serious problems with my mother's Medicare and Medicaid benefits, the Clintons graciously provided us with relief that literally rescued our family from declaring bankruptcy. Our paths also continued to cross occasionally. In October 2008, Ellen and I were invited to a Democratic fundraising party in Baldwin County where President Clinton was the honored guest, and we had a good visit with him.[84]

In early April 2019, we journeyed back to Little Rock for the first time since our departure twelve years earlier. We attended the dedication of the "Bobby L. Roberts Library of Arkansas History & Art," named in honor of my dear friend who recently had retired as the CALS Executive Director. President Clinton was the keynote speaker for this event. He paid tribute to Roberts, who had served during Clinton's governorship, in recognition of his distinguished career of public service in Arkansas. The President also called for spiritual reconciliation among all Americans during this current era of bitter political divisiveness and "tribalism." After Clinton spoke and most of the audience had departed, I approached to shake his hand. He genuinely was surprised to see me and asked, "What are *you* doing here?" He knew the distance between Little Rock and Mobile. I responded that we returned to Little Rock to honor Roberts and to visit with my former staff members at the Clinton Library. The President next inquired about my health, and I said, "Well, it's pretty good, considering my age, but as you know, you and I are the same age, and we're all

---

[83] DA notes, 14 May 2007, telephone conversation with President Bill Clinton, DA Collection.

[84] President Bill Clinton to DA, 8 October 2008, 6 January, 4 February 2009; DA to President Bill Clinton, 15 March, 23 December 2008, 21 March 2011, 10 November 2016, DA Collection; Rhoda A. Pickett, "Clinton attends fundraiser in Daphne," *Mobile Press-Register*, 3 October 2008, 1B, 6B.

getting older." He laughed and pointed to his brother, who was standing next to me. "Roger's about the same age as us," he said, "and he's still here."[85]

This trip to Little Rock reminded me that anyone who is accorded the honor and privilege of serving former presidents and first ladies remains forever within their universe. In his remarks at the twentieth anniversary of the opening of his presidential library, Jimmy Carter mentioned my name as one of the original staff who had achieved "national prominence."[86] When I left the Bush Library in August 2000, President Bush wrote, "I will never forget the masterful way that you handled our papers long before the library was there to house them…. Thanks for all you did to get us off to such a great start."[87]

President Bush and I continued to communicate in writing until his death in November 2018.[88] After attending the Clinton Library dedication in November 2004, he graciously wrote, "It was good seeing you again. I want to thank you for your key role in making the Clinton Library the wonder that it is. Well Done…." [89] In January 2005, after personally greeting our museum visitors, he contacted me again: "You've done a great job. I really like that Library."[90] After my retirement from NARA in 2007, President Bush wished me "the very best in all that lies ahead," adding, "As one who continues to benefit directly from the outstanding work you and your colleagues at NARA do, I am particularly grateful."[91] The

---

[85] Invitation, dedication of Bobby L. Roberts Library of Arkansas History & Art, 5 April 2019; DA to Bobby Roberts, 8 April 2019; DA email to Bobby Roberts, 8 April 2019; Bobby Roberts to DA, 14 April 2019; Bobby Roberts emails to DA, 8, 9 April 2019; David Stricklin email to DA, 8 April 2019; DA to President Bill Clinton, 7 April 2019. All in DA Collection.

[86] Jay E. Hakes to DA, 23 October 2006, DA Collection.

[87] President George H. W. Bush to DA, 28 August 2000, DA Collection.

[88] President George H. W. Bush to DA, 7 February 2001; Bush to Trustees Selection Committee, Auburn University, 10 June 2011; DA to President George H. W. Bush, 2 February 2001, 29 November 2004, 12 January 2005, 21 March 2011, DA Collection.

[89] President George H. W. Bush to DA, ca. 19 November 2004, DA Collection.

[90] President George H. W. Bush to DA, 17 January 2005, DA Collection.

[91] President George H. W. Bush to DA, 16 May 2007, DA Collection.

nobility of public service creed seldom was far from his thoughts.

When I reflect on the presidents and first ladies who touched and blessed my own life, the haunting lyrics of Gene Scheer's "American Anthem" fill my heart and soul. I also can hear Norah Jones's beautiful musical rendition from the soundtrack of Ken Burns's documentary film *The War*. Although only one of *my* presidents and first ladies served overseas in uniform, "American Anthem" is a fitting tribute to all of them:

> For those who think they have nothing to share. Who fear in their hearts there is no hero there. Know each quiet act of dignity is that which fortifies the soul of a nation that never dies…. What shall be our legacy; what will our children say? Let them say of me, I was one who believed in sharing the blessings I received…. Let me know in my heart when my days are through—America, America, I gave my best to you.[92]

---

[92] Gene Scheer, "American Anthem," http://www.lyricsreg.com/lyrics/norah+jones/American+Anthem (accessed 5 July 2019).

Chapter 7

My Fall from Grace:
A Cautionary Tale of Redemption
and Second Chances

Welcome to Aggieland—The Greatest Place on Earth!
You're Leaving Aggieland—The Greatest Place on Earth!
—Arrivals and Departures signage
at airport, College Station, Texas

On 14 April 1997, Archivist John Carlin, after consultation with President George H. W. Bush, appointed me as the Bush Library's first director. Citing my experience with Bush and Carter presidential materials, Carlin wrote, "Dr. Alsobrook is uniquely qualified to be the director of the Bush Library.... I am confident that under his direction, the Bush Library will be an active and vital research center."[1] Although Carlin was NARA's designated "selecting official" for my appointment, President Bush was the primary "decision-maker." Several months earlier, he shockingly labeled me as "our greatest living archivist." Ellen and I smiled at Bush's rhetorical hyperbole and speculated about the identity of "our greatest *dead* archivist."

After applying for the position, I was cautiously hopeful but not overly sanguine about my possible selection as the Bush Library's director. I had not actively campaigned for the job and realized that the selection process would be highly competitive. Consequently, when a local reporter solicited my reaction to the appointment, I frankly admitted, "The reality of it hasn't set in yet. I've been here four years. I'm still trying to get used to the idea. I'm real excited about it."[2]

---

[1] "David E. Alsobrook Appointed as Director of the Bush Library," NARA news release, 14 April 1997, DA Collection.

[2] "U.S. archivist names head of Bush Library," (Bryan-College Station TX) *Eagle*, 15 April 1997, A1.

With the Bush Library's dedication scheduled for early November 1997, I was too busy to consider "the reality" of my new job. At a party in Bryan, Texas, on the eve of the dedication, Bush Library Foundation Executive Director Don Wilson whispered to my wife, "David will be a *great* director!" Since Wilson had given me the opportunity in 1991 to transfer from the Carter Library to work on Bush materials at the EOB, his personal vote of confidence was encouraging. Under Wilson's leadership, the foundation supported all of our programs. His presence in College Station was essential to the Bush Library's development, especially during our formative years.

Between 1993 and 1997, I tried to cultivate positive professional and personal relationships with Wilson, the Bushes, and their respective staffs. I also recruited and selected our entire staff, including five graduates of the Auburn University Archival Training Program. I was extremely proud of our young staff's work ethic, productivity, professionalism, and *esprit des corps*. By autumn 1997, we had advanced exponentially beyond January 1993, when Warren and Mary Finch and I first arrived at the Bush Project.[3]

The Finches and I worked alone during most of the Bush Project's first year. We needed additional staff to meet the inexorable demands of the 1978 Presidential Records Act and implement design planning for the future Bush Library and Museum. Like all fledgling presidential materials projects, we primarily depended on NL and NARA for our funding. The allocation of NARA's overall congressional appropriations generally was the purview of the Archivist of the United States.

---

[3] Alsobrook, "A Portrait of the Archivist as a Young Man," 285–87; Alsobrook, "The Birth of the Tenth Presidential Library," 36–41; Michael Precker, "The Trip Down Memory Lane Starts Humbly in Old Bowling Alley," *Dallas Morning News*, reprinted in *Washington Post*, 30 August 1993, A17; David E. Alsobrook, "An Update from College Station," *The Record: News from the National Archives and Records Administration* 3/1 (September 1996): 7, 15; "Three Alabamians to Serve at Future George Bush Presidential Library," draft news release, 3 January 1993; DA to Kathleen Gillespie, 25 December 1992; Wayne Flynt to DA, 14 January 1993; DA to Wayne Flynt, 2 February 1993; DA to Dave and Marlee Horrocks, 10 February 1993; DA to William Warren Rogers, 22 March 1993. Draft press release and correspondence all in DA Collection.

After Robert Warner and Don Wilson retired, they were succeeded by several "acting" Archivists, some of whom were vocal opponents of presidential libraries, such as Trudy Peterson, my first NL supervisor, who hired me in 1977. To ensure adequate and equitable funding for the libraries, in the mid-1990s Don Wilson, my former NL boss John Fawcett, Ford Library Director Richard Norton Smith, and I supported Kansas Governor John Carlin's candidacy for Archivist. Carlin promised to champion presidential libraries—a pledge he promptly discarded after his nomination and confirmation.[4]

Despite NARA's squeeze on the libraries' budgets, the Bush Project was authorized in spring 1993 to hire two additional archivists, two archives technicians, and an office automation clerk.[5] Acknowledging our staff's activities, Auburn historian Wayne Flynt wrote to us, "Please congratulate Warren and Mary Finch for me. They are delightful people and will do first-rate work for you."[6] I wholeheartedly agreed: "I do feel very fortunate to have them as the first members of our staff. They've already performed admirably.... Over the next few months, I may try to recruit a few other Auburn folks, including Jimmie Purvis, who now works for [Senator] Lloyd Bentsen in DC."[7] I also informed my parents that without the Finches, "I simply couldn't have done the job.... If the rest of the people I hire are only half as good as them, I'll be lucky."[8]

Weighing my staffing priorities, I remembered lessons learned at the Carter Project, particularly the advisability of hiring a curator who could be involved in the earliest stages of the museum exhibits planning. In fall 1993, Patricia Burchfield, the LBJ Library's registrar, joined our staff as the curator. Similarly, I added an experienced facility manager to ensure our direct input in all construction issues, from groundbreaking through

---

[4] Misc. correspondence, memos, and notes, ca. 1993–1995, Archivist of the United States Selection Files, DA Collection.

[5] DA to Allen W. Jones, 29 March 1993; DA to Dave and Marlee Horrocks, 10 February 1993; DA to Paul M. Pruitt, Jr., 20 April 1993, DA Collection.

[6] Wayne Flynt to DA, 14 January 1993; "A Presidential Task," *Auburn Alumnews,* clipping, ca. winter-spring 1993, DA Collection.

[7] DA to Wayne Flynt, 2 February 1993, DA Collection.

[8] DA to "Dearest Mother & Daddy [Frances & Thomas Alsobrook]," 23 April 1993, DA Collection.

dedication day. In July 1996, Oklahoman Steve Samford filled this essential position. Despite budgetary restrictions on hiring, we eventually built an excellent archival, museum, and administrative team of thirty-one professionals, all of whom worked well together.[9]

During their embryonic project phases, presidential libraries typically experience various growing pains, such as malfunctioning equipment, leaky roofs, and fluctuations in temperatures and humidity. Security violations and personnel grievances also occasionally occur at projects, which is not surprising since the staffs are drawn from other NARA and federal units and the private sector, which are governed by different laws and regulations.

During our four years on the Bush Project, we encountered systemic problems with a porous roof that required periodic patching, air conditioning units that produced heavy volumes of condensation, and unpredictable spikes in temperatures and humidity. Remarkably, we did not incur any security violations that I can recall. However, in 1995, several anonymous complaints earned us an investigation by the NARA Inspector General (IG).

Much of the IG's final report addressed allegations that I had violated federal statutes in the use of our government vehicle. Since we did not have a petty cash or imprest fund to cover incidental expenses, in two instances I drove the van overnight to my home for washing and cleaning. On four other occasions, I temporarily authorized the Finches and Debbie Bush to drive the vehicle after their cars broke down. Although the IG and NL ruled that I should have obtained permission from NARA in advance, they understood the reasons for my decisions:

> Clearly, Dr. Alsobrook did not benefit from taking the vehicle home to wash and clean. He did so to save the government the money of having to pay for the vehicle to be cleaned at a local car wash…. Dr. Alsobrook did not personally benefit when he permitted staff employees to use the vehicle…. NLBP [the Bush Project] benefited by having these employees present at the facility to work

---

[9] DA to Estelle Owens, 13 August 1993; Michael Graczyk, "Preserving lifetime of material," *Mobile Press-Register*, clipping, ca. 3 July 1994; Steve Samford text message to DA, 11 August 2019, DA Collection; Alsobrook, "The Birth of the Tenth Presidential Library," 40.

instead of…having to remain at home for the day due to automobile problems.[10]

Another anonymous complaint alleged that I improperly allowed staff without the requisite security clearances to photocopy classified records responsive to a federal court order in the case *Armstrong v. Executive Office of the President.* The complainant, however, was unaware that NARA routinely authorized such photocopying under the close supervision of an employee with a Top-Secret clearance, which I had ordered, thereby preventing NARA from being charged with contempt by a federal judge for failing to produce the documents. Dick Jacobs, the acting head of NL, wrote, "I am fully aware of the tremendous pressure you were under to comply with a court order and that…your quick management decision got the job done."[11]

In reacting to the IG report in its entirety, Jacobs further recognized that the director of a project or a library was "entrusted with a broad range of responsibilities and wide discretion to manage effectively a highly sensitive program in remote sites, far from any other federal entity."[12] Firmly rejecting any disciplinary action such as a suspension or reprimand, Jacobs concluded, "[Y]ou have my full support in your management of the project and I believe you made management decisions based on your best judgment for the good of the project…. I continue to have complete faith in your ability to manage the Bush Project. You have done an excellent job in working toward the establishment of the Bush Presidential Library."[13]

A battled-scarred veteran of internecine wars between presidential libraries and other NARA divisions and offices, Jacobs distinguished himself in various posts in the field and in Washington. He knew everything about NARA's often dysfunctional bureaucracy and his colleagues' personal ambitions, agendas, and vendettas. Drawing upon his own management experience, he intuitively understood my dilemma in serving many

---

[10] Memo, Richard A. Jacobs, NL, to DA, NLBP [Bush Presidential Materials Project], 3 April 1995, RE: "Management of Bush Project/Recent Complaint to IG," DA Collection.

[11] Ibid.

[12] Ibid.

[13] Ibid.

masters: NARA/NL, the former President and First Lady and their families, friends, and associates; White House veterans, the Bush Library Foundation, local community leaders, and TAMU. In addressing these entities' disparate needs, I also had to navigate strictly within the boundaries of federal laws and regulations.

TAMU's bureaucratic thicket proved to be as formidable as any in the federal government. The university's administrative power grid was heavily wired with vice presidents, deans, and other ambitious administrators. In our first meeting with Aggie officialdom in December 1992, we learned, "*Everybody* pays for parking here." Our rejoinder that presidential libraries' patrons and staff traditionally have access to free parking fell on deaf ears.

Nevertheless, NARA attorneys subsequently negotiated a "joint use agreement" with TAMU that exempted Bush Library visitors and staff from parking fees during "operating hours." By mid-February 1998, however, TAMU students were parking illegally in our reserved lot. When I telephoned Jerry Gaston, Vice President for Administration, about this problem, he issued a forceful warning in bold-faced type to all TAMU department heads: "[T]he University has a formal and contractual obligation to maintain the Library/Museum parking lot for patrons and Library employees." "Anything less" than rigid enforcement of these parking restrictions, he cautioned, "will risk the University's being out of compliance with agreements with the National Archives and Records Administration."[14]

I thanked Gaston for his proactive approach. Yet, in July 1998, students and unauthorized campus visitors again were supplanting library patrons and staff from our lot. So I voiced my complaint in writing to Gaston. I noted that attendees at a recent TAMU Extension Service conference had occupied our entire parking lot. I also mentioned that "during the extremely hot weather we have experienced, some of the parking enforcement staff have been observed in the shade of the Library

---

[14] Misc. correspondence, memos, draft contracts, and notes, ca. January–February 1997; memo, Jerry Gaston to [TAMU] Department Heads and Directors, Academic Building West, 16 February 1998, RE: "Parking at Bush Presidential Library Complex," DA Collection.

building, visiting with the maintenance people, rather than enforcing the parking restrictions."[15] I stated that unless "this frustrating problem" can "be resolved locally," the joint use agreement's terms required us to seek a resolution from NARA's attorneys.[16]

Five days elapsed without any written or verbal reply from Gaston. TAMU parking enforcement officers failed to appear for two days, and on 15 July they allowed students to park without any deterrence. I contacted Sheran Riley, TAMU President Ray Bowen's special assistant, who had assisted us with several campus issues since 1993. I explained that since this parking problem was rapidly escalating, our only recourse was to seek action from NARA's General Counsel. She agreed to look into the matter.[17]

Within a few days, to my relief and amazement, our parking problem vanished. Sheran Riley's efforts were successful. Unfortunately, Gaston was furious that I had gone above him to the TAMU president's office. He curtly instructed me by phone to cease airing any grievances in writing, specifically memoranda to Bowen's office. Gaston later dropped by my office, ostensibly to inquire about our daughter Meredith's oral surgeries and to express his "personal concerns" to me and Ellen. Yet, before leaving, he repeated his recent warning about the inherent dangers of our written communications being routed up TAMU's chain of command.[18] Surely, I thought, Gaston knew that archivists are not merely records custodians— they habitually create and preserve written documentation of their own activities.

Despite incurring Gaston's wrath, I was pleased that our parking kerfuffle had been resolved, if only temporarily. Yet I knew that our bureaucratic head-butting with the Aggies was far from over. After one particularly contentious session with TAMU officials, I shared an elevator with Robert E. "Bob" Wiatt, the campus police and security director. A legendary Texas lawman and former FBI Special Agent, the laconic Wiatt had been wounded in naval combat during World War II and again while

---

[15] Memo, DA to Jerry Gaston, 10 July 1998, RE: "Persistent Parking Problems at Bush Library," DA Collection.

[16] Ibid.

[17] Memo, DA to Sheran A. Riley, 15 July 1998, DA Collection.

[18] DA email to Sheran A. Riley, 19 March 1999, DA Collection.

serving with the FBI. He puckishly grinned at me and said, "You really don't cut these Aggies much slack, do you?" As a "Fed," I answered, I eschewed undeliverable promises or violations of the law. A wily survivor of countless federal and TAMU turf squabbles, Wiatt smiled knowingly and wished me well in the future. He knew that I would need some good fortune to prosper in Aggieland.[19]

By 1999, Wiatt already had logged fifteen years at TAMU and was much more adept than I was in circumventing potential bureaucratic minefields. His mythical heroic status undoubtedly struck fear into even the most powerful Aggies. Of course, I lacked Wiatt's experience and armor that were forged over his many decades of faithful service to our nation.

In spring 1999, we co-hosted an Easter egg hunt with the College Station Police Department on the Bush Library grounds. Although we had scheduled our public event with TAMU officials several months in advance, they continually complained that the egg hunt would "disrupt the campus calendar." Each of their bureaucratic "spike strips" reminded us that TAMU would determine which events were worthy of consideration or conflicted with other campus activities. Following a disrespectful, unprofessional harangue, one minor TAMU official angrily said if I had a problem with his scheduling procedures, take it up with Jerry Gaston. I futilely indicated that as a federal employee, my chain of command was not linked to Gaston.[20] This was neither the first nor the final time that an Aggie erroneously assumed that I was on the TAMU payroll.

Soon after our Easter egg hunt in April 1999, we partnered with the

---

[19] Robert Eugene Wiatt (1926–2010), a native Ohioan, enlisted in the US Navy at age seventeen in 1944. He was wounded aboard an ammunition ship during the Okinawa invasion. After the war, he played varsity football at the University of Cincinnati. Following his graduation, he joined the FBI, where he served with distinction for three decades. Several of his FBI exploits became documentaries and movies, most notably, Stephen Spielberg's *Sugarland Express* in 1974, in which actor Ben Johnson's character was based on Wiatt. See "Texas A&M University Police Leadership," 1964–2013, https://upd.tamu.edu/sitecollectiondocuments/UPD_History.pdf (accessed 10 August 2019); "Robert Eugene 'Bob' Wiatt," *Find a Grave*, memorial no. 57049207, https://www.findagrave.com/memorial/57049207 (accessed 11 August 2019).

[20] DA email to Sheran A. Riley, 19 March 1999, DA Collection.

local Lions Club to sponsor a Fourth of July fireworks celebration near the library. TAMU decided to charge $2.50 per vehicle for anyone who parked on the large grassy field adjacent to our lot. Not surprisingly, the Lions Club moved the event down to the track and field area—some distance from the library—where free parking was available.

By June 1999, Roman Popadiuk, a former State Department diplomat and National Security Council spokesman, had succeeded Don Wilson as the Bush Library Foundation Executive Director. Warren Finch and I told him that we were exhausted from battling with TAMU in advance of every scheduled public event in the vicinity of the Bush Library. Popadiuk shared our frustration and promised to parley soon with Jerry Gaston.[21]

I did not learn if this meeting ever materialized. Meanwhile, ignoring Gaston's earlier warning about written communications, I regularly briefed President Bush's staff about our deteriorating relationship with TAMU. For example, in March 1999, I reported to Jean Becker, Bush's chief of staff: "[TAMU] desperately wanted this Presidential Library and they promised GB a hell of a lot....All we want is a friendly cooperative attitude on their part and evidence that they want to work with us. Other than Sheran Riley, Bob Wiatt, and our cleaning staff, we aren't met by many smiling A&M faces, and this situation really begins to wear us down after a few years."[22]

Since the 1992–1993 transition, I had communicated frequently with Jean Becker and her team in Houston. I rarely minced any words with Becker—our relationship rested on mutual trust and truth-telling. I always provided my unexpurgated views on any issue, which sometimes frustrated her. Once when she asked for my "guarantee" that the Bushes would be pleased with historian Herbert Parmet's *Lone Star Yankee*, his biography of the President, I politely demurred. I said that Parmet was a fine historian and would produce a comprehensive, objective account of President Bush's life. I believed that this honest approach best served her and the Bushes. She allowed me to vent whenever I wished and was not judgmental about my "Scotch-Irish" moments of anger or frustration. In return,

[21] DA email to Jean Becker, ca. June 1999, DA Collection.
[22] DA email to Jean Becker, 22 March 1999, DA Collection.

whenever she was burdened with the crushing weight of her job, I quietly listened to her for hours on end.

I was particularly attentive to Becker whenever she adopted "The Tone"—serious words of personal advice and concern. Before retiring with his wife, Patsy, to their home in Virginia's pastoral Shenandoah Valley, Don Wilson said, "Although I thought you would be a good library director, I've always been worried about your temper." But he delivered this message without offering further guidance about any corrective measures I should pursue.

Rather than commenting on my personality, Becker—usually partnering with attorney James Cicconi—specifically counseled me about my "relationship with Archives and A&M.... [I]n A&M's eyes, you represent President Bush and must act accordingly."[23] In April 1999, Becker left no doubt about where we all fit within President Bush's world:

> Please do not think for a moment that I am siding with A&M. I am not. I hate bureaucracy almost as much as anyone and I'm glad I don't have to deal with it. However, Jim [Cicconi] is right when he says in A&M's eyes, you are no different than Roman [Popadiuk], or me, or Michael [Dannenhauer], or any of us. You are a George Bush person. That does not mean that you need to bend over and let them kick you in the ass. But...you need to do whatever possible to get along. If there's anything I can do to help on this front, please let me know. I want to help fix this before it gets worse instead of better.[24]

Throughout spring and summer 1999, I agonized over Becker's advice—was I a federal employee or "a George Bush person"? I shared President Bush's belief in the nobility of public service, but as a civil servant, where should I draw the line in doing "whatever possible" to placate TAMU?

My reverie was interrupted by an actual example of the conflicting nature of this conundrum. A prominent local businessman, who also was an Aggie, requested a meeting with Administrative Officer Johnna Arden to discuss our contracting procedures for acquisitions and "services

---

[23] Jean Becker email to DA, 3 April 1999, DA Collection.
[24] Ibid.

rendered." We carefully explained to our guest that as a unit of the federal government, the Bush Library's contracts were all subject to a standard competitive bidding process. We invited him to submit a bid for his company's services. He vehemently objected to bidding because TAMU already had selected him as the sole source for his particular product. We then explained that the Bush Library was not part of the TAMU administrative system.[25]

A few days later, he inquired by phone if his people could "assist" our staff in evaluating or interpreting the bids we received. Although I knew the answer to his question, I glanced at Johnna Arden, who was listening closely to my end of the conversation and vigorously shaking her head, "no." I said to him, "Absolutely not." He stubbornly insisted that the Bush Library Foundation had given him a contract and promised a similar arrangement with us. He asked, "Why was the Bush Library any different than the foundation?" We repeated that the federal government operated the Bush Library. Since he argued relentlessly with us, I finally said, "I simply refuse to violate federal laws for you and risk losing my job and the ability to support my family. I'm not going to the federal pen for you."[26]

This tortuous, redundant exercise in futility crystallizes the pressures I regularly faced in College Station. Jean Becker, James Cicconi, and Don Wilson insulated me to some extent from these forces. Yet, by June 1999, Wilson had retired to Staunton, Virginia, over a thousand miles from College Station; and Cicconi and Becker were preoccupied with other matters. Cicconi, as President Bush's designated PRA representative, was deluged with records issues. Becker was deeply immersed in editing a compendium of Bush letters, scheduled for completion in August 1999. They both also devoted many hours to policy and management issues related to TAMU's Bush School of Government and Public Service.

By late summer 1999, I fully realized that our foundation's top priority was the "care and feeding" of the Bush School, which relied on a combination of university and private funding. Of course, the library also needed the foundation's financial support for exhibits, our volunteer program, educational outreach, publicity, and special events. Popadiuk argued

<hr>

[25] DA Journal, 7 February 2000, DA Collection.
[26] Ibid.

that from "a business and visitors' angle," locating the Bush Library in an isolated corner of Texas was "a very bad idea." When I suggested that presidential libraries were designed to educate and serve the public rather than turn a profit, he said this philosophy deviated from the foundation's "new direction."[27]

Since I believed that the foundation's prime mission was equitably supporting the Bush School, the library, and the President's activities, some clarification was needed from Becker. "If the Foundation is taking us in a 'new direction,'" I wrote, "I hope someone will tell me where we're going....I don't want the Library to develop into a puny, scrawny, little undernourished bastard step-child because money is needed to revive the Bush School and other A&M programs."[28] Although exhausted from working on *All the Best, George Bush*, Becker reassured me that they would not neglect the library's funding. I thanked her and added a final plea: "We need money for all of our programs, but I cannot continue to sweet-talk, beg, cajole, etc....Whenever our Foundation balks on funding, I simply will come to you or Andy [Card] or somebody who will give us some measure of relief."[29]

Just before Labor Day 1999, I briefed the Bush Library Advisory Council in Kennebunkport, Maine, about our recent activities and projected funding needs. Bush aide Linda Poepsal, whom I first met at the White House around 1991, urged me to give Andy Card a "pre-briefing" by phone prior to our gathering in Maine, which I did. This was probably the third or fourth time I had attended the council's meetings in Kennebunkport, Houston, and College Station. I always enjoyed these sessions, which typically featured lively, substantive discussions.

I reminded council members that federal appropriations specifically paid for staff salaries, building maintenance, utilities, contracted services, and renovation of the permanent museum exhibits. Since some staff positions were supported by our trust fund, I also noted that this account currently was $83,000 in the red. I again highlighted the Bush Library's pro-

---

[27] DA email to Jean Becker, 30 August 1999, DA Collection.

[28] Ibid.

[29] Memo, DA to Jean Becker, 30 September 1999, RE: "Foundation Funding for Library Programs," DA Collection.

grams that required the foundation's support, emphasizing our volunteers, temporary in-house and traveling exhibits, public outreach, and advertising. Thanks to retired Admiral David Jeremiah's timely question, I elaborated on presidential libraries' funding "successes and failures." Wrapping up my briefing, I recommended adoption of an annual budget line item for our exhibits and programs and a fundraising campaign earmarked solely for the library.[30]

After we returned to College Station, Popadiuk told me that the Kennebunkport meeting accomplished very little of importance because the council failed to reach any definitive decisions.[31] Yet my subsequent communications with council members revealed a different picture. Andy Card, for example, succinctly assessed the meeting as "constructive" and asked for a "time-line of cash-flow needs" for the next eighteen months. He also offered some personal words of encouragement:

> Your participation was important and motivating. Thank you for your passionate commitment to the Bush Library! I appreciate the particular concern you have about the immediate resource needs of the Library and the competing interests of the Bush School. My hope is that both institutions, important to the legacy of President Bush, can be funded to optimal viability. That will require a well developed plan of expectation and action. I will work with Roman, Brent [Scowcroft], and Jim [Cicconi] to bring focus to the challenge. Obviously, your counsel is critical.[32]

Echoing Card's sentiments, Tom Collomore pledged that "the School will not interfere in any way with funding for the Library," asserting further, "I know for certain that both the Board & the Council are *very* supportive of the Library and what *you* are doing and am confident you will have the financial support you need and deserve. As you put so well, the *Library* is GB's legacy and front line of same—all of us involved are committed to its success."[33]

While the council's dedicated support for the library was gratifying

---

[30] DA Remarks to Bush Library Advisory Council, 29 August 1999, Kennebunkport, ME; DA to Admiral David Jeremiah, 30 August 1999, DA Collection.

[31] DA email to Jean Becker, 30 August 1999, DA Collection.

[32] Andrew H. Card, Jr., to DA, 13 September 1999, DA Collection.

[33] Thomas J. Collomore to DA, 4 October 1999, DA Collection.

and inspiring, Becker brought me back down to earth with a reminder that I was preaching to the wrong group—the board of directors retained final approval authority for all fundraising decisions.[34]

In the wake of my advisory council briefing, the Bush Foundation gradually, if reluctantly, became more receptive to our funding pleas. As per Andy Card's directive, in late September 1999, I submitted a programs budget for the coming year to Popadiuk. Upon its receipt, he recommended an emphasis on more traveling exhibits to garner positive national publicity for the Bush Library. While pleased with his apparent change of heart toward library funding, I suspected that Andy Card, Jean Becker, or someone else—possibly General Scowcroft—had spoken with Popadiuk. However, he frequently complained about living in College Station and threatened to resign. More ominously, after I vehemently challenged one of his arbitrary demands, with a tight smile he threatened, "David, you shouldn't get cross-ways with me."[35]

In early October 1999, the foundation peevishly balked at inviting our entire staff to the President's public launch for *All the Best, George Bush*. This decision seemingly was a symbolic gesture in behalf of fiscal austerity. I objected to Jean Becker in Kennebunkport that although the foundation finally agreed to include a few library staff members who actually had worked on the book, "We had to crawl on our hands and knees on broken glass to get them to do what they should do on their own accord."[36]

Like the mythological Icarus, by clumsily disturbing a celebratory day at Walker's Point, I now was flying dangerously close to the sun. Becker swore "to try to fix what apparently has been broken when I get home.... But the book came out today and we're all on a real high around here, and I just can't let anything ruin this day for me." She ended apologetically, "I'm sorry....But for today—just today—I am going to be selfish and just rejoice in what has been a fun day."[37]

---

[34] DA to Marlin Fitzwater, 29 August 1999, DA Collection.

[35] DA email to Jean Becker, 3 September 1999; memo, DA to Jean Becker, 30 September 1999, RE: "Foundation Funding for Library Programs"; DA to Andrew H. Card, Jr., 21 September 1999; DA to Thomas J. Collomore, 13 October 1999. All in DA Collection.

[36] DA email to Jean Becker, 5 October 1999, DA Collection.

[37] Jean Becker email to DA, 5 October 1999, DA Collection.

As they popped champagne corks up at Kennebunkport, I recalled that Becker had carried a lot of water for me over the past year, and I was chagrined to have crashed her book party. Since Archivist John Carlin had authorized Senior Executive Service (SES) ratings for the JFK, Ford, Carter, and Reagan Libraries, Becker, Cicconi, and Don Wilson unanimously agreed that my position merited a comparable grade.[38] Ellen and I gratefully welcomed this proposed salary upgrade—Meredith's oral surgeries had devastated our personal finances.

On 30 October 1998, Becker drafted a gracious, diplomatic letter from President Bush to John Carlin: "My main purpose for writing is to let you know of my high regard for David Alsobrook. He is a great example of a dedicated public servant, and I feel very blessed that he was assigned to the George Bush Library. I hope I am not overstepping my bounds when I ask if there is any way you can reward or recognize his hard work and service, I would be very appreciative."[39] The President added a handwritten postscript: "Warm *personal* regards."[40]

Carlin's tardy reply failed to match the graceful tone of the President's letter. A month later, Carlin stiffly responded, "I appreciate your good opinion of David Alsobrook." He then recognized his other units that contributed to the Bush Library's opening, "one of NARA's major achievements in the past year." His letter also was addressed incorrectly to "The Honorable George W. Bush," the President's eldest son.[41]

Former presidents and first ladies routinely write letters such as Bush's. Despite Carlin's reacting as if he did not understand the President's cordial request, he privately stated, "Dave Alsobrook and Don

---

[38] DA to Jean Becker, 21 June 1999; Jean Becker emails to DA, 8 September 1998, 3 April, 29 June, 10 August, 1, 8 September 1991; DA emails to Jean Becker, 9 September 1998, 23 March, 23, 29 June, 4, 6 August, 8 September 1999; DA emails to James W. Cicconi, 8, 16 September 1999; James W. Cicconi emails to DA, 1, 11, 16 September 1999; memo, DA to James W. Cicconi, 15 December 1998, RE: "Background for Your Meeting with John Carlin." All in DA Collection.

[39] President George H. W. Bush to John Carlin, 30 October 1998, DA Collection.

[40] Ibid.

[41] John W. Carlin to "The Honorable George W. Bush" [sic], 20 November 1998, DA Collection.

Wilson cooked up this idea." Carlin, who had only served as Archivist for four years, told Cicconi that I had not earned an SES position. By 1998, I had served at NARA for over twenty years. Yet Carlin objected that this recognition was "a few years too early" and would necessitate moving my name above other career employees with longer NARA tenures.[42] Cicconi was convinced that the Archivist had to "save face" and not appear that the President's letter had influenced him in any manner. Therefore, Carlin wanted some time to elapse between the letter and SES authorization.[43]

Between January and September 1999, Carlin and his leadership team "slow-walked" the SES approval paperwork. Meanwhile, at the White House, President Clinton's advisers voiced their support for a Bush Library SES position. They were aware that Carlin already had approved identical positions for several other presidential libraries and wanted the future Clinton Library director to have the same rating.[44]

In late June 1999, almost seven months after receiving President Bush's letter, Carlin asked Cicconi for an additional written recommendation in my behalf. After Cicconi drafted this letter, the Archivist again mentioned that I was being promoted before "my time" ahead of other employees on "the list." Citing NARA's "huge rumor mill," Cicconi and Becker instructed me, "Not to say anything to anyone at Archives about this, even if you trust them and consider them good friends.... [I]f Carlin has any inkling this is being talked about in any way, it will be a huge setback."[45]

Soon after the Carter and Reagan Libraries' SES positions were approved and posted in August 1999, I learned from NL that my

---

[42] DA notes, 23 November 1998, telephone conversation with Skip Rutherford; Jean Becker email to DA, 3 April 1999; James W. Cicconi email to DA, 11 September 1999, DA Collection.

[43] Jean Becker email to DA, 29 June 1999; DA emails to Jean Becker, 23 March, 29 June 1999; DA to Skip Rutherford, 3 August 1999, DA Collection.

[44] "Chronology [of SES Appointment]," October 1998–January 2000; DA notes, 23 November 1998, telephone conversation with Skip Rutherford; DA email to Jean Becker, 5 April 1999; DA to Skip Rutherford, 4 February, 7 September 1999, DA Collection.

[45] James W. Cicconi to John W. Carlin, 14 July 1999; Jean Becker email to DA, 29 June 1999, DA Collection.

appointment paperwork would be dispatched to the White House Personnel Office (WHPO) "right away." On 1 September, Carlin advised Cicconi that my SES authorization was "on track." That same day, Richard Norton Smith jokingly called from Michigan: "Is this the only presidential library of a living former President that doesn't have an SES director?"[46] Smith obviously was closely monitoring our situation from Grand Rapids.

A week later, David F. Peterson, Assistant Archivist for Presidential Libraries, requested a copy of my vita for inclusion with the SES paperwork for WHPO. On 15 September, Carlin phoned to see if I would accept a Non-career SES appointment. Although unlike Career SES appointees, I could be terminated "without cause," I accepted his offer. He explained that after WHPO "signs off" on his authorization, it will go to OPM (Office of Personnel Management) for final approval and then back to NARA for "some internal vetting." He estimated that the entire procedure would require thirty to sixty days. WHPO approved Carlin's request on 30 September 1999; the final check-offs and vetting by OPM and NARA were pushed forward into January 2000.[47]

As the SES saga proceeded at its proscribed, glacial pace, I pondered the impact of my own NARA history. In one frank exchange with Jean Becker, I admitted, "Sometimes it's virtually impossible to represent the former POTUS's best interests, while simultaneously adhering to NARA's company line, esp. when that line will be harmful to GB and the Library." Despite being "placed in a tough situation by NARA, ...I've always tried to do what was right and...the best course of action for the Library." However, NARA expected me to prove my loyalty as a "team player" by distancing myself from President Bush and his family. "But I can't do that," I concluded, "even if it means NEVER being promoted. I love GB and BPB like my own parents, and that feeling will never change."[48] Becker answered, "I would always rather you be loyal to GB and BPB than anyone else!"[49]

---

[46] "Chronology [of SES Appointment]," August–September 1999; DA email to Jean Becker, 1 September 1999, DA Collection.

[47] "Chronology [of SES Appointment]," September 1999–January 2000; DA email to Jean Becker, 16 September 1999, DA Collection.

[48] DA email to Jean Becker, 5 April 1999, DA Collection.

[49] Jean Becker email to DA, 5 April 1999, DA Collection.

In November 1999, Ellen and I enjoyed a brief respite from the NARA melodrama with an overseas trip to Germany for the tenth anniversary of the Berlin Wall's collapse. The Bush Library partnered with the Allied Museum in mounting an exhibit to commemorate the collegial relationship between President Bush and Chancellor Helmut Kohl. We attended a rollicking party near the Brandenburg Gate that lasted until 1:00 a.m. After President Bush was named *Ein Ehrenburger vom Berlin* ("An Honored Citizen of Berlin"), I spoke briefly with him and Mrs. Bush.[50]

Back in College Station, still heavily jet-lagged and caffeinated after our overseas adventure, I prepared for a live C-SPAN tour of the Bush Library, scheduled for mid-December. After a leisurely stroll through our exhibits with host Susan Swain, historian John Robert Greene and I fielded viewers' phone calls. As the calls rolled in, we pointed out relevant documents and artifacts in the exhibits.[51] I always will remember that glorious night because it marked my final appearance as the Bush Library's director at a televised public event.

On 7 January 2000, I learned from NARA General Counsel Gary Stern that his office's portion of my SES background paperwork was finished and ready to be returned to WHPO. Just before hanging up, he casually added that NARA might have an "SES ceiling problem," but they hoped "to squeeze" my paperwork through WHPO. David Peterson followed up on 14 January that because of this "small glitch," the Archivist would reexamine his options and consult with OMB regarding congressional authority to expand NARA's SES pool. Peterson said this issue was a "top priority" and should be resolved within a few weeks. John Fawcett, who formerly held Peterson's NL position, left a brief phone message: "Sounds like Carlin is wanting to let you know that he controls your future—Son of a bitch."[52]

---

[50] DA email to Jean Becker, 15 November 1999; misc. speech drafts, itineraries, and notes, ca. October–November 1999, Allied Museum—Berlin, DA Trip to Germany File, DA Collection.

[51] DA email to Jean Becker, 15 November 1999; misc. memos and notes, ca. November–December 1999, C-SPAN File, DA Collection.

[52] DA notes, 14 January 2000, telephone conversation with David Peterson; DA email to James W. Cicconi, 14 January 2000; "Chronology [of SES

Another week passed without any resolution. On 20 January, Sharon Fawcett (Peterson's NL deputy and John Fawcett's ex-wife) said that the Archivist had directed Henry "Hank" Leibowitz, NARA personnel chief, to draft a comprehensive options memorandum on the entire SES issue. While Leibowitz was reluctant to increase the number of Non-career SES positions, he thought that an official request for such action to OMB and Congress might be the only available option. NARA also had two Career SES slots that had been vacant for several years, but Leibowitz and Carlin did not want to touch those positions. Sharon Fawcett surprisingly confided to me that the NL staff had been excluded from "this process since the beginning."[53]

I stood at a crucial crossroads—should I "be patient" as Cicconi counseled or seek assistance elsewhere? As usual, I thoroughly briefed Cicconi and Becker on the latest NARA developments. I told Becker, "We're in a very tough situation, Jean, and it won't do any good for Cicconi to pat me on the head and tell me to be patient because Carlin is really a good guy and loves the Libraries. Nothing could be further from the truth." "I'm so sorry, David," she replied, "I'm at a loss to understand how all this works, but this certainly has been torturous for you."[54] Meanwhile, Cicconi went "radio-silent" and ignored my latest plea.[55]

Ellen and I talked long into the night about our remaining options. "Do you think I should reach out to Skip Rutherford in Little Rock?" I asked. Without pausing, she said, "Why not? Carlin can't hate you more than he already does." I brought Rutherford up to speed with a detailed summary of recent events and asked for any assistance he could lend. He quickly volunteered to call his OMB contacts and seek additional background information on SES positions. After I apologized for bothering him with "this kind of crap," Rutherford replied, "I'm ready, willing and

Appointment]," January 2000; John Fawcett telephone message, 14 January 2000, DA Collection.

[53] DA notes, 20 January 2000, telephone conversation with Sharon Fawcett; DA emails to Sharon Fawcett, 20, 21 January 2000; DA emails to Diana Carlin, 20, 21 January 2000, DA Collection.

[54] DA email to Jean Becker, 15 January 2000; Jean Becker email to DA, 17 January 2000, DA Collection.

[55] DA email to James W. Cicconi, 25 January 2000, DA Collection.

able....Just let me know."[56]

In January 2000, I also contacted US Congressman Kevin Brady's staff and Governor George W. Bush, who was deep into presidential campaigning. I shared the details of my SES problem with Brady's staff but did not broach this topic with the governor. I instead sent him a short list of my favorite historical and fictional works for suggested reading on the campaign trail. I also requested a meeting with him after the election to discuss "the future of Presidential libraries."[57] I knew that Don Wilson and political guru Karl Rove also were interested in this topic and probably would speak over the coming months with the governor. As a courtesy, I wrote Wilson about my contacting Bush: "I wanted to let you know that I plan to do this, but I didn't want to steal any of your thunder."[58]

Receiving no reply from Wilson, I assumed that he had no objection to my meeting with the governor in the fall. However, on 28 January 2000, after speaking with Don and Patsy Wilson, John Fawcett called me: "Not an easy time in Staunton, Virginia—DW doesn't like idea of you going to GB."[59] Thus, I unwittingly had stumbled over a hidden "trip-wire" protecting the Bush inner sanctum. Although nobody other than Wilson expressed their displeasure with my indiscretion, I apparently had committed an unpardonable offense. Because of my previous history of perceived transgressions, a swift, decisive punishment lay ahead—ostracism, followed by banishment, from the Bush kingdom.

My journey along the "road to perdition" began precisely at 10:00 a.m. on 4 February 2000. David Peterson phoned to let me know that he would fly down to College Station in three days to discuss a "confidential, somewhat sensitive matter." Since he refused to offer any further details, I

---

[56] DA emails to Skip Rutherford, 14 (quote), 15, 19, 20 January 2000; Skip Rutherford emails to DA, 14, 15 2000; DA to Skip Rutherford, 25 January 2000, DA Collection.

[57] DA to Carol Thobae, Rep. Kevin Brady's Press Secretary, 27 January 2000; DA emails to Carol Thobae, 24, January, 1 February 2000; Carol Thobae email to DA, 1 February 2000; DA to Governor George W. Bush, 21 January 2000, DA Collection.

[58] DA to Don Wilson, 25 January 2000, DA Collection.

[59] DA notes, 28 January 2000, telephone conversation with John Fawcett, DA Collection.

did not ask any questions.[60] Later that day, I called Sharon Fawcett, whom I had known since the late 1970s, when she and her husband had transferred to NL from the LBJ Library. Since we had been friends for several years, I hoped that she would provide additional details about Peterson's upcoming visit. She nervously repeated—almost verbatim—Peterson's earlier message. Several days later, she apologized and expressed a fear that Peterson would have retaliated against her if she said "too much" to me.[61]

Since the Clinton Library architects were scheduled to visit College Station the following week, I thought that Peterson's trip might be related in some way. I contacted Skip Rutherford about my strange conversation with Peterson. Rutherford and I talked for about twenty minutes, and he surmised that his recent discussion with Alan Lowe in Little Rock might have triggered Peterson's action. Kentuckian Alan Lowe was an NL archivist involved in the selection and preparation of the Clinton Project site. He questioned Rutherford about whether or not I would be a candidate to replace Carlin as Archivist after the upcoming presidential election. Rutherford said that although he doubted that I wanted to leave the Bush Library, "David would be an excellent candidate." Lowe then apparently reported this conversation to Peterson. I promised to call Rutherford again after my upcoming session with Peterson.[62]

On the following Monday, 7 February 2000, Peterson arrived at my office shortly after 4:00 p.m. He did not shake my hand, which I thought was somewhat strange. He wore a finely tailored, navy blue suit, crisp white shirt, and a tightly knotted dark tie. Since Peterson usually traveled in casual clothes, his business attire looked odd. With his closely shaved scalp and towering physical presence, Peterson could be quite intimidating. Yet, on this occasion, I was more puzzled than awed by his unusual demeanor—not anger but a frenetic, highly charged eagerness.[63]

---

[60] DA Journal, 4 February 2000, DA Collection.

[61] DA notes, 9 February 2000, telephone conversation with Sharon Fawcett; DA Journal, 4, 9 February 2000, DA Collection.

[62] DA to Skip Rutherford, 4 February 2000; DA notes, 4 February 2000, telephone conversation with Skip Rutherford, DA Collection.

[63] DA Journal, 7 February 2000; "Libraries' Peterson is Retiring," *NARA Staff Bulletin*, clipping, ca. September 2001; "Peterson, David Frederick," biography, *Who's Who in America*, clipping, ca. 1996, DA Collection. Peterson earned

Sitting in a chair parallel to mine, Peterson wasted little time with any social pleasantries. He excitedly said that John Carlin had received phone calls from two "serious, very important" friends of President Bush. These unnamed individuals charged that I was "obstinate, obstructionist, and highly unprofessional" in all of my interactions with TAMU, the Bush office in Houston, and the Bush Library Foundation. Peterson asked, "What is all this about?" I suggested that perhaps he could provide more specifics or context for these complaints. He said that Carlin had not told him anything else. Because of the seriousness of these charges, Carlin was obligated to conduct a full investigation. Peterson eagerly pressed forward, adding that since I now had lost President Bush's "confidence, trust, and respect," the Archivist and NARA would "open up" competition for the SES position I was "interested in" and scheduled to receive.[64]

Peterson paused and appeared to be waiting for my reaction to his last comment, but I remained silent. He again repeated—more emphatically—the tenor of the complaints to Carlin and asked me what could have precipitated these calls. Peterson was well acquainted with the recent history of our parking squabble with TAMU, but I revisited it in minute specificity. I also added a summary of our meeting in 1999 with the Aggie businessman who pressured us to skirt our bidding procedures for his contract. After about fifty minutes, Peterson instructed me to spend the next two or three days thinking about what could have prompted these two phone calls. When I again asked about the specifics of these allegations, he said, "John might have mentioned something about emails or other communications that were highly unprofessional on your part." Once more

---

an AB at Harvard University in 1959, followed by an LLB at Cornell University. After law school and brief service in the US Army, he was employed at Metromedia, Inc., in New York City and Los Angeles. In 1970–1976, he served as Director of the Consumer Information Center and later as GSA's Director of Consumer Affairs. In 1982, during the Reagan administration, he transferred from GSA to NARA as an Associate Archivist for Management. The following year, he became Assistant Archivist for Federal Records Centers, a position he held until John Carlin appointed him as Assistant Archivist for Presidential Libraries. Ellen and I first met Peterson in Atlanta around 1984 at a dinner hosted by Carter Project Director Don Schewe. Peterson retired from NARA in October 2001.

[64] DA Journal, 7 February 2000, DA Collection.

declining to shake my hand, Peterson asked where our computer specialist's office was located and abruptly left.[65]

Debbie Wheeler, my administrative assistant, silently looked at me
after Peterson's departure. I said, "Well, it looks like I'm in a lot of trouble,
but I'm not exactly sure why." I phoned my friend Linda Poepsal at the
Bush office, and she seemed to be expecting my call. As I began to speak,
she broke in, "Dave, I'm sorry, but the Boss is calling us into a meeting.
Talk to you later." I did not ask her to identify "the Boss." Ellen picked
me up at the rear of the library, and I gave her a brief encapsulation of the
meeting. She was as dumbfounded as I was; we rode home in silence. I
then attempted for over an hour to reach Jean Becker on her home phone,
but there was no answer or recorded message. I left a message for Michael
Dannenhauer, who promptly returned my call and promised to locate
Becker. Another hour passed. He called back with the news that her an-
swering machine appeared to be shut off or malfunctioning. Tormented
by the unknown, Ellen and I spent a miserable, sleepless night.[66]

The following morning, 8 February, Jean Becker and I had a tense,
emotional phone conversation. Choking up and crying, she asked how I
was doing, and I said, "Not very good." She replied, "I know you must be
devastated," and suggested that I go home and enjoy the backyard scenery
"with your pipe." She admitted knowing that Peterson was coming to College Station to talk with me, but "was instructed to stay out of it." If I
would relate what Peterson had said, she promised to tell "the truth." After
I summarized the conversation, she asked if he had mentioned the possibility of a transfer for me. I replied, "No."[67]

After a minute or two of silence, I expressed my disappointment in
learning that I no longer had the President's "confidence, trust, and respect." She began softly crying again and said that was untrue; President
Bush "always liked you and the library" and would help me now and not
let NARA fire me. She also added that I always was totally professional in
all of my dealings with the President's office. I now knew that the com-

---

[65] Ibid.

[66] Ibid.

[67] DA notes, 8 February 2000, telephone conversation with Jean Becker; DA
Journal, 8 February 2000, DA Collection.

plaints focused on my relationships with TAMU and the foundation. She then confessed, "I had done a bad thing"—those two calls were placed to Carlin, and she had trusted someone at NARA she regarded as a friend.[68]

She regretted not talking with me over the previous summer when she "was worried about me" and suspected I might have marital or other problems because I was "depressed, moody, angry, and very unhappy." She said that some of my staff concurred with her diagnosis of my behavior. President Bush was "taken aback" after she told him I "might not be his library director much longer." She recommended to him that I might be happier and "a better fit elsewhere." He agreed they would allow the "NARA process or procedure" to move forward. I responded to Becker with disbelief—she remembered the trauma we suffered after our daughter's accident, oral surgeries, and sexual assault. I wondered aloud why she had not called me with her concerns about my happiness and well-being, and she agreed that perhaps that should have happened. Finally, she promised "to sort everything out" and call me again later that afternoon or the next day.[69]

Although I was uncertain how much President Bush actually knew about the "NARA process," on 8 February I decided to offer him another option. I drafted a personal letter to the President, emphasizing my desire in playing "a positive role" in the transition to "your next director." "Jean mentioned to me yesterday that you might be willing to assist me," I continued, "Therefore, it is in this spirit I would like to suggest a proposal for your consideration."[70]

I asked him for an opportunity to remain at the Bush Library for two years, until reaching retirement eligibility with twenty-five years' service. As the library's assistant director, I could focus on archival and museum supervisory duties, thus allowing my successor to concentrate on TAMU and Bush Foundation issues. This "quick, calm resolution," I stressed, "will benefit all interested parties," adding, "I want to finish my career in the Library which I helped build and will always love."[71]

---

[68] DA notes, 8 February 2000, telephone conversation with Jean Becker, DA Collection.

[69] Ibid.

[70] DA to President George H. W. Bush, 9 February 2000, DA Collection.

[71] Ibid.

Although the Bushes already knew about our difficulties over the past year, I told the President, "I also want to have some semblance of control over my family's future. We just need a small break at this point."[72] I presented specific examples of how my proposal would advance this goal:

This…also will allow me enough time to find a job outside the government to help pay our daughter's medical bills. Moreover, this time will allow our daughter, Meredith, to graduate from high school (she's currently a junior). Also, our son, Adam, will finish his architectural studies at UT next year. If we have to move sooner, we'll have to pay out-of-state tuition for Adam's last year. Ellen and I don't want to move our family again if we can possibly avoid it. I think you and Barbara understand how important our children's happiness is to us.[73]

I finished my letter by asking the President to contact John Carlin. I realized that Carlin might reject my proposal because I was a grade higher than the other presidential libraries' assistant directors. However, the LBJ Library's assistant director was a GS-15 and had served at that grade for many years. "In other words," I noted, "Carlin can approve this request if he wants to because of the precedent established by the LBJ Library. But Carlin will only do it with your blessing."[74]

The following morning, 9 February, I presented the gist of my letter by phone to Jean Becker. She began to weep. When I asked, "Why the tears?" she said, "Because you're just being so wonderful about this, just like the old David that I used to know, not the angry one of last summer."[75] I wanted her to read my letter before passing it on to President Bush to ensure that it did not contain "anything silly or stupid." I signed off by mentioning "one small hurt" to Becker—if she had told me a year ago that I needed a "change of scenery," I could have applied for the Carter Library's SES position. But I refrained "out of loyalty" to the Bushes.[76]

I thought our conversation was finished, but Becker added some

---

[72] Ibid.

[73] Ibid.

[74] Ibid.

[75] DA notes, 9 February 2000, telephone conversation with Jean Becker, DA Collection.

[76] Ibid.

additional context to the "NARA process." Since General Brent Scowcroft was the Bush Library Board's chairman, she asked him to call Carlin about Peterson's visit with me. Scowcroft supposedly told the Archivist, "You had no right to send your man down there to tell Dave Alsobrook that he didn't have the President's support and confidence." According to Ginny Lampley, Scowcroft's assistant, she "had never seen the General so angry on the phone with anyone."[77] Becker finally said, "If it's any satisfaction to you, if George W. becomes President, Carlin will be out on his ass!"[78]

That night at home, I tried to process everything that Becker had revealed during our conversation. Sharon Fawcett called—like Becker, she also was crying. Fawcett said it was terrible what President Bush's "close friends" were doing to me. She promised to fight for me and asked if anyone had provided any specific reasons why I had to go. I answered, "Not yet." She said that I should expect to receive that call within the next day or so. Even Carlin apparently was not sure of exactly what I allegedly had done. Fawcett added that no possibility existed for my being fired; I would be allowed to finish my career—hopefully "somewhere nice," but "maybe not."[79]

On 10 February, Linda Poepsal in Houston emailed me with an emotional message titled "Friendship!" We had been friends for a decade, and I deeply appreciated her anguished attempt to console me without being disloyal to the Bushes:

> I hope you're doing okay, David—Ellen, too. Just know that there are a lot of us out here who really care and who have the highest personal and professional regard for you. Anyway, David, I don't know what to say. Personally, I really, truly hate to see you and Ellen leave. I can't even imagine that we'll ever get anyone nearly as capable or amiable as you two. Sometimes, though, change is a good thing, and maybe this change will be the SECOND best thing to happen to you in your career, heading up our library, of course, THE best thing![80]

[77] Ibid.

[78] Ibid

[79] DA notes, 9 February 2000, telephone conversation with Sharon Fawcett; "Chronology of Recent Events," 9 February 2000, DA Collection.

[80] Linda Casey Poepsal email to DA, 10 February 2000, DA Collection.

Bidding farewell to an old friend who is being removed to a distant, unknown "penal colony" required a courageous act, and I admired Poepsal's bravery. She risked her own job security simply by acknowledging our friendship.

Over the next two days (10–11 February), Jean Becker and I chatted via a lengthy email chain that proved to be our final communications during the "NARA process." On 10 February, she wrote, "I did not want to leave you in limbo, so just to let you know I have the letter and have shown it finally to President Bush. He was very touched by it, David. He wants to think about your proposal. He wonders if it's really best for you, if you would feel comfortable staying on as No. 2. He asked me to ask you to really think about that…. He has much on his mind today but I promise you, he has taken your letter to heart."[81] That evening Ellen raised a disquieting question: "George and Barbara Bush know you; they know us, and they have our phone numbers—Why haven't they called you directly to inquire about what's going on?" I was unable to answer her question.

On 11 February, I told Becker that my proposal was "the best means of providing me with some distance from my agency in the coming days. Right now I just need time—not very much, but some breathing space, …and this is the most valuable gift that President Bush can give me now."[82] I explained that NARA probably would pressure me to accept the first available vacancy, regardless of its location. Although I presently was "too young" to retire from NARA with a full pension, "I don't plan to stay here any longer than necessary" and merely needed enough time to find another job. I pleaded with Becker to remember that my message was "for you and for nobody outside your office. Please protect it for me."[83]

"We are not going to let your agency send you [to] some dreadful place," Becker promised. "I need to speak very carefully as it is not my place to tell you what is going on and have been told not to. But a plan is in the works that I think you'll be VERY happy about, allow you to keep your family intact, [and] give you new challenges." She expected that I would

---

[81] Jean Becker email to DA, 10 February 2000; "Chronology of Recent Events," 10 February 2000, DA Collection.

[82] DA email to Jean Becker, 11 February 2000, DA Collection.

[83] Ibid.

receive a call on the following Monday. "I am so sure about this," she continued, "that I feel in good faith I can tell you to have a great, relaxing weekend with your family and discuss what you might want for what I truly believe is a very bright future."[84]

Becker's optimistic forecast for my future sounded promising, but Ellen and I did not experience "a great, relaxing weekend." That night Sharon Fawcett alerted me that David Peterson was attempting to reach me. I appreciated her warning but asked, "Hasn't he already done enough damage? Does he really need to harass me and my family at home?" Shortly afterward, around 6:00 p.m., Peterson rang and immediately said, "Dave, can you talk?" "Of course," I replied but did not indicate that Ellen was listening on our extension phone. I wanted her to witness the ensuing conversation. Peterson had met that afternoon with the Archivist of the United States before his two-week vacation in Hawaii. Peterson said that their discussion had yielded what "should be good news, candidly and frankly."[85] I briefly anticipated hearing the news about my "very bright future," as described by Jean Becker.

Not surprisingly, Peterson's call was neither uplifting nor friendly—it was threatening. He informed me that *all* of my communications with the Bush office, including the recent personal letter to the President, were now in the Archivist's possession. My stomach churned when I recalled all of the notes, letters, and email messages I had shared with Jean Becker, Linda Poepsal, Michael Dannenhauer, and the Bushes about Meredith's medical history and emotional trauma. Peterson said that my proposal to serve as the Bush Library's assistant director was a "non-starter" and "Frankly, ain't going to happen." A reassignment elsewhere, "somewhere in Texas or even in College Station, is possible, …but it is counterproductive to write the President's office or to make phone calls—Don't do anything to piss off Carlin anymore."[86]

Peterson then outlined what he and Carlin immediately expected from me. First, I must write a letter requesting a reassignment to an

---

[84] Jean Becker email to DA, 11 February 2000, DA Collection.

[85] DA memo for the record, 11 February 2000, RE: "Dave Peterson Telephone Call," DA Collection.

[86] Ibid.

unspecified new duty station. He would furnish "guidance and advice" for my letter's language. He next stated that I could not communicate or transact any business with the Bush office, Bush Library Foundation, or TAMU, without first seeking his approval.[87]

He asked if I had any questions. I replied, "Do I correctly understand that my private correspondence and other personal communications with President and Mrs. Bush and their staff have been forwarded to a third party without my prior knowledge or consent?" "Yes," he answered. I next asked if he would record that fact and his new directive to me in writing, and he said, "No. A supervisor can provide a subordinate with an oral directive, and I have done so."[88]

Peterson grudgingly agreed that as a federal career employee I was entitled to request specifications of any allegations against me. "I would think so," he said. When I briefly mentioned "conferring with my lawyer" about these matters, Peterson stated, "It will be counterproductive to this process if you contact an attorney or seek any legal guidance in this matter."[89] These chilling words were delivered by a trained lawyer who once belonged to the District of Columbia Bar.

Peterson's frightening call left us virtually speechless for the rest of the night. His egregious disregard for my basic constitutional rights was shocking. How could this nightmare happen in a democracy? In ninth-grade civics, Ellen and I had learned that all US citizens were guaranteed certain legal rights and protections. At that early stage in the NARA process, we were not well versed in the intricacies of federal personnel regulations. However, we had no doubt that even a career federal employee was entitled to seek and retain counsel. Therefore, we disregarded Peterson's bullying threat that I should not speak with an attorney. Since we were financially unable to afford full-time legal services, immediately after Peterson's visit to my office, Ellen had contacted several attorneys who graciously volunteered pro bono legal guidance.[90]

---

[87] Ibid.

[88] Ibid.

[89] Ibid.

[90] Memos, EA [Ellen Alsobrook] to Ben Erdriech, 8, 9 March 2000; EA notes, 8 March 2000, telephone conversation with Ben Erdriech; EA notes, 14,

John Fawcett and Claudine Weiher, two close friends in Washington, DC, who personally had survived the NARA process during the twilight of their distinguished careers, counseled me from February through August 2000. Unlike my wife and I, they assuredly were experts in NARA and federal personnel regulations. They functioned as two highly skilled pro bono paralegals—editing my written communications with NARA, advising me of employee rights, and interpreting my agency's Byzantine personnel practices. They also bolstered my depleted spirits during those dreary, lonely months. Before Peterson's arrival in College Station on 7 February 2000, Weiher counseled, "Be cool—You're smarter, brighter, and more conniving than he is—Let *him* talk. Provoke him if you can— Don't get mad and leave!"[91]

Another trusted friend, JFK Library Director Bradley Gerratt, connected me with Lis Gordon, an expert in federal employees' law in Boston, who formerly had served at OMB. After reviewing my case, she enumerated NARA's multiple violations that fell under the category of "prohibited personnel actions." With my dedicated pro bono defense team of Gordon, Weiher, and Fawcett and several attorneys in Texas and South Carolina, I avoided bankruptcy and also gave NARA the impression of being "lawyered up." Nancy Smith, a good friend at NL, later said, "We always wondered if you had an attorney, or maybe more than one."[92]

While my legal consultants buttressed my defense against NARA, a "Kafkaesque" drama unfolded in College Station. One afternoon Meredith came home in tears from school because her classmates pointedly asked about our departure date from Aggieland. On 16 February 2000, John Kirsch, a self-styled "investigative reporter" for the Bryan-College

---

25 February 2000, telephone conversations with Fritz Jekyl; EA to Brenda Cramer, 16, 20 March, 4 April 2000, DA Collection.

[91] DA notes, 7 (quote), 11, 13 February 2000, telephone conversations with Claudine Weiher; Claudine Weiher telephone message, 14 February 2000; DA email to John Fawcett, 3 March 2000; John Fawcett email to DA, 7 March 2000; DA notes, 3 March 2000, telephone conversation with John Fawcett; DA Journal, 22 March, 11, 17 April, 2 May 2000, DA Collection.

[92] Bradley Gerratt telephone message, 24 April 2000; Lis Gordon telephone message, 25 April 2000; DA to Lis Gordon, 26 April, 16 May 2000; DA Journal, 26 April 2000, DA Collection.

Station *Eagle*, launched a relentless series of harassing visits and phone calls to my office and home. At 6:20 p.m. that evening, he appeared at our front door, and Ellen quickly sent him away.[93]

The next day, Kirsch lied to a TAMU security officer at the Bush Library, saying that I had invited him to my office. After Debbie Wheeler said I was out of the building, Kirsch asked if he could "wander around" our staff offices. On 18 February he refused to leave the library's reception area and was escorted from our building by Facility Manager Steve Samford and TAMU Security Sergeant Jason Alexander. That afternoon Kirsch attempted to interrogate Ellen by phone about "What's going on at the library?"[94]

In the midst of Kirsch's feverish activity, Deputy Archivist Lewis Bellardo called me at work. He commended us for our professionalism in handling the press in recent days. He repeated this message several times, which probably indicated that Kirsch also was incessantly pestering him. Bellardo said that he had spoken with the Archivist in Hawaii, who was concerned that Peterson had not delivered the "second part" of his message to me. Carlin, according to Bellardo, wanted me to know that if NARA's investigation produced any basis for my alleged problems, I would be given an opportunity "to work these things out" during the SES selection process. Bellardo further clarified that my job was not in jeopardy; I was entitled to apply for the new SES position, and if not selected, I would not be fired.[95]

I thanked Bellardo for filling in the omitted portion of the Archivist's message. Bellardo then said we all can second-guess what happened, adding, "Sometimes I get pissed off with Carlin." I had no idea exactly what that statement meant. Bellardo confirmed that my recent personal letter to President Bush in Houston was routed to General Brent Scowcroft and then to Carlin. Denying any firsthand knowledge of my letter's

---

[93] "Chronology of Recent Events," 14, 16 February 2000; DA Journal, 16 February 2000; DA notes, 16 February 2000, RE: "John Kirsch's Rude Behavior," DA Collection.

[94] DA Journal, 17, 18 February 2000; "Chronology of Recent Events," 18 February 2000, DA Collection.

[95] DA notes, 18 February 2000, telephone conversation with Lewis Bellardo, DA Collection.

transmission, Bellardo speculated that as a retired general, Scowcroft was furious about my violation of the chain of command. He and Cicconi presented my letter to Carlin as the latest evidence that "it wasn't working out" at the Bush Library and another reason why "We have to get him out of there."[96] So now I knew the identities of the two "serious, very important" people "close to President Bush" who had complained to Carlin.

I did not tell Bellardo that all of my communications with President Bush went through Jean Becker—General Scowcroft was not in my chain of command. Bellardo stated that Peterson would "plod along" with the NARA investigation, and they would contact me again at some point.[97] When I briefed Skip Rutherford about Bellardo's call, he advised against assuming that Peterson was no longer involved; they were merely playing "good cop, bad cop."[98] As usual, Rutherford's instincts were quite accurate.

The day after my conversation with Bellardo, Kirsch released his "exposé" in the *Eagle*, under a prominent headline: "Bush Library job due upgrade." Kirsch emphasized that I would have to reapply for my own position, and I "did not return [his] phone calls."[99] Bellardo was not quoted in the article—that chore fell to NARA spokeswomen Susan Cooper and Laura Dischenko and LBJ Assistant Director Patrick Borders. The combined gist of their comments was that an SES position was highly coveted among career federal employees. Borders said, "It's at the top of the career ranks."[100] Kirsch's article, despite its lack of insight into the Bush Library's intrigues, featured a flattering photograph of the incumbent director in happier times.

Since my previous discussion with Bellardo had focused on media inquiries and NARA press guidance, I was disappointed but not surprised that he failed to provide a "heads-up" on the *Eagle* story. On 18 February he stated that NARA would not discuss our SES position with any specificity other than to indicate it was a "personnel matter" and not subject to

---

[96] Ibid.; "Chronology of Recent Events," 18 February 2000, DA Collection.

[97] DA notes, 18 February 2000, telephone conversation with Lewis Bellardo, DA Collection.

[98] DA Journal, 20 February 2000, DA Collection.

[99] John Kirsch, "Bush Library job due upgrade," (Bryan-College Station TX) *Eagle*, 19 February 2000, A9.

[100] Ibid.

public disclosure and that I was still the Bush Library director.[101]

With input from my legal team, on 22 February I sent memoranda on two separate topics to Bellardo and Peterson. I pointed out to Bellardo the obvious discrepancy between the *Eagle* article and NARA's press guidance that we discussed several days earlier. I asked him to clarify this matter and to furnish me with any future NARA press advisories on the SES topic.[102] I sought permission from Peterson to amend my official Performance Plan to conform with his "oral directive" of 11 February that prohibited my dealing with the Bush office, Bush Library Foundation, and TAMU.[103]

Bellardo and Peterson did not address the issues raised in my memoranda. However, Peterson later referenced my conversation on 18 February with the deputy archivist: "According to Mr. Bellardo, he did not promise you an opportunity to work on any specific problem areas" with the Bush office, Bush Library Foundation, and TAMU. Since these matters "involve your demeanor" in dealing with these three entities, "This would be very difficult for you to do" within the limits of the "oral directive."[104]

Parsing Peterson's twisted syntax, I thought of Joseph Heller's brilliant satirical novel on the absurdity of war, *Catch-22*, that probed the bureaucratic madness surrounding "Section 8" discharges for World War II pilots suffering from "combat fatigue." Peterson's responses to my requests for information about the specific allegations against me rivaled *Catch-22*. For example, while acknowledging that I was entitled to such information, he added, "I understand your desire to learn about these, but I must clarify that I did not suggest you would be provided them in writing."[105] He puzzlingly concluded with a cheery, congratulatory note: "I am pleased that you

---

[101] "Chronology of Recent Events," 18 February 2000; DA notes, 18 February 2000, telephone conversation with Lewis Bellardo, DA Collection.

[102] Memo, DA to Lewis J. Bellardo, 22 February 2000, RE: "Press Information," DA Collection.

[103] Memo, DA to David F. Peterson, 22 February 2000, RE: "Amendment of Performance Plan," DA Collection.

[104] Memo, David F. Peterson to DA, 17 March 2000, RE: "Your request for clarification," DA Collection.

[105] Ibid.

and your staff continue to ensure that the George Bush Library provides museum patrons, students, and researchers an excellent experience and exemplary service."[106] I wondered whether NARA was preparing to issue me a stern reprimand or a generous cash award.

Replying to my multiple written queries for information between February and June 2000, Peterson produced only one memo on 17 March. However, he frequently telephoned during those four months, usually with the same question: "Have you given any more thought to where you want to go?"[107] In each instance he became more insistent that I expeditiously choose a new duty station. On 1 March Peterson called Supervisory Archivist Warren Finch and said he wanted to "open a dialogue" with me. When I spoke later in the day with Peterson, he again asked about my preferred relocation site. Other than the "Alaska Federal Records Center," I would consider any "reasonable options for reassignment." But I needed "specific options" before committing to leave the Bush Library. Multiple times he offered the possibility of my transferring back to Washington or an unspecified "federal agency in Texas." Several weeks later, we had a similar conversation in which he recommended two options: Washington or "elsewhere." When I asked him to define the second choice, he replied, "Anywhere in the country." Preparing to apply for the upgraded Bush Library SES position, I adamantly rejected any vague, unidentified location offer.[108]

I always will remember March through May 2000 as the "spring of our discontent," full of extraneous white noise and false flags. Almost daily, I had to squelch rumors about my departure from the Bush Library. On 3 March, Curator Patricia Burchfield inquired when I would issue an announcement about leaving. I explained that I still did not know much about my situation and might stay in College Station for months or even years. I assured her that any decision would be on "my own schedule." She looked disappointed and quickly left my office.[109] Two weeks later, during

---

[106] Ibid.

[107] DA emails to Skip Rutherford, 1, 2 March 2000, DA Collection.

[108] DA email to Skip Rutherford, 1 March 2000; DA Journal, 1 March, 11 April 2000, DA Collection.

[109] DA Journal, 25 February, 3 March (quotes) 2000; "Chronology of Recent Events," 25 February 2000, DA Collection.

a meeting with Warren Finch and me, she kept staring at my empty book-shelves—which perhaps indicated that "an announcement" was coming soon. On 27 March at a wedding shower for Debbie Wheeler's daughter, Burchfield refused to speak to my wife.[110]

Although I had given her an opportunity in 1993 to finish her thesis and to advance in her career as a museum professional, Burchfield now saw me as a detriment to her future. Ellen and I had befriended Burchfield and her husband, Brent Maxwell, an artist and high school instructor. They in turn were very kind to our children. To our great disappointment, that was all ancient history in spring 2000.

Burchfield's reaction was symptomatic of the virus that raged throughout my entire staff. Although I had recruited, hired, and nurtured all of them over the preceding seven years, they now faced an unpleasant choice—either support me or disavow my existence. Since I had painstak-ingly built my staff as a team, each of whom had unique skills and talents, it was heartbreaking to witness the disintegration of this once-proud, finely tuned unit.

From speaking privately with Debbie Wheeler and Johnna Arden, I fully comprehended the paralyzing fear that gripped my staff. They were terrified about losing their own jobs by remaining loyal to me. And their terror produced some strange, unexpected results. For example, when I conveyed my distress about the staff's deteriorating morale to one of my supervisors, he said, "Morale isn't important; all that matters is that they do their jobs." I replied, "I'll pretend I didn't hear you say that, because you sure as hell didn't learn it from me."

In addition to their nagging fear, several staff members were frus-trated and angry. In May 2000, Johnna Arden wrote to a friend at NI:

> We are going to lose good people over what I believe is a pissing contest with John Carlin…, which, by the way, MY Dave did not start. The Bush Library is going to have a MAJOR personnel over-haul in the coming months. People are looking for transfers and outside jobs because of what is happening to Dave…. It's very dis-couraging. Dave built a good, strong, loyal, dependable staff here and it is being torn apart. I just keep my fingers crossed that the

---

[110] DA Journal, 14, 27 March 2000, DA Collection.

lottery pays off for me. Unfortunately, that is my only option. But what I'd like to do is walk out the day Dave is forced to leave.[111]

While Arden's bravery was heartening, I worried that she someday would pay a heavy price after my departure. She and Facility Manager Steve Samford were steadfast in supporting me and later were consigned to their own special "purgatories" at the Bush Library.[112]

During spring 2000, several archivists and archives technicians became so disillusioned that they sought immediate transfers, including Debbie Carter, Debbie Bush, and Gary Foulk. They appeared individually or together at my door, and we discussed their career options. Foulk, whom I originally hired at the Carter Library from NARA's Declassification Division, returned to his old position. He and Bush were interested in someday joining me in Little Rock at the Clinton Project if I landed there.[113]

The cohesive bond that once united the "Auburn Mafia"—my staff who were graduates of the Auburn University Archival Training Program—also began to erode. Jimmie Purvis, Bill Harris, John Laster, and Laura Spencer transferred from the Bush Library after 2000. I might add one note of personal pride—today they are all engaged in productive archival careers.[114]

In addition to those among my staff who fiercely supported my cause in 2000, I discovered that many of my friends across the country had not abandoned me—James Kratsas, Martin Elzy, Robert Bohanan, Tina Houston, Nancy Smith, Jacque Wood, and Doug Thurman.[115] However,

---

[111] Johnna Arden email to Betsy Cristaudo, 3 May 2000, DA Collection.

[112] Johnna Arden email to DA, 4 October 2000; Johnna Arden to DA, ca. 21 October 2000; DA Journal, 4, 16 October 2000, 10 February, 9, 27, 29 March 2001, DA Collection.

[113] DA Journal, 23, 27, 28 March, 7 April, 2, 9 June 2000, 29 March 2001, DA Collection.

[114] Purvis currently is approaching retirement at the Clinton Library. Laster is serving as director of the Presidential Papers Staff at NL. Harris is the FDR Library's assistant director. Spencer is a records management officer at the Center for Disease Control in Atlanta, GA.

[115] James R. Kratsas email to DA, 14 February 2000; DA to James R. Kratsas, 23 February 2000; Martin Elzy emails to DA, 20 March, 19 June 2000;

only two presidential libraries directors remained in close touch with me throughout the spring—Richard Norton Smith and Bradley Gerratt.[116] Hoover Library Director Timothy Walch later explained that when our peers learned of "my situation" and the SES position was posted, they all were frightened because they knew "the same thing could happen to them."[117] Walch's explanation was comforting to hear—if our positions had been reversed, I probably would have reacted in the same manner.

My colleagues certainly had ample evidence to fear for their own positions. In mid-February 2000, Mark Hunt, the Reagan Library director, voluntarily transferred to the FDR Library. As one reporter accurately observed, Hunt's new position as assistant director was "technically a step down" after serving as the "Reagan Library's top administrator."[118] John Fawcett interpreted the "Mark Hunt model" as exemplifying a NARA pattern in which they targeted any directors for removal who fell out of favor with their former presidents or support groups. He suggested that if Carlin and Peterson were applying the same model to me, I would be in College Station for several months until NARA found a new home for me.[119] I subsequently warned Bradley Gerratt that when NARA "finishes with me, they may come after him," and he should seek protection from his strongest advocate, Paul Kirk.[120]

The Mark Hunt case dragged on for almost two years; I was not eager to repeat that scenario in College Station. Since I still had not received a bill of particulars about my offenses from NARA by March 2000, John Fawcett, Claudine Weiher, and Lis Gordon all recommended "hunkering down" in College Station. They did not deviate from this message over the

Tina Houston emails to DA, 18, 29 February 2000; Robert Bohanan email to DA, 3 March 2000; Nancy Smith email to DA, 23 February 2000; DA Journal, 9, 24, 29 February 2000, DA Collection.

[116] DA Journal, 17 March 2000, DA Collection.

[117] DA Journal, 4 October 2000, DA Collection.

[118] Tony Lystra, "Reagan Library Chief Leaves for FDR Museum Post," *Los Angeles Times*, 24 February 2000, clipping, DA Collection.

[119] DA Journal, 25 March, 15 May, 16 June 2000, DA Collection.

[120] DA Journal, 7 March 2000, DA Collection.

next three months.[121]

Gordon, who had seen many OPM cases similar to mine, was amazed at NARA's recalcitrant obsession with my "demeanor," despite the fact that I earned an "Outstanding" performance appraisal in 1999. She asserted that even if any undocumented problems existed in my performance since 1999, NARA was obligated to provide counseling and an opportunity for correcting any perceived deficiencies. She stressed that without any "performance-related" issues, I had to decide how much more abuse to endure. She firmly believed that I could "sit tall" in College Station for several years until reaching an eligible retirement age.[122]

Meanwhile, the pressure in Aggieland intensified. Popadiuk periodically dropped by my office to "express his concern" and conveyed messages to me through Debbie Wheeler, Johnna Arden, and Warren Finch. Popadiuk's diplomatic communiques sounded familiar—"Have you decided where you want to go? Remember that GB is willing to help you." Like Scowcroft, Cicconi, Becker, and others in his chain of command, Popadiuk apparently wanted everything resolved before departing for his annual summer sabbatical.[123]

John Kirsch, the *Eagle* reporter, also ratcheted up his relentless pursuit of "the truth," as he viewed it—appearing at our front door at dinnertime or silently staring at our house from his vehicle while parked across the street. Sometimes he stood motionless like stone statuary in our yard. Meredith nicknamed him "pyscho-boy."[124] Ellen finally ended Kirsch's visits to our residence after agreeing to speak with him if he correctly answered a single question: "Who operates the Bush Library?" When Kirsch predictably replied, "Texas A&M," she politely said, "Good afternoon," and closed the door in his face. Frustrated in his efforts in stalking my family, Kirsch doubled down on phone calls to my friends and former colleagues in Atlanta and Auburn—Robert Bohanan, Jeff Jakeman, David

---

[121] DA email to Allen W. Jones, 27 March 2000; DA Journal, 22, 23 March, 17, 26 April, 8 May 2000, DA Collection.

[122] DA Journal, 26 April, 8 May 2000, DA Collection.

[123] DA Journal, 25, 28 February, 27 March, 2, 30 May, 21 July 2000, DA Collection.

[124] DA Journal, 6, 14, 16, 24 March, DA Collection.

Rosenblatt, and Allen W. Jones.[125]

Kirsch probably was unprepared for Jones's impassioned defense of the Auburn University Archival Training Program and my professional career. Jones advised Kirsch to seek "the truth" from John Carlin ("a political pimp"), TAMU, and President Bush's "rich and powerful friends."[126] Suspecting that Kirsch was "in the pocket" of TAMU, Jones later wrote, "If he does not print the truth of what I said, I will write a letter to his paper and force them to print it." He also included some personal advice: "All we can do here is tell them how good you are and what a great career you have had as a professional archivist.... You just keep your mouth shut and keep your cool. Let your friends defend your reputation and we will do that."[127]

On 18 March 2000, four days after Jones's *Eagle* interview, I responded to him: "Kirsch hasn't printed another story on this situation.... You actually gave him all of the key areas to investigate; he's just not perceptive enough to connect the dots for himself...[and] didn't get what he was looking for from you. He seems to think that the big story is that I'm being pressured to leave my job. I'm just a very small part of a much bigger story, and he doesn't realize that and probably won't until somebody tells him or another newspaper gets the story."[128]

Undeterred in his quixotic quest for "the big story" about me, Kirsch filed an FOIA request with NARA, which, in strict accordance with federal statutes, was required to produce copies of any relevant records. As with all FOIA cases, NARA responded expeditiously and comprehensively to Kirsch. Having personally handled FOIA requests, I knew that Kirsch was legally entitled to see every document (with redactions) in my official personnel file, including records about my federal Thrift Savings Retirement Plan and security clearance. Unfortunately, in their haste to release all responsive records, NARA staff improperly redacted several

[125] Robert Bohanan email to DA, 24 February 2000; Jeff Jakeman email to DA, 14 March 2000; Allen W. Jones emails to DA, 14, 15 March 2000; DA emails to Allen W. Jones, 14, 18 March 2000; DA Journal, 14, 15 March 2000, DA Collection.
[126] Allen W. Jones email to DA, 14 March 2000, DA Collection.
[127] Allen W. Jones email to DA, 15 March 2000, DA Collection.
[128] DA email to Allen W. Jones, 18 March 2000, DA Collection.

items, such as my Social Security number, which was clearly visible beneath the black ink. Adhering strictly to the federal Privacy Act, NARA also redacted President Bush's laudatory comments in my file.[129]

By April 2000, suffocating beneath the combined pressure from NARA and TAMU, Ellen and I were physically and emotionally exhausted. I wrote in my journal, "I'm essentially having to reply on people who aren't reasonable & certainly aren't interested in a resolution that has a lot of positives for me & my future."[130] Our Auburn support network and a few Aggie friends gave us the strength to persist. Moreover, from the outset of our struggle, Skip Rutherford and Stuart Eizenstat never abandoned us. Without their timely intervention, I doubt that any salutary resolution ever would have occurred.

Since I had solicited Eizenstat's support for John Carlin's candidacy for Archivist in 1994, he was dismayed when first learning about my situation in February 2000. "Do you want me to call Carlin?" he asked. Fearing that his call would infuriate Carlin, I explained why it would not be helpful to my cause. Eizenstat agreed to do everything he could in my behalf. I prepared briefing papers for him and suggested that he touch base with Skip Rutherford.[131]

Eizenstat recently had moved from a senior State Department position to become the Deputy Secretary of the Treasury. Despite a heavy load of new responsibilities, he somehow found time to write to David Peterson, recommending my SES appointment at the Bush Library: "I have a great deal of confidence in David and hope that you will accept him for this position."[132] Although Eizenstat realized the unlikelihood of my being

---

[129] Memo, Ellen Alsobrook to Brenda Cramer, 4 April 2000; memo, DA to Mary Ronan, 22 May 2000, RE: "FOIA Question"; memo, DA to Gary M. Stern, 11 May 2000, RE: "FOIA"; Mary Ronan email to DA, 12 May 2000; Mary Ronan telephone message, 3 April 2000, Kirsch FOIA File; DA Journal, 3, 4, 26 April, 15 May 2000, DA Collection.

[130] DA Journal, 11 April 2000, DA Collection.

[131] DA to Stuart E. Eizenstat, 8 February 2000; DA Journal, 24, 25, 28 February 2000; Ellen Alsobrook to Stuart E. Eizenstat, 28 February 2000; DA email to Skip Rutherford, 28 February 2000, DA Collection.

[132] Stuart E. Eizenstat to David F. Peterson, 24 April 2000; DA to Stuart E. Eizenstat, 8 May 2000, DA Collection.

selected for this job, he grasped the importance of having his letter in the official application file.[133]

Skip Rutherford, like Eizenstat, supported me during the earliest stages of the NARA process. In mid-February 2000, Rutherford twice proposed to Peterson a resolution to the "awkward" Bush Library imbroglio that would be beneficial to all parties. Since the Clinton Project needed an experienced manager to assist the museum exhibit designers and architects, Rutherford suggested transferring me to Little Rock, where I would "be up here among friends." Peterson was noncommittal to this proposal. Afterward, Rutherford predicted that Carlin and the White House might reject his plan, but said, "First, we need to get you out of purgatory—Nothing good will happen to you in College Station."[134] Ellen and I deeply appreciated his honest assessment and thoughtful proposal. "Who wouldn't like such a reasonable, mutually beneficial resolution?" we asked ourselves, but we knew the answer.

To preserve a semblance of mental and emotional equilibrium, I focused on aspects of our lives that were controllable—Meredith's recuperation and well-being and my private-sector job opportunities. We had to face the realistic possibility that NARA would veto Rutherford's proposal. So I applied for a vacant archivist's position at Mississippi State University in Starkville. I also looked seriously at jobs at the Robert Dole Institute in Kansas, the Georgia Department of Archives and History, and the North Carolina Outer Banks Historical Museum. I also submitted an application for the Clinton Project director's position.[135]

Meanwhile, John Fawcett and Claudine Weiher thought that NARA was "clueless" about what to do with me and might let the next Bush Library director deal with this problem. Fawcett also believed that Carlin probably favored the Rutherford proposal for detailing me to Little Rock. After Peterson objected and pitched one of "his legendary temper tan-

[133] DA Journal, 8, 12 May 2000, DA Collection.

[134] DA notes, telephone conversations with Skip Rutherford, 13, 15 (quotes) February 2000; DA to Skip Rutherford, 25 February 2000; DA email to Skip Rutherford, 2 March 2000; DA Journal, 15, 16, 20, 28 February 2000, DA Collection.

[135] DA Journal, 25, 30 March, 31 May, 2, 4, 16, 19, 21, 25, 26, 30 June 2000, DA Collection.

trums," however, Carlin instructed him to clean up the mess.[136]

By May 2000, the Bush camp was growing impatient with the situation in College Station. Don Wilson informed Richard Norton Smith that "they" were very displeased with the performances of Carlin and Peterson, who "better pray that Gore wins" the presidency in November.[137] About a month later, General Brent Scowcroft solicited Smith's assistance in solving the Bush Library's problem. While supporting Smith's potential intervention as beneficial, I was prepared to remain indefinitely in College Station unless NARA allowed me to retire with my full pension.[138] Perhaps this reaction merely reflected my bravado after the exhausting struggle with NARA. Yet I was certain that those who personally attacked me had anticipated a quick, "bloodless" surgical removal process and were frustrated by my survival. Nevertheless, as summer approached, I was still a "dead man walking" at the Bush Library.

In June 2000, a pinpoint of sunlight pierced our gloomy existence in College Station. I learned on the twelfth that my name was among three candidates on NARA's register for the Clinton Project's "Program Manager" (Director). Despite everything that had transpired since February, I was cautiously optimistic about this position, primarily because of my previous experience with two presidential materials projects.[139] However, I anticipated that the selection process would be rigorous—Terry Sullivan, a distinguished political scientist and presidential scholar at the University of North Carolina in Chapel Hill, also was an attractive candidate.[140] Even so, I remained hopeful that Eizenstat and Rutherford were quietly supporting my candidacy.[141]

---

[136] DA Journal, 3, 22 March, 17 April 2000, DA Collection.

[137] DA Journal, 20 May 2000, DA Collection.

[138] DA Journal, 10 July 2000, DA Collection.

[139] DA Journal, 13 June 2000, DA Collection.

[140] Terry O. Sullivan email to DA, 27 August 2019; DA email to Terry O. Sullivan, 26 August 2019; DA Journal, 16 June 2000, DA Collection; Terry Sullivan vitae, Department of Political Science, University of North Carolina, Chapel Hill, NC, https://politicalscience.unc.edu/staff/terry-sullivan/ (accessed 26 August 2019).

[141] DA to Stuart E. Eizenstat, 19 June, 28 September 2000; Stuart E. Eizenstat to DA, 10 July, 18 September 2000; DA Journal, 19 June 2000, DA Collection.

On 20 July 2000, David Peterson offered me the Clinton Project position in Little Rock. I immediately accepted his offer, with the caveat that I wanted to discuss it with Ellen and Meredith. I also asked several specific questions about relocation allowances and my grade. Finally, I wanted to brief my staff prior to NARA's official announcement. Peterson surprisingly acquiesced to all of my demands and said that I would keep my GS-15 rating. As an extra inducement, after the Clinton Library director's appointment, there "might be a possibility" for me to remain in Little Rock until I retired. Last, he inquired if there was "any possibility" that I would change my mind over the weekend, and I said, "That's highly unlikely." Peterson sounded relieved. He apparently wanted this long, debilitating stalemate over as much as I did. On 24 July, I officially accepted the appointment.[142]

I quickly passed on the good news to my faithful advocates. John Fawcett said that regardless of any future comments about my "demeanor," this appointment gave "positive closure" to my Bush Library tenure and entire NARA career. Claudine Weiher agreed, adding her own personal touch: "The most important thing now is to save your ass, leave that place and get on with your life." Allen W. Jones, my Auburn professor who introduced me in 1972 to the wondrous possibilities of an archival career, exclaimed, "You might not have won the war, but you won a big battle!" When I thanked Stuart Eizenstat for his unwavering support, he modestly replied, "[Y]ou got this because of your own abilities and talents."[143]

I spoke several times with Skip Rutherford during those joyous days. Expressing my deep gratitude to him, Bruce Lindsey, and "the other Clinton folks" for the chance "to start over," I promised not to disappoint them. Rutherford reiterated that I would "be among friends" in Little Rock. He recently had explained to Lindsey that TAMU had "cratered" around me, and it could have happened to anyone in a university setting.[144]

Nineteen years later, I asked Rutherford which factors led to the final decision on the Clinton Library's location in downtown Little Rock. He

---

[142] DA Journal, 21, 24 July 2000; DA notes, telephone conversation with David F. Peterson, 20 July 2000, DA Collection.

[143] DA Journal, 21, 22, 24 July 2000; Stuart E. Eizenstat to DA, 18 September 2000, DA Collection.

[144] DA Journal, 21 July 2000, DA Collection.

succinctly noted, "[A]ccessible to and easily seen from the interstate; close to convention center, hotels, restaurants and public library; on the river; near the airport."[145] Today, even the most casual observer can see the visible fruits of that fateful decision—much of the downtown area near the Clinton Library has evolved into a lively tourist destination, sporting an array of historical, educational, cultural, artistic, and entertainment venues. Based on my own experience in College Station, if anyone in Little Rock had asked for my opinion, I would have agreed wholeheartedly with the decision to locate the library downtown rather than on a university campus.[146]

In August 2000, I was ready to move on to my new challenges in Little Rock. However, a few last-minute anomalies surfaced. For some inexplicable reason, Hank Leibowitz, the NARA personnel chief, blocked approval of my retaining a GS-15 rating as the Clinton Project director. Since both the Carter and Reagan Project directors were GS-15s, his objection quickly evaporated. NARA and the Bush camps also wanted to delay a public announcement of my new assignment until the appointment of a successor in College Station.[147]

When the selection of the next Bush Library director bogged down, NARA finally moved ahead with a press release about my appointment on 16 August 2000. Sharon Fawcett quickly emailed me: "The nightmare is over. Congratulations on your new assignment finally being official! I'm looking forward to the Clinton Project and delighted to have a professional and a friend in charge."[148] Her NL colleague, Alan Lowe, expressed his satisfaction to have someone of "my ability and experience" on board. He and Sharon Fawcett were eager to brief me on current preparations for the Clinton White House move, renovations at the Clinton Project site, and

---

[145] Skip Rutherford email to DA, 12 August 2019, DA Collection.

[146] DA Journal, 21 July 2000, DA Collection; Leslie Newell Peacock, "Ten years after the Clinton library opened," (Little Rock AR) *Arkansas Times*, 13 November 2014, https://arktimes.com/news/arkansas-reporter/2014/11/13/ten-years-after-the-clinton-library-opened (accessed 20 September 2019).

[147] DA notes, telephone conversation with David F. Peterson, 2 August 2000; DA Journal, 1–2, 4, 7–8, 14–15 August 2000; memo, DA to David F. Peterson, 9 August 2000, RE: "Relocation to Little Rock," DA Collection.

[148] Sharon Fawcett email to DA, 17 August 2000, DA Collection.

recruitment of archivists and other staff.[149]

Scheduled to report to Little Rock in mid-October 2000, I had one final official duty left as the Bush Library's director. At 3:00 p.m. on 15 August, I met for about fifteen minutes with my staff and volunteers. I announced that the following week, Warren Finch would become their acting director; he would serve in this capacity until my successor was named, probably within thirty days. I had recommended to NL that Finch was the best choice for this task, and they fully concurred.

"This is a bittersweet day for me," I said. I spoke about the past and the future, emphasizing the latter. Although my brief remarks were not very inspirational or imaginative, I spoke directly from the heart. I had not campaigned for my position; President Bush picked me. Readily admitting stepping on some "big toes" since 1993, I asked rhetorically, "Would I do anything differently now?" Then I continued, "Maybe, but probably not," since I still did not know the specific "errors of my ways." I always simply tried to do my job. Pointing toward the exhibits gallery, I concluded, "We worked our butts off, and the tangible results are outside that door."[150] Having completed my mission in Aggieland, I looked northward to a new beginning in Arkansas.

During August and September 2000, I shuttled between College Station and Little Rock. I also traveled twice to NARA for briefings and training on issues related to the Clinton Project, which were quite informative. Sharon Fawcett, Nancy Smith, Alan Lowe, and NARA Security Chief Stephen Hannestad all ensured that I was well prepared for my new duties and the logistics of the impending Clinton White House move.[151]

Since we all knew each other well, my NARA briefings were thorough but quite informal. My colleagues welcomed me back to the NARA fold like a "prodigal son" who briefly had strayed off the family reservation. To the NARA brass, however, I resembled a species of untamed "feral creature" to be "housebroken" before being released back into "the wilds of

---

[149] DA Journal, 31 July (quote), 4 August 2000, DA Collection.

[150] DA Remarks to Bush Library Staff, 15 August 2000; DA Journal, 15 August 2000, DA Collection.

[151] DA Journal, 25 September 2000; misc. memos and notes, ca. August–September 2000, Clinton Presidential Materials Project Files, DA Collection.

Arkansas." Nancy Smith sardonically characterized my indoctrination as "Vietnamese Re-education." Walch, my Iowa friend, labeled me as "NARA's Dung Beetle," who had become "a legend" by not only surviving "the process" but also having the unique career opportunity of launching three presidential libraries.[152]

Following my second trip to Washington, DC, in September Ellen and I dropped by the Bush Library to check the mail and pick up some personal items from my desk. Entering my old office, we discovered that it had been stripped of my few remaining personal belongings. The furniture was polished to a high gloss, and the windows were spotless. The TAMU security guards thought someone had pilfered my personal items while I was gone. We then looked inside the adjacent assistant director's office, which always had been vacant, and found my missing possessions, neatly arranged on the desk. It was Saturday morning; the other staff offices were empty. I called Facility Manager Steve Samford to inquire about what was afoot. He said that since my successor was arriving soon, David Peterson ordered Warren Finch to remove my belongings so the office could be cleaned. Ellen and I gathered up my meager personal items and left the library. I worked from home until my departure for Little Rock in October.[153]

After my eviction from the Bush Library, I concentrated along with Ellen on selling our home and moving to Little Rock. During our quieter, more introspective moments, usually when Meredith was asleep, we reflected on our seven years in Aggieland. We were leaving behind some good friends—Harry and Nelda Green, Emily Evins, Marty Medhurst, and Ellen's boss, safety engineer Jack Madeley. More importantly, Meredith was bidding farewell to her high school compadres.[154]

Several of our Aggie acquaintances, including Bush Library volunteers Emily Evins, Glinn White, and Anne Simms, wanted us to stay in College Station. I explained that my original plan was to retire at the Bush

---

[152] DA Journal, 31 July, 4 October 2000, 16 January 2002, DA Collection.

[153] DA Journal, 25 September 2000, DA Collection.

[154] Nelda and Harry Green to DA and EA, 21 September 2000; DA to Nelda and Harry Green, 28 September 2000; Emily Evins to DA, 13 October 2000; DA to Emily Evins, 20 October 2000; Jack Madeley telephone message, 10 February 2000; DA Journal, 9, 16 March 2000, DA Collection.

Library, "but that decision was taken away from me."[155] Two of our staunchest allies, Nelda and Harry Green, wrote, "The news of your moving came as a great disappointment to us. We have enjoyed your friendship, and you have been a delightful and important addition to the Bryan/College Station/Texas A&M community. We just hope that the folks in Arkansas will appreciate you both half as much as we do and that you will be very happy there.... [W]e shall miss you and remember you always."[156] I answered, "[S]ome very powerful people decided that they didn't want me to stay here...; nevertheless, I'm very proud of the Bush Library & what we accomplished...; your support & loyalty were essential to the success we had here."[157]

Ellen and I would miss the Greens and the other Aggies who befriended us in College Station. Those relationships underscored for us an important lesson—you do not need a *large* circle of friends to be happy and contented in this life. But if you are fortunate enough to acquire a few faithful friends, they will sustain you during the difficult times that will surely come.

I learned many life lessons during our sojourn in Aggieland—perhaps most importantly, the true meaning of the nobility of public service. George and Barbara Bush undoubtedly believed in this principle and exemplified it through their own selfless devotion to our nation. Yet they somehow failed to notice that I was a living, breathing example of a career federal civil servant, at work right under their noses. While I forever will love and revere the Bushes, sadly, they both vanished from my life when I most needed them. Although I never expected them to extricate me from my troubles, I anticipated that they would at least listen to my version of events. They both visited the Bush Library several times during the NARA process, and we could have spoken face to face. But that never happened.[158]

---

[155] DA to Anne Simms, 3 September 2000; Anne Simms to DA, 22 August 2000; DA Journal, 9, 16 March 2000, DA Collection.

[156] Nelda and Harry Green to DA and EA, 21 September 2000, DA Collection.

[157] DA to Nelda and Harry Green, 28 September 2000, DA Collection.

[158] DA Journal, 12, 27 March, 10 April, 12, 25 May 2000, 20 June 2001, DA Collection.

Moreover, the Bushes, like many former presidents and first ladies, willingly allowed themselves to be insulated and isolated by impenetrable layers of faithful gatekeepers. Unfortunately, some of their former White House advisers apparently had forgotten about the nobility of public service. In April 2000, Tim McBride, a member of the Bush Library Advisory Council, visiting with me at the library, candidly remarked, "Someone hasn't served the President well."[159] He was not referring to me. McBride was ashamed of his Bush colleagues' roles in the NARA process, and I appreciated his support for my efforts at the library. However, I did not press him about why President Bush failed to circumvent his aides and intervene in my behalf.

About a year later, in June 2001, Ellen and I dined in Little Rock with Billy Mac and Sally McKenzie, who were visiting their daughter and son-in-law, Martha and French Hill. The McKenzies, who had known the Bushes for many years, were distraught that we were no longer in Texas. When they inquired about why I had left the Bush Library, I related the entire story. Mr. McKenzie sadly replied that he and his wife loved George and Barbara, "but the Bushes were funny people because they've allowed those around them to do some pretty horrible things to other people."[160]

Although our luncheon with the McKenzies revived some bitter memories of the late unpleasantness in Aggieland, by June 2001 Ellen and I were deeply ensconced in Little Rock's Heights neighborhood. We were living in a cozy Depression-era grey brick bungalow on Blair Street. We already were acquainted with many of our neighbors: the Runnells, Henrys, Andersons, Bourys, and Arnolds. Prior to our moving to Little Rock, a resident provided a preview for us: "I think you'll like what you find here…, a handsome and livable city with decent amenities, a real cultural life, some beautiful landscape (in town and, especially, in the nearby Ouachitas), good food, and best of all, friendly people."[161]

Ellen and I loved living in Little Rock and still have many pleasant memories of the city and its people who warmly welcomed and accepted

---

[159] DA Journal, 22 April 2000, DA Collection.
[160] DA Journal, 2 June 2001, DA Collection.
[161] David Ware to DA, 24 August 2000, DA Collection.

us from the beginning as if we were native Arkansans. Regardless of their personal political affiliations and sympathies, virtually everyone we met was excited about the prospects of the future Clinton Library. They also understood that the Clinton Project staff were all federal employees and not connected with the University of Arkansas. Banker J. French Hill, whom I knew from his service as a Bush domestic policy adviser, welcomed us before we left College Station: "Martha and I are so excited to know that you will be moving to our great city. We hope you will enjoy Little Rock as much as we do. It is a terrific place to live and work…. Martha and I are supportive of the library and think it will be a wonderful addition to our city's many educational and community institutions."[162]

As a Republican, Hill added that the fact that his bank, Delta Trust, had provided financing for the renovation of the Clinton Project site was a source of much "local amusement." As the Clinton Project opened its doors in autumn 2000, we found friends like French Hill throughout the city—business leaders Rett Tucker and Fred Balch III, physician Dean Kumpuris, Mayor Jim Dailey, City Manager Bruce Moore, Alan Sugg and Pat Torvestad at the University of Arkansas System headquarters, former US Senator David Pryor, and academics Bobby Roberts, Tom Dillard, Johanna Miller Lewis, David Stricklin, Harri Baker, and Peggy Scranton. Skip Rutherford's team paved the way for our association with all of these Little Rock residents.

Back in Washington, Sharon Fawcett and Nancy Smith had organized the core Clinton Project staff—Richard Stalcup, Rhonda Wilson, John Keller, Marlene Ware, and Ed Quick. During the Clinton White House move, Stalcup and Keller were stationed at NL; the rest of us were on the receiving end of the Clinton materials in Little Rock. Debbie Bush transferred to the Clinton Project from College Station in December 2000. In 2001–2002, several other former colleagues joined our staff—Jimmie Purvis, Gary Foulk, Steve Samford, and Kathleen Gillespie. We also hired additional key staff members from Little Rock and elsewhere, including Emily Robison, Denise Persons, Audra Oliver, Rob Seibert, Dana Simmons, Kathleen Pate, Stephen Charla, and Adam Bergfeld. When the Clinton Library was dedicated in November 2004, we had

---

[162] J. French Hill to DA, 25 August 2000, DA Collection.

thirty-one staff members.[163]

As with my Carter and Bush Library colleagues, I was proud of the Clinton Library team's accomplishments. Long after I retired in 2007, they perpetuated an exceptional performance standard for their successors. They will be memorialized in historical annals as the Clinton Library's first staff. For me personally, I will fondly remember them as the professional family that replenished my heart and soul and restored my faith in the nobility of public service.

Ellen and I also are indebted to Bill and Hillary Clinton for many gifts. First and foremost, they gave us an opportunity to begin our lives anew in the beautiful city of Little Rock. They also unfailingly supported me throughout my service at the Clinton Project and Library.

Despite the comfort of being "among friends" in Little Rock in 2000–2001, I still bore "a lot of scar tissue," in the words of my veteran archivist Gary Foulk. Pat Torvestad at the University of Arkansas System offices lamented, "You'll probably have a lot of trouble ever trusting anybody again." While agreeing with her, I said, "That may be true, but I'll try." However, after unloading the Clinton materials during the transition, we had little time for hand-wringing. The Clinton Project staff immediately was inundated with subpoenas for records from Congressman Dan Burton's office and the US Attorney for the Southern District of New York. These subpoenas primarily dealt with President Clinton's controversial pardon of wealthy financier Marc Rich.[164]

Although the subpoenas absorbed much of our time in 2001, I knew that John Carlin's ferocious personal assault against me was not over. During the transition, Carlin sought to curry favor with the incoming George W. Bush administration, in a desperate attempt to keep his position as

---

[163] Deborah Bush email to DA, 23 July 2019; memo, Dana Simmons to Clinton Library Staff, 15 December 2004, RE: "Staff Directory," DA Collection. My sincere apologies to everyone else who served at the Clinton Library during its formative years—due to space limitations, I was unable to include each of your names. Be assured that such omissions do not minimize in any way the significant contributions that you made to the Clinton Library's accomplishments or my personal admiration and respect for you.

[164] DA Journal, 23 July, 29 October, 19 November 2000, 27 February, 3, 12 March 2001, DA Collection.

Archivist. Simultaneously, he pressured the "Clintonistas" to appoint a permanent Clinton Library director—anyone but me. Although Carlin stubbornly lobbied Bruce Lindsey, Stephanie Streett, and Skip Rutherford for an audience with President Clinton, they stifled his requests. To support his argument for immediately selecting a library director, Carlin widely circulated a fabricated story that my "problems" at the Bush Library originated because I had not been present "at its creation."[165]

Since both the "Clintonistas" and the "Bushies" knew that I had arrived in College Station in January 1993, Carlin's false narrative gained little traction. However, if President Clinton refused to meet with him, Carlin threatened to appoint a permanent library director without any further consultation. Carlin thus alienated *both* the Clinton and Bush camps—no easy task.[166]

Meanwhile, Sharon Fawcett periodically warned, "John Carlin is not your friend," which, of course, was not surprising to hear. In late July 2001, she described Carlin's seething frustration and anger with my "presence in Little Rock," despite his concerted efforts to end my career. He was particularly incensed that I had performed well over the past year and had earned favorable reviews from the Clinton family and associates. Bruce Lindsey and Skip Rutherford assiduously protected me from Carlin's more aggressive attacks and seemed unconcerned about my reluctance to campaign for the Clinton Library director's position.[167]

In February 2002, President Clinton inquired, "Now, what is it that Carlin wants?" After a senior adviser responded that Carlin wanted to get rid of me, the President said, "Well, I like David, and all of the reports I get on him are very good."[168] Similarly, at another meeting that winter, Clinton added, "I like David and the work he has done over the past year, I want him to stay here."[169]

Two years later, in early February 2004, I attended a museum design

[165] DA Journal, 8, 14 November 2000, 2 January, 6 February, 31 May, 7 June, 21 July, 7, 27 November 2001, DA Collection.

[166] DA Journal, 16, 17 July 2002, DA Collection.

[167] DA Journal, 29 July, 7 November 2001, 20 February, 13 March, 12 April 2002, DA Collection.

[168] DA Journal, 20 February 2002, DA Collection.

[169] DA Journal, 22 January 2002, DA Collection.

meeting at the Clintons' residence in Chappaqua, New York. A wet snow was falling as we prepared to leave for the airport. Outside his back door, President Clinton waved me over to his side and said, "Go on back down there and keep working hard. I want you to know that we'll be tenacious in our efforts to stabilize your career. And we're 100 percent behind you."[170] Several days later, back in Little Rock, I thanked him for allowing me "to put down permanent roots anywhere" for the first time in over a decade: "You, Senator [Hillary] Clinton, and your entire Clinton team have changed our lives dramatically, and Ellen and I will never forget what you've done for us."[171]

Our "permanent roots" in Arkansas only lasted three years—Ellen and I returned to Alabama to be closer to our elderly mothers. After I retired as his first library director in May 2007, President Clinton phoned me at home. We discussed many different topics, most memorably, "so-called Christians" who by their actions did not exhibit strong beliefs in "forgiveness" and "second chances." I again thanked him for giving me a "second chance" in Little Rock, and he said, "Everyone deserves a second chance."[172]

---

[170] DA Journal, 4 February 2004, DA Collection.

[171] DA to President Bill Clinton, 8 February 2004, DA Collection.

[172] DA notes, telephone conversation with President Bill Clinton, 14 May 2007, DA Collection.

Epilogue

We Few Who Dwell in the People's House: The Clinton Presidential Library and Museum Dedication

Arkansas is a state that knows political skill when you see it. A fellow in Saline County was asked by his son why he liked Governor Clinton so much. He said, "Son, he'll look you in the eye, he'll shake your hand, he'll hold your baby, he'll pet your dog—all at the same time."
—from remarks by President George W. Bush,
18 November 2004

Driving before dawn through Little Rock's deserted, rain-slicked streets on 18 November 2004, I was alone with my thoughts and memories. Twelve hours earlier, the weather was sunny, cool, and crisp—a perfect autumn day in the Natural State. The overnight forecast called for severe thunderstorms covering the entirety of Pulaski County. As predicted, chilly, heavy rains and gusty winds blanketed Little Rock throughout the night. Other than ice storms and tornadoes, this was the worst weather I had seen over the past three years and did not bode well for attendance at the Clinton Library dedication.

However, my concerns extended beyond meteorological developments—I fretted about the personal chemistry among the first families and their invited guests at the dedication. With the exception of Jimmy and Rosalynn Carter, these former presidents and first ladies shared a political history fraught with considerable rancor, and these wounds were still quite raw. Bill Clinton had evicted George H. W. Bush from the White House in 1992 after both candidates had waged personal attacks for several months. At the Bush Library dedication in 1997, then-Governor George W. Bush delivered some "edgy" partisan comments that deeply offended current White House staffers in attendance. Without specifically mentioning Bill Clinton's name, the governor praised the elder Bush as a "war hero, loving husband, world leader, dedicated father, and incurable optimist, and a President who brought dignity and character and honor to the White House..., a man who entered the political arena and left with his integrity intact."[1] The underlying meaning of Governor Bush's clever presentation was not lost on his audience.

In the 2000 presidential election, in which the US Supreme Court ultimately was the final arbiter of contested Florida ballots known as "hanging chads," George W. Bush was declared the winner over Vice President Al Gore. Gore and his wife Tipper would be in Little Rock for the dedication, along with John Kerry, whom Bush had vanquished two weeks earlier in earning a second presidential term. So our event was unfolding the midst of some visceral, bitter tensions among the first families and honored guests.

President Carter, who was well known for his irascible independence within the inner circle of the "former presidents' club," added another unpredictable element to this gathering. Carter's closest friend in this exclusive club, Gerald R. Ford, aged ninety-one, was physically unable to travel to Little Rock. President Ford's absence possibly meant that Carter would be even more aloof than usual. I also was somewhat apprehensive about seeing the Bushes for the first time since my exile from College Station four years earlier. However, I soon discovered that my worries were ill founded.

That day held many surprises for me. To my utter amazement, around twenty-five thousand intrepid souls braved the miserable weather to attend the festivities. Many guests were clad in camouflage or bright orange rain gear as if it was the opening day of Arkansas duck-hunting season. They were packed tightly in the rain-swept bleachers—their boisterous enthusiasm unfazed by the weather. The scene reminded me of gridiron crowds "Calling the Hogs" at Reynolds-Razorback Stadium at the University of Arkansas in Fayetteville.

---

[1] "George W. Bush Remarks," Bush Presidential Library Dedication, 6 November 1997, videotape, C-SPAN, https://www.c-span.org/video/?95003-1/bush-presidential-library-dedication (accessed 3 October 2019); Maureen Dowd, "Young Bush lacks his father's manners," *Salina (KS) Journal*, 11 November 1997, 4.

Marty Allen, the Ford Library Foundation's seasoned leader, who was seated next to me, marveled at the crowd's "undampened" good cheer. I said to him, "Arkansans are a very hearty bunch of folks." My friend and guest, Lynn Scott "Scottie" Cochrane, then serving as the Denison University Library director in Ohio, observed that despite the "rip-roaring rain and falling temperatures…, it was a very festive mood, everyone was there to celebrate."[2]

Spectators who were nestled down on the pavilion below the stage were all wrapped in ponchos and sheltered under large red, yellow, and blue umbrellas. The only people I saw who lacked any protection from the downpour were young military escorts stationed around the stage and seating areas. I wore a heavy trench coat and my trusty weather-resistant L. L. Bean hat. When attorney Bruce Lindsey half-jokingly offered me $300 in cash for my hat, I replied, "No way!" Lindsey's compatriot, Skip Rutherford, who had arrived at dawn for media interviews, noticed the event staff's team removing the protective cover from above the speakers' platform. He asked, "Why are you doing this? It's supposed to pour down." They told him that the Air Force One crew had radioed ahead that "there would be a 'window' of no rain during the ceremony." But Rutherford recalled, "There was a 'window' all right—the heaviest rain of the day."[3] I heard that Jimmy Carter, as the senior member in attendance among the former presidents, ordered the cover to be removed prior to the ceremony.

The first ladies appeared first—Senator Hillary Clinton led Rosalynn Carter, Laura Bush, and Barbara Bush in single file to the stage. The wind and rain whipped at their umbrellas. As a military band struck up "Hail to the Chief," the presidents casually strolled out four abreast—all bareheaded and without umbrellas. I speculated that perhaps President Carter had convinced the others to discard their umbrellas. Scottie Cochrane, seated with her husband Louis Middleman in the tall bleachers, thought, "These people are old; some of them could die."[4]

After the presidents joined their wives on the slick platform, military

---

[2] Evelyn Frolking, "Presidents' united front at Clinton dedication impresses libraries scholar," *Granville (OH) Sentinel,* 3 February 2005, 4B.

[3] Skip Rutherford email to DA, 29 September 2019, DA Collection.

[4] DA notes, 1 October 2019, telephone conversation with Lynn Scott "Scottie" Cochrane and Louis Middleman, DA Collection.

aides with huge black umbrellas assumed positions over the group like motionless sentinels, seemingly impervious to the torrents of rain. When an officer accidentally dropped his umbrella on First Lady Laura Bush's head, my friend French Hill quipped, "There's the Air Force's newest enlisted man." Jimmy Carter and George W. Bush chivalrously brushed the pooling rainwater from their wives' chairs. Bush tapped Skip Rutherford on the shoulder and gestured at the audience, asking, "Where did all these people come from?" Rutherford, who had guided the earliest discussions about the Clinton Library's location, nodded toward the nearby intersecting interstate highways, I-30 and I-40, and said, "Access is a very important consideration."[5] George W. Bush already was thinking about his presidential library's location and its accessibility in Texas.

America's version of political royalty was assembled on the pavilion just below the podium—members of the Eisenhower, Kennedy, Johnson, Nixon, Ford, Carter, Reagan, and Bush families. First Lady Nancy Reagan, like President Ford, was too frail to attend the festivities. As expected, Al and Tipper Gore were in the VIP section, and John Kerry arrived a few minutes before the ceremony began and walked past me to his assigned seat. Foreign dignitaries gathered from around the world, including Israel's former Prime Minister Shimon Peres and the late Yitzhak Rabin's children. Hollywood entertainers also were there—Barbra Streisand, Robin Williams, Morgan Freeman, Joan Baez, Kevin Spacey, Ed Begley, Jr., and Irish rock icon Bono. With the rain pelting an exquisite black Steinway piano on the stage, Bono delivered a truncated repertoire of Beatles songs, including one appropriate selection, "Rain." That performance probably was the beautiful Steinway's final appearance—the rain obviously ruined it.[6]

---

[5] French Hill email to DA, 24 November 2004, DA Collection; C. S. Murphy, "Bush library finalists seek out Rutherford," *Arkansas Democrat-Gazette*, 18 May 2006, 1A.

[6] Marie Newman, "Thousands Attend Dedication of Clinton's Presidential Library," *New York Times*, 18 November 2004, https://www.nytimes.com/2004/11/18/politics/thousands-attend-dedication-of-clintons-presidential-library-html (accessed 3 October 2019); Lynn Scott "Scottie" Cochrane email to DA, 2 October 2019, with attached Lynn Scott "Scottie" Cochrane email to "All,"

The ceremony's preliminaries grew so lengthy that Scottie Cochrane and her husband returned to their comfortable quarters at the Old Capitol Hotel to view the remaining festivities on TV: "It was much more pleasant to be warm & dry, eating BBQ while we watched the speeches."[7] Meanwhile, back on the stage, President Clinton peeked from beneath his umbrella and asked Skip Rutherford, "Who made this program so long?" "You did," Rutherford smilingly replied.[8]

Finally, the four presidents spoke—each delivered lively, conciliatory remarks. Scottie Cochrane, a serious student of presidents and their libraries, later commented, "Despite a bitterly fought election two weeks earlier, they were polite, civil and cordial. This should send a message to the rest of the world. Our system goes on—we don't shoot each other because of political differences."[9]

President Carter set the tone for the day in remarks that carefully blended seriousness and humor. He laughingly remembered a visit to Little Rock thirty years earlier when he mistook Bill Clinton, a youthful congressional candidate, for a messenger. In another humorous aside, Carter paid homage to the unique fellowship of former presidents: "[N]either the news media nor any member of the House or Senate can tell us how to do our job unless you happen to be married to one of them, like Bill is."[10] Quickly pivoting toward more serious themes, he hailed Clinton as an inspirational figure who "brought insight, wisdom, and determination to bear on the issues he addressed" and led "other people to go beyond…their own limits" to reach "great goals." In closing, he also paid special tribute to his contemporary, George H. W. Bush, for his national service, "almost

20 November 2004, DA Collection; "Clinton library, museum dedicated," *Milwaukee* (WI) *Journal Sentinel*, 19 November 2004, 3A.

[7] Lynn Scott "Scottie" Cochrane email to "All," 20 November 2004, DA Collection.

[8] Skip Rutherford email to DA, 29 September 2019, DA Collection.

[9] Frolking, "Presidents' united front…," *Granville Sentinel*, 3 February 2005, 4B.

[10] "Remarks of Former U.S. President Jimmy Carter at the Dedication of the Clinton Presidential Library," 18 November 2004 (released 17 November 2004), Carter Presidential Center, https://www.cartercenter.org/news/documents/doc1897.html (accessed 2 October 2019).

unmatched in history." Carter recognized that regardless of the rigors of "a very difficult political year—more difficult for some of us than others—it is valuable for the world to see two Democrats and two Republicans assembled together all honoring the great nation that has permitted us to serve."[11]

Smoothly transitioning from President Carter's message, George H. W. Bush invoked the "inseparable bond that binds together all who have lived in the White House." He lauded Bill Clinton as "one of the most gifted American political figures in modern times," adding in his inimitably droll, deadpan style, "Trust me, I learned this the hard way.... He was a natural, he made it look easy, and oh, how I hated him for that.... He devoured ideas with an insatiable curiosity and then pursued them with unbounded energy and infectious enthusiasm."[12] President Bush thus had masterfully walked an emotional, rhetorical tightrope in which he simultaneously praised Clinton's talents and described the agony of defeat in 1992. His remarkably generous, self-effacing words left many in the audience hopeful that the Bush-Clinton chasm could be bridged in the near future.

Twenty years had elapsed since a Republican president had won a second term. George W. Bush, fresh off his reelection win over John Kerry, had every reason to be cocky and take a victory lap. He instead chose a more magnanimous route, eloquently speaking about his predecessor's accomplishments and thereby erasing any lingering recriminations from his speech in College Station in 1997. In perhaps one of his most endearing public addresses, Bush honored Clinton as "an able and energetic American" who "led our country with optimism and a great affection for the American people.... In all of his actions and decisions, the American

---

[11] Ibid.

[12] "Transcript: Former President George H. W. Bush Comments at Clinton Library Dedication," *Washington Post*, 18 November 2004, http://www.washingtonpost.com/wp-dyn/articles/A60354-2004Nov18.html (accessed 3 October 2019); "Clinton library, museum dedicated," *Milwaukee Journal Sentinel*, 19 November 2004, 3A; "George H. W. Bush speech at opening of Clinton Presidential Library," 18 November 2004, videotape, C-SPAN, https://www.c-span.org/video/?c4444491/user-clip-george-hw-bush-speech-opening-clinton-presidential-library (accessed 3 October 2019).

people sensed a deep empathy for the poor and the powerless."[13]

Bush also thoughtfully added that the Clintons' "greatest achieve-ment" was the manner in which they reared their daughter: "It's not easy to be a teenager in the White House, it's a lot easier when you have a loving mother and a loving father that Chelsea Clinton had."[14] His com-ments also included the funniest anecdote of the day: "Arkansas is a state that knows political skill when you see it. A fellow in Saline County was asked by his son why he liked Governor Clinton so much. He said, 'Son, he'll look you in the eye, he'll shake your hand, he'll hold your baby, he'll pet your dog—all at the same time.'"[15]

The Clinton Library's namesake, of course, was the featured speaker. Barely two months after his heart bypass surgery at age fifty-eight, Presi-dent Clinton looked gaunt and weak, and his ordinarily "puffy grey hair was flattened by the rain." Scottie Cochrane observed that although "quite pale and thin, ...once he began to speak, he seemed like himself."[16]

In comparison with his other speeches, President Clinton's address was relatively brief (about twenty minutes), undoubtedly because of the rapidly deteriorating weather. In his usual conversational tone, Clinton ex-plained how as a "New Democrat" in the 1990s, he wanted "to prepare America" for the new century by combining conservative and progressive values in a coherent series of domestic and foreign policies as "our bridge to tomorrow." He summed up with an appeal for national unity: "What shall our shared values be? Everybody counts. Everybody deserves a chance. Everybody has got a responsibility to fulfill. We all do better when we work together. Our differences do matter, but our common humanity

[13] "President's Remarks at the Clinton Presidential Center Dedication," 18 November 2004, news release, Office of the Press Secretary, The White House, https://georgewbush-whitehouse.archives.gov/news/re-leases/2004/11/print/20041118-3.html (accessed 1 October 2019).

[14] Ibid.

[15] Ibid.; "Transcript: President Bush Speaks at Clinton Library Dedication," *Washington Post*, 18 November 2004, http://www.washingtonpost.com/wp-dyn/articles/A60352-2004Nov18_2.html (accessed 3 October 2019).

[16] Frolking, "Presidents' united front...," *Granville Sentinel*, 3 February 2005, 4B.

matters more."[17]

President Clinton's comments concluded the public portion of the ceremony. The drenched, frozen audience quickly dispersed to seek shelter and sustenance. The first families and their guests retreated inside the museum and gathered in the Oval Office replica, where I joined them. They all were looking around and excitedly speaking in hushed whispers like school children on a field trip. This precise re-creation of the Oval Office apparently had triggered many personal memories. I stood silently off to the side. George and Barbara Bush and their son warmly greeted me. "The first time I've seen the Bushes in over 5 years," I recorded in my journal, adding cryptically, "Both GB & GWB seemed to be interested in how long I planned to stay in LR. I really didn't understand why."[18] At home that night I wearily reflected that perhaps the "Bush Boys" planned to "pick my brain" in planning the next presidential library.

Leaving the Oval Office, I accompanied the first families on a leisurely tour of the entire museum. Barbara Bush pulled me aside and asked, "David, where did you find all of these incredible toys? There's so much more here than you gave us at the Bush Library." While her tone was not menacing or accusatory in any way, I immediately realized that she seriously was inquiring why the Clinton Library's interactive exhibits exceeded the number at the Bush Library. She smiled thinly, pursing her lips and waiting for my explanation.

That moment seemed like an eternity. I knew that bureaucratic exculpatory jargon would not be advisable. In the past, I always found that unexpurgated truthfulness was the best policy in conversations with her and other members of first families. So I said, "Ma'am, to be brutally

---

[17] "Transcript: Former President Clinton Speaks at Library Dedication," *Washington Post*, 18 November 2004, http://www.washingtonpost.com/wp-dyn/articles/A60393-2004Nov18.html (accessed 3 October 2019); John F. Harris, "Unity Shines in the Rain at Clinton Library Dedication," *Washington Post*, 19 November 2004, http://www.washingtonpost.com/wp-dyn/articles/A60914-2004Nov18.html (accessed 3 October 2019); Louis Middleman notes/summary of President Clinton's Remarks, 18 November 2004, in Louis Middleman email to DA, 1 October 2019, DA Collection; "Clinton library, museum dedicated," *Milwaukee Journal Sentinel*, 19 November 2004, 3A.

[18] DA Journal, 22 December 2004, DA Collection.

honest with you, electronic technology in museum exhibits has advanced light years since we designed the Bush Library in the mid-1990s. That's about all that I can offer you in the way of an explanation." She appeared to be satisfied with my answer and nodded, saying, "Okay, that's fine," or words to that effect. Although relieved by her response, I expected that the Bush Library soon would upgrade and expand its museum exhibits. A few months later, three Bush Library and Foundation staff members visited with us in Little Rock and carefully examined our new exhibits.[19]

After my exchange with Barbara Bush, I noticed that Jimmy Carter was huddled in a corner of the museum with the other presidents. He insisted that they restrict the number of signed dedication group photographs. Although Carter did not specifically say so, I assumed that he wanted to enhance the intrinsic value of these unique images for future presidential memorabilia collectors. The three other presidents silently acquiesced to Carter's proposal, but I always wondered if they ever reached a consensus as to a specified quantity of signed group photographs, which today are highly coveted by collectors. President Carter abruptly announced that an evening event at the Carter Center in Atlanta awaited him and Rosalynn; they said a perfunctory farewell to all and departed for the airport.

After the Carters' departure, our entourage drifted into the museum's Cabinet Room. They all were intrigued by the electronic devices that instantaneously retrieved bits and pieces of documents and speeches about domestic and foreign policy issues. President Clinton later inscribed a photographic image from this moment: "David, You've got three Presidents doing 'research' in your library—Not bad!"[20]

We spent over an hour in this corner of the museum, with the Clintons serving as the proud hosts amid much lighthearted banter—somewhat reminiscent of a cocktail party or backyard barbeque. One slightly somber note intruded when a crestfallen Al Gore said to me, "The National Archives really does a lot for these former presidents, but not so

[19] Warren Finch email to DA, 8 March 2005; Roman Popadiuk to DA, 21 March 2005; Patricia Burchfield to DA, 29 March 2005, DA Collection.

[20] Inscribed photograph, Presidents George H. W. Bush, George W. Bush, and William J. Clinton, with DA, 18 November 2004, William J. Clinton Foundation (in author's possession).

much for vice presidents." After I indicated that NARA also preserves and processes vice presidential records, photographs, and memorabilia, he perked up somewhat. Yet my words rang hollow—how do you console someone who came within only a few thousand "hanging chads" of becoming the forty-third president of the United States?

Meanwhile, President George H. W. Bush circulated throughout the crowd, paying his respects to everyone, including Secret Service agents, architects, museum designers, and our staff. As always, on this occasion, he comported himself with good manners, grace, and inclusiveness. He grabbed my shoulder and pointed across the room: "That's a White House photographer over there. He'll take any shots we want. Let's get some pictures of you with the 'Bush Boys'!" And we did—Bush 41 and Bush 43, with me in the middle.[21]

Soon after our "photo op," Bush 41 asked when lunch would be served: "The President is hungry." I had no doubt which president he was referring to—his son, Bush 43, next asked me the same question. I responded to both "Bush Boys" that dining was scheduled within the next half hour or so. They resumed their socializing in the Cabinet Room. According to Skip Rutherford, he had "to interrupt a private conversation between Bush 41 and Clinton because Bush 43 was ready for lunch."[22]

I accompanied the "Bush Boys" and our other guests to the large white luncheon tent adjacent to the museum, and we said our good-byes there. Needing to go home and change into dry clothes and return to greet our media and public visitors, I skipped the lunch. By all accounts, it was a leisurely affair, dominated by story-telling, reminiscences, and toasts.

Mike Allen, a *Washington Post* reporter, chronicled the scene inside the tent, where guests feasted on Arkansas trout and barbequed chicken beneath eight gleaming chandeliers. Bush 43, a reformed teetotaler, toasted Bill Clinton without a wine glass. He referred to Clinton's story as one of "talent recognized early and lifelong friendships and hard work that was rewarded." Bush's final comments came straight from his father's hymnal:

---

[21] Photograph, Presidents George H. W. Bush and George W. Bush, with DA, 18 November 2004, George W. Bush Presidential Library and Museum, Dallas, TX.

[22] Skip Rutherford email to DA, 29 September 2019, DA Collection.

"Americans look to our former Presidents as elder statesmen. In the case of President Clinton, the elder statesman is about one month younger than I am. His public service came early, and his service to America has not ended."[23] Bush was on his way to an international economic summit in Chile and would spend that night at his ranch in Crawford, Texas. "Moments after the glasses clinked, his limousine was rolling."[24]

That evening I was exhausted and still somewhat chilled and water-logged from my day outside in the bitter weather. But realizing that this was my third and final presidential library dedication, I savored every moment of this day—particularly seeing all of *my* presidents and first ladies gathered together in Little Rock. Three years later, my long journey ended, and we returned home to Alabama, where my life as an archivist had begun thirty-five years before.

Over the years, friends have inquired if the circuitous arc of my professional life has been worthwhile. Would I do it all over again, they asked. Then, as now, I always answer, "In a heartbeat."

---

[23] Mike Allen, "Bush, former president swap praise at ceremony," *Washington Post,* 18 November 2004, reprinted in *Milwaukee Journal Sentinel,* 19 November 2004, 3A.

[24] Ibid.

Appendix

Glossary of Acronyms

ABD—All But Dissertation
A&D—Accessioning and Disposal
ADAH—Alabama Department of Archives and History
ADP—Automated Data Processing
ALA—American Library Association
API—Alabama Polytechnic Institute
AU—Auburn University
CALS—Central Arkansas Library System
CIA—Central Intelligence Agency
C-SPAN—Cable-Satellite Public Affairs Network
DNC—Democratic National Committee
EOB—Old Executive Office Building
FARC—Federal Archives and Records Center
FBI—Federal Bureau of Investigation
FOB—Friends of Bill [Clinton]
FOIA—Freedom of Information Act
FPS—Federal Protective Service
FRC—Federal Records Center
GAH—Georgia Association of Historians
GDAH—Georgia Department of Archives and History
GNS—Global Navigation System
GSA—General Services Administration
HRS—Historical Records Survey
IG—Inspector General
I&NS—Immigration and Naturalization Service
MARAC—Mid-Atlantic Regional Archives Conference
MARC—MAchine-Readable Cataloging
MARTA—Metropolitan Atlanta Rapid Transit Authority
NARA—National Archives and Records Administration

NARS—National Archives and Records Service
NHPRC—National Historical Publications and Records Commission
NL—Office of Presidential Libraries
NLBP—Bush Presidential Materials Project
NLCP—Carter Presidential Materials Project
NLE—Eisenhower Presidential Library and Museum
NLR—FDR Presidential Library and Museum
NSC—National Security Council
OCD—Obsessive Compulsive Disorder
OCLC—Online Computer Library Center
OCS—Officer Candidates School
OPAC—Online Public Access Catalog
OPM—Office of Personnel Management
PBS—Public Broadcasting System
PDB—President's Daily Brief
PHM—Presidential Historical Materials
PRA—Presidential Records Act of 1978
Q&A—Questions and Answers
RIF—Reduction in Force
RLIN—Research Libraries Information Network
ROTC—Reserve Officer Training Corps
SAVAK—Anagram of Persian Words for Organization of Intelligence
    and National Security in Iran
SES—Senior Executive Service
SF-171—Standard Form No. 171 (Federal Job Application)
SGA—Society of Georgia Archivists
SLIS—School of Library and Information Science
TAMU—Texas A&M University
UAB—University of Alabama-Birmingham
VISTA—Volunteers in Service to America
WHCA—White House Communications Agency
WHCF—White House Central Files
WHORM—White House Office of Records Management
WHPO—White House Personnel Office
WPA—Works Progress Administration

Bibliography

ARCHIVAL SOURCES

David Alsobrook Collection, Auburn University Special Collections and Archives, R. B. Draughon Library, Auburn AL, ca. 1967–2019.

Jimmy Carter Presidential Library and Museum, Atlanta, Georgia, Donated Historical Materials, 1978–1991.

Federal Records of Temporary Committees, Commissions, and Boards, 1977–1981.

Oral Histories, 1978–2004.

Presidential Handwriting File, Staff Secretary's Office, 1977.

Records of White House Office of Administration, 1977–1981.

William J. Clinton Presidential Library and Museum, Little Rock, Arkansas, White House Office of Records Management Subject File, 2000.

NEWSPAPERS

Atlanta Journal-Constitution, 2002.

(Auburn University) *Plainsman,* 1974.

Austin (TX) *American Statesman,* 1990.

Birmingham (AL) *Post-Herald,* 1979.

(Bryan-College Station TX) *Eagle,* 1997, 1999–2000.

Dallas Morning News, 1993, 1996, 2000.

(Denver CO) *Rocky Mountain News,* 1977.

(Fayetteville AR) *Morning News,* 2000.

Granville (OH) *Sentinel,* 2005.

(Harlingen TX) *Valley Morning Star,* 1994.

(Little Rock AR) *Arkansas Democrat-Gazette,* 2004–2006.

(Little Rock AR) *Arkansas Times,* 2014.

Los Angeles Times, 2000.

Milwaukee (WI) *Journal Sentinel,* 2004.

Mobile (AL) *Press-Register,* 1994, 1996, 2008.

New York Times, 1979, 1985–1986, 1991, 2002, 2004, 2009.

Opelika-Auburn (AL) *News,* 1979.

Salina (KS) *Journal,* 1997.

Washington Post, 1977, 1987, 1993, 2004, 2015.

Washington Star, 1977.

BOOKS

Alsobrook, David E. *Southside: Eufaula's Cotton Mill Village and Its People, 1890–*

1945. Macon GA: Mercer University Press, 2017.

Assessing Alabama's Archives: A Plan for the Preservation of the State's Historical Records. Montgomery AL: Alabama Historical Records Board, 1985.

Brinkley, Douglas. *The Unfinished Presidency: Jimmy Carter's Journey Beyond the White House*. New York, Viking, 1998.

Bush, George. *All The Best, George Bush: My Life in Letters and Other Writings*. New York: Scribner, 1999.

Clinton, Bill. *My Life*. New York: Alfred A. Knopf, 2004.

Daniels, Maygene, and Timothy Walch, editors. *A Modern Archives Reader: Basic Readings in Archival Theory and Practice*. Washington DC: National Archives and Records Administration; corr. repr., 2002.

Eanes Teens—1961. Volume 6. Yearbook. Mobile AL: Mae Eanes Junior High School, 1961.

Eizenstat, Stuart E. *President Carter: The White House Years*. New York: St. Martin's Press, 2018.

Hufbauer, Benjamin. *Presidential Temples: How Memorials and Libraries Shape Public Memory*. Lawrence KS: University Press of Kansas, 2005.

Jacoway, Elizabeth, and Dan T. Carter, Lester C. Lamon, and Robert C. McMath, Jr., editors. *The Adaptable South: Essays in Honor of George Brown Tindall*. Baton Rouge LA: Louisiana State University Press, 1991.

Jernigan, Mike. *Auburn Man: The Life & Times of George Petrie*. Montgomery AL: The Donnell Group, 2007.

Kirkland, Scotty E. *We the People: Alabama's Defining Documents*. Montgomery AL: Alabama Department of Archives and History, 2019.

Meacham, Jon. *Destiny and Power: The American Odyssey of George Herbert Walker Bush*. New York: Random House, 2015.

Olliff, Martin T., editor. *The Great War in the Heart of Dixie: Alabama during World War I*. Tuscaloosa AL: University of Alabama Press, 2008.

Owen, Thomas McAdory. *History of Alabama and Dictionary of Alabama Biography*. 4 volumes. Chicago: S. J. Clarke Publishing Company, 1921.

Parmet, Herbert S. *George Bush: The Life of a Lone Star Yankee*. New York: Scribner, 1997.

Thornton, J. Mills, III. *Dividing Lines: Municipal Politics and the Struggle for Civil Rights in Montgomery, Birmingham, and Selma*. Tuscaloosa AL: University of Alabama Press, 2006.

Webster's Seventh New Collegiate Dictionary. Springfield MA: Merriam-Webster, Inc., 1963.

ARTICLES
Alsobrook, David E. "The Auburn University Archival Training Program." *Provenance: Journal of the Society of Georgia Archivists* 2/2 (Fall 1984): 49–53.

———. "The Best Years of Their Lives: Alabama Polytechnic Institute's World War II Veterans Era, 1946–1950." *Alabama Review* 70/4 (October 2017): 316–62.

———. "The Birth of the Tenth Presidential Library: The Bush Presidential Materials Project, 1993–1994." *Government Information Quarterly* 12/1 (January 1995): 33–41.

———. "A Portrait of the Archivist as a Young Man." *Alabama Review* 71/4 (October 2018): 283–319.

———. "An Update from College Station: The Future Bush Presidential Library." *The Record: News from the National Archives and Records Administration* 3/1 (September 1996): 7, 15.

"Alsobrook named director of Clinton Library." *NARA Staff Bulletin* 529 (May 2004): 6.

Beasley, Gerald. "Curatorial Crossover: Building Library, Archives, and Museum Collections." *RBM: A Journal of Rare Books, Manuscripts, and Cultural Heritage* 8/1 (Spring 2007): 20–28.

Bohanan, Robert D. "The Presidential Libraries System Study: The Carter Project's Experience." *Provenance: Journal of the Society of Georgia Archivists* 2/2 (Fall 1984): 32–38.

Choi, Youngok, and Edie Rasmussen. "What Qualifications and Skills are important for Digital Librarian Positions in Academic Libraries?" *Journal of Academic Librarianship* 35/5 (September 2009): 457–67.

Conniff, Richard. "What the Luddites Really Fought Against." *Smithsonian Magazine* (March 2011), https://www.smithsonianmag.com/history/what-the-luddites-really-fought-against-264112/ (accessed 16 February 2018).

Cox, Richard J. "America's pyramids: Presidents and their libraries." *Government Information Quarterly* 19/1 (January 2002): 45–75.

Gandy, Amy. "Library Commemorates Tenth Anniversary." *The Centerpiece* [Carter Center Newsletter] 4/2 (February 1991): 3–4.

Geselbracht, Raymond, and Timothy Walch. "The Presidential Libraries Act After 50 Years." *Prologue* 37/2 (Summer 2005): 49.

Geselbracht, Raymond H., and Daniel J. Reed. "The Presidential Library and the White House Liaison Office." *American Archivist* 46/1 (Winter 1983): 69–72.

Ginsburg, Wendy, and Erika K. Lunder and David J. Richardson. "The Presidential Libraries Act and the Establishment of Presidential Libraries." CRS Report, 6 February 2015. Washington DC: Congressional Research Service, 2015.

Hufbauer, Benjamin. "Billion-Dollar Boondoggle?" *Inside Higher Ed*, 4 June 2013, https://www.insidehighered.com/views/2013/06/04/essay-questions-push-put-presidential-libraries-campuses (accessed 5 March 2020).

———. "Turning Presidents into Pharaohs." *POLITICO Magazine*, 1 May

2015, https://www.politico.com/magazine/story/2015/05/obama-presidential-library-116695 (accessed 4 May 2015).

Jost, Kenneth. "Presidential Libraries." *CQ Researcher* 17/11 (16 March 2007): 243–54.

Leuchtenburg, William E. "R. D. W. Connor and the Creation of Presidential Libraries." *Carolina Comments* 51/4 (October 2003): 130–39.

Levy, Steven. "The Luddites Are Back." *Newsweek*, 15 June 1995, 55.

Lowry, Angie. "All the President's Stuff." *Auburn Magazine* 5/1 (Spring 1998): 15–18.

McMillen, David. "Moving Out, Moving In: The National Archives' Important Role When the Presidency Changes Hands." *Prologue* 48/4 (Winter 2016): 36–46.

Mitchell, Catherine C. "Computers Are Only Machines." *Chronicle of Higher Education*, 16 January 1985. "Opinions" page.

Morris, Edmund. "A Celebration of Reagan." *New Yorker*, 16 February 1998, 50–57.

Reynolds, Regina, and Mary Elizabeth Ruwell. "Fire Insurance Records: A Veritable Resource." *American Archivist* 38/1 (January 1975): 15–21.

Ruwell, Mary Elizabeth, and Eleanor M. King. "From the Archives: Rediscovering the Eskimo." *Expedition* [Journal of the University of Pennsylvania's Museum of Archaeology and Anthropology] 25/2 (Winter 1983): 2–4.

Samuelson, Mark. "Interns Help Out, Discover Careers." *On the Record: A Newsletter of the National Archives and Records Service* (April 1978): 4.

Sarasohn, David. "Zero Historian Growth." *Harper's Magazine*, July 1975, 92.

Schewe, Donald B. "Establishing a Presidential Library: The Jimmy Carter Experience." *Prologue* 21/2 (Summer 1989): 125–33.

Schultz, Charles R. "Personality Types of Archivists." *Provenance: Journal of the Society of Georgia Archivists* 14/1 (January 1996): 15–35.

Sewall, Gil, and Elliott D. Lee. "The Ph.D. Meat Market." *Newsweek*, 4 February 1980, 74.

Warner, Robert M. "The Prologue Is Past." *American Archivist* 41/1 (January 1978): 5–15.

Weldon, Edward. "Archives and the Challenges of Change." *American Archivist* 46/2 (Spring 1983): 125–34.

Wilson, Don W. "Presidential Libraries: Developing to Maturity." *Presidential Studies Quarterly* 21/4 (Fall 1991): 771–79.

———. "Presidential Records: Evidence for Historians or Ammunition for Prosecutors." *Government Information Quarterly* 14/4 (October 1997): 339–49.

MISCELLANEOUS ONLINE SOURCES

"2002 Nobel Peace Prize Awarded to President Carter." Press release, 10

October 2002, Carter Presidential Center, https://www.carter-center.org/news/documents/doc1235.html (accessed 29 May 2019).

Berlin, Ira. "In Memory of Sara Dunlap Jackson," https://www.archives.gov/publications/prologue/1997/summer/sara-dunlap-jackson.html (accessed 14 December 2018).

"Call Me Bar: Remembering Former First Lady Barbara Bush." Transcript, David Alsobrook's interview with Stan Ingold, Alabama Public Radio, 19 April 2018, http://apr.org./post/call-me-bar-remembering-former-first-lady-barbara-bush#stream/0 (accessed 21 April 2018).

"Chairman's Notebook on Presidential Records Act." US House of Representatives Government Operations Committee, https://history.house.gov/HouseRecord/Detail/15032450288 (accessed 3 March 2019).

Craven, Jackie. "The Architecture of Presidential Library Buildings." *ThoughtCo*, 3 July 2019, https://www.thoughtco.com/presidential-library-buildings-178464 (accessed 5 March 2020).

"Dr. Daniel John Reed," (1922–2012). *Find a Grave*, memorial no. 98429639, https://www.findagrave.com/memorial/98429639 (accessed 23 September 2019).

"Dr. Sara Dunlap Jackson," https://scafricanamerican.com/honorees/dr-sara-dunlap-jackson/ (accessed 14 December 2018).

"George H. W. Bush Speech at opening of Clinton Presidential Library," 18 November 2004, videotape, C-SPAN, https://www.cspan.org/video/?c4444491/george-hw-bush-speech-opening-clinton-presidential-library (accessed 3 October 2019).

"George W. Bush Remarks." Bush Presidential Library Dedication, 6 November 1997, videotape, C-SPAN, https://www.c-span org/video/?95003-1/bush presidential-library dedication (accessed 3 October 2019).

"Martin Luther King, Jr. Federal Building, Atlanta, GA." GSA, US General Services Administration, http://www gsa.gov/historic-buildings/martin-luther-king-jr-federal-building-atlanta-ga (accessed 7 May 2019).

McDaid, Jennifer Davis. "Alternatives to the Academic Job Market —Archival Work," August 2006, http://thesawh.org/wp content/uploads/2012/06/Alternatives_to_the_Academic_Job_Market.pdf (accessed 26 February 2019).

Nicolow, Jim, and Susan Turner. "GSA Rehabilitates Historical King Federal Building in Atlanta." *FacilitiesNet Newsletter*, October 2012, https://www.facilitiesnet.com/green/article/-GSA-Rehabilitates-Historic-King-Federal-Building-in-Atlanta--13583 (accessed 7 May 2019).

"Presidential Records Act (PRA) of 1978." *44 USC* §2201-2209, https://www.archives.gov/presidential-libraries/laws/1978-act.html (accessed 3 March 2019).

"President's Remarks at the Clinton Presidential Center Dedication," 18 November 2004, news release, Office of the Press Secretary, The White House, https://georgewbush-whitehouse.archives.gov/news/releases/2004/11/print/20041118-3.html (accessed 1 October 2019).
"Remarks of Former U.S. President Jimmy Carter at the Dedication of the Clinton Presidential Library," 18 November 2004 (released 17 November 2004), Carter Presidential Center, https://www.cartercenter.org/news/documents/doc1897.html (accessed 2 October 2019).
"Robert Eugene 'Bob' Wiatt." *Find a Grave*, memorial no. 57049207, https://www.findagrave.com/memorial/57049207 (accessed 11 August 2019).
Scheer, Gene. "American Anthem," http://www.lyricsreg.com/lyrics/norah+jones/American+Anthem (accessed 5 July 2019).
"Sullivan, Terry." Vitae, Department of Political Science, University of North Carolina, Chapel Hill, NC, https://politicalscience.unc.edu/staff/terry-sullivan/ (accessed 26 August 2019).
"Texas A&M University Police Leadership," 1964–2013, https://upd.tamu.edu/sitecollectiondocuments/UPD_History.pdf (accessed 10 August 2019).
"Trudy Huskamp Peterson," https://www.trudypeterson.com/resume (accessed 15 January 2019).
"William Alton "Uncle Buddy" Carter." *Find a Grave*, memorial no. 35275427, https://www.findagrave.com/memorial/35275427 (accessed 2 March 2019).

UNPUBLISHED THESIS
Alsobrook, David E. "William Dorsey Jelks: Alabama Editor and Legislator." MA thesis, West Virginia University, 1972.

Index

Index

Peck, Ralph, 97
Pendleton, Debbie, xviii, 32, 38-41, 60
Penn, Mark, 186
Pennsylvania, University of, 7-8, 81, 89
Perdue, Judy, 55-56
Peres, Shimon, 248
Perkinston Junior College (MS), xi
Perrett, Geoffrey, 183
Persian Gulf War, the, 170
Persons, Denise, 140
Peters, Gayle Patrick, 36-38
Peters, Ralph, 140
Peterson Air and Space Museum (CO), 8
Peterson, David F., 209-10, 212-15, 218, 220-22, 225-26, 229, 233-35
Peterson, Trudy Huskamp, 5, 67, 69, 74, 82, 85, 195,
Petrie, George, 34, 54
"PhD glut," 4, 33, 43, 47, 72, 105
Plains, GA, 127, 132, 145
Playhouse 90, xii
Podesta, John, 186
Poepsal, Linda, 204, 215, 218-20
Popadiuk, Roman, 201-206, 230, 253n.19
Posner, Ernst, 1
Powell, Jody, 89-90, 102-103, 107, 115, 136, 150, 164, 168
Powers, Willow, 10
Presidential Daily Diary, 83
Presidential "Handwriting File," 136-37
"presidential historical materials," 93, 99
presidential libraries, 2, 47, 56-57, 77, 80-82, 86, 99, 119-20, 123n.1, ch. 5, *passim. See also* names of individual libraries
Presidential Libraries, Office of (NL), 37, 43, 45-47, 56-57, 66-67, 71, 80, 87, 96, 127-28, 150, 211-12
presidential materials projects, 124, 156, 194. *See also* names of individual projects

Presidential Papers Staff, 85. *See also* National Archives White House Liaison Office
"Presidential Papers Task Force," 101-102, 104
Presidential Records Act (PRA) of 1978, 99-102, 104, 119-20, 138-39, 194, 203
President's Daily Brief (PDB), 137
Pruitt, Paul M. Jr., xviii, 13-14, 104, 109, 120, 132
Pulaski County, AR, 245
Purvis, Jimmie, xviii, 16-17, 38, 195, 228, 241
Quick, Ed, 241
Rabin, Yitzhak, 248
Raines, Howell, 165
Rapport, Leonard, 76
Rea, Robert, R., 35, 48, 58n.27
Reagan, Nancy, 248
Reagan, Ronald, 7, 101, 108, 112-13, 115-17, 120, 130, 134, 142, 155, 159, 175
Reed, Daniel J., 5, 37, 43, 45-47, 45n.1, 56, 66-68, 82-87, 90-92, 100, 103, 111, 156
Rhoads, James B. "Bert," 68-69, 82-83, 85-86, 100, 111
Rice, Bradley, 148
Rich, Marc, 242
Rich's department store, 125
Rickover, Adm. Hyman, 162, 166
RIF (Reduction in Force), 133-35
Rikard, Marlene, xviii
Riley, Sharan, 199, 201
RLIN (Research Libraries Information Network), 60
Roberts, Bobby, 184, 186, 188-89, 241
Roberts, William, 154
Robison, Emily, xviii, 241
Rockefeller Foundation, the, 43
Rockford, IL, 70
Rockville, MD, 65
Rodham, Dorothy, 189
Rogers, William Warren, 43